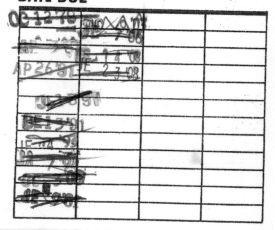

The Poetry of American Women from 1632 to 1945

The Dan Danciger Publication Series

from 1632

The Poetry of American Women to 1945

by Emily Stipes Watts

University of Texas Press, Austin and London

The publication of this book was assisted by a grant from the Andrew W. Mellon Foundation.

Library of Congress Cataloging in Publication Data

Watts, Emily Stipes.
  The poetry of American women from 1632 to 1945.

  (The Dan Danciger publication series)
  Bibliography: p.
  Includes index.
  1. American poetry—Women authors—History and criticism.
I. Title.
PS147.W3   811'.009'352   76-43282
ISBN 0-292-76435-9

Design by Eiichi Kono

Second Printing, 1977

Grateful acknowledgment is made to the following for permission to quote copyrighted materials:

WILLIAM L. CLEMENTS LIBRARY: 8 lines from THE GROUP: A FARCE, by Mercy Otis Warren, facsimile edition (1953).

CONSTABLE & CO., LTD.: "Pear Tree" and lines 1–2 of "Orchard," from SEA GARDEN, by H. D. (Hilda Doolittle Aldington) (1916).

NORMA MILLAY ELLIS: Line 1 of "I will put Chaos in fourteen lines," by Edna St. Vincent Millay. From COLLECTED POEMS, Harper & Row. Copyright, 1954, by Edna St. Vincent Millay and Norma Millay Ellis.
15 lines from *Conversation at Midnight* by Edna St. Vincent Millay. From COLLECTED POEMS, Harper & Row. Copyright, 1937, 1964, by Edna St. Vincent Millay and Norma Millay Ellis.

FABER AND FABER LTD.: "To a Snail" and four short quotations from other poems, by Marianne Moore. Reprinted by permission of Faber and Faber Ltd from THE COMPLETE POEMS OF MARIANNE MOORE.

DAVID R. GODINE, PUBLISHER: 2 poems by Sarah Kemble Knight. From *The Journal of Madam Knight*. Reprinted by permission of David R. Godine, Publisher.

HARVARD UNIVERSITY PRESS.: Nos. 657, 212, 732, 520, 284, 848, 1583, 1129, 801 (line 7), 271 (lines 13–16), 1158 (line 2), 1115 (line 10), 250 (line 8), and 214 (line 16). Reprinted by permission of the publishers and the Trustees of Amherst College from THE POEMS OF EMILY DICKINSON, edited by Thomas H. Johnson, Cambridge, Mass.: The Belknap Press of Harvard University Press, Copyright © 1951, 1955 by the President and Fellows of Harvard College.
Fragment from THE LETTERS OF EMILY DICKINSON, edited by Thomas H. Johnson, Cambridge, Mass.: The Belknap Press of Harvard University Press, 1958.
Material from THE WORKS OF ANNE BRADSTREET, edited by Jeannine Hensley, Cambridge, Mass.: The Belknap Press of Harvard University Press, 1967.
Poems by Anna Tompson Hayden (or Haiden), from HANDKER-CHIEFS FROM PAUL, edited by Kenneth B. Murdock, Cambridge, Mass.: Harvard University Press, 1927.

HOUGHTON MIFFLIN COMPANY: Emily Dickinson, lines 1–2 of poem no. 1158, "Best Witchcraft," from EMILY DICKINSON FACE TO FACE: UNPUBLISHED LETTERS WITH NOTES AND REMINISCENCES, edited by Martha Dickinson Bianchi.
Louise Imogen Guiney, HAPPY ENDING: THE COLLECTED LYRICS: section XII of Fifteen Epitaphs; lines 1–8 of "The Still of the Year."
Louise Imogen Guiney, A ROADSIDE HARP: line 1 of "Spring Nightfall."
Amy Lowell, A CRITICAL FABLE: from THE COMPLETE POETICAL WORKS OF AMY LOWELL. 22 lines beginning "For the men . . ." and ending "He answered at once." Copyright 1955 by Houghton Mifflin Company.
Walt Whitman, COMPETE POETRY AND SELECTED PROSE, edited

For Virginia Schenck Stipes

Contents

Preface

Had American women written no original poetry, or had they said nothing important, or had they followed no special course, a book such as this would be unnecessary. However, it is clear that American women poets have developed their own themes, prosodic techniques, types of poems, and particular images—all elements essential to a vigorous and original poetry.

For reasons that will be made clear in the body of this work, major studies of American poetry have dealt almost exclusively with the poetry of American men. In this book, I hope to delineate and define the poetic contributions of American women, so that someday we will be able to perceive the interrelationships and tensions between the poetry of American men and women and thus more accurately judge the achievement of American poetry.

I am grateful to the John Simon Guggenheim Memorial Foundation for a twelve-month grant to complete this book.

Several of my Americanist colleagues at the University of Illinois at Urbana-Champaign have helped me with both concepts and research problems: George Hendrick, Keneth Kinnamon, Carol Kyle, and John T. Flanagan. Elizabeth Klein Shapiro, herself a poet, gave me valuable suggestions concerning contemporary women poets. The librarians at the University of Illinois have been ever patient and helpful, especially Eva Faye Benton, Martha Landis, and Mary Ceibert.

To my colleague Nina Baym, I offer my sincere gratitude for her several important suggestions and for her advice in matters of research. Her continual interest and encouragement and her thorough reading of this book in manuscript are indicative of her generosity.

Carolyn Cates Wylie, associate editor at the University of Texas Press, is a thorough and intelligent reader and critic. Her aid was significant in the final stages of this book.

To our sons, Ben, Ned, and Tom, thank you for your consideration. I hope that you will someday enjoy this book.

My husband Bob has had to live the last two years not only with me, but also with American women poets. For sixteen years, he has encouraged me to find my own way as a scholar.

The Poetry of American Women from 1632 to 1945

Introduction

From the time that Anne Bradstreet defied "each carping tongue," set aside her "needle," and picked up her "poet's pen," American women have been writing poetry. In addition to the many women whose verse appeared in local newspapers and pamphlets, several hundred women published poetry in books or in journals with national distribution, even before 1900.[1] For a time, it appeared that the women poets would be like Prufrock's mermaids: that they would sing only "each to each." From 1900 to 1945, however, a number of women poets—H. D., Gertrude Stein, Marianne Moore, Amy Lowell, Edna St. Vincent Millay, and Muriel Rukeyser—appeared: women whose verse not only is valuable in itself, but also has significantly altered the course of American poetry.

The poetry written by American women from 1945 to the present is more diverse, more profound, and more sophisticated in large part because of the rich tradition of preceding women's verse from which it has developed. In fact, a study of the poetry written by women during the past thirty years would require a volume in itself. Therefore, it is upon the historic backgrounds of contemporary poetry, that is, upon verse written by American women from 1632 to 1945, that I will concentrate.

In following this course of investigation, I do not mean to imply that poetry by American men and poetry by American women are two separate kinds of poetry, although they have at times been so treated in the past. Ultimately, our common problem is to understand that larger subject—American poetry. In a number of other studies which center almost exclusively on poetry by men,[2] certain contributions, themes, prosody, and images have already been examined. We need now to understand the historical contributions of women poets.

In the course of Western civilization, poetry by American women is one of the first bodies of verse written by many women over an extended period. Sappho's group (of whose works we have only scraps remaining) was limited to a few women over a far shorter period of time. The only comparable body of verse has been written by women in England, beginning in significant numbers about the same time Bradstreet set aside her needle. The vitality of the verse of American women has been more consistent, however, especially in the last century (perhaps because, very early, poetry was written and published in America by women of all colors, classes, and religious persuasions; by women who lived in the cities, the civilized countryside, and the wilderness; by women who, while they were rejecting traditional female stereotypes, lived in a land dominated economically, governmentally, and religiously by men and thus had not even the image of Queen Elizabeth I to help in the formation of their own self-images). Moreover, at least before 1900, a good many of the most intelligent and sensitive women in America expressed themselves in literature: practically nothing else was open to them. The same cannot be said of the men, who had many other outlets for their creative energies.

The verse of American women does not conveniently fall into the pattern of a "thesis." The best women poets have been too individualistic to allow themselves or their poetry to conform to any one theme or image. In their best work, their topics have been various, their images their own, their modes of expression as original as necessary. The vitality of their thought and feeling has dictated their poetic development. It is clear, however, that the most obvious and significant difference between the poetry of American men and that of the women is their choice of theme and, correspondingly, of dominant images and personae. Moreover, at particular times, for example, 1860–1910, it was the women who were at the outer edge of prosodic experimentation and innovation.

Consistently, however, two charges have been directed by critics against female poets. The first is that women tend to write "popular" or "public" poetry, that they appeal to a broad readership. The second is that women poets are "realistic," that they express no sense of cosmic optimism or transcendence (a complaint directed also against women prose writers). It is a fact that women have tended to be popular, that they have found an audience—most often, admittedly, other women. (The law of supply and demand has greatly benefited the woman poet in America.) [3] The popular poet has been critically scorned since the early nineteenth century, when the sales of men's verse first fell behind the women's. Thus we have developed a school of criticism devoted to distinguishing the difference between "public" or "popular" and "private" poetry. For example, one difference, as defined by William Charvat (*The Profession of Authorship in America, 1800–1870*), is in the approach of the public and private poets to the conflicts of the past and present and to the poet's own conflicts with the present environment and with a personal past. The public poet preserves these conflicts (perhaps is even unaware that they are conflicts); the private poet tries to resolve them in a language the world must "learn." "Public poet" is still a derogatory term, often directed at women poets.

If our private poets have resolved these conflicts, it has been through the nationalistic Adamic myth with its cosmic (mystical) implications and the admitted egocentrism of the male hero. [4] Thus the Adamic image developed by our private poets must resolve conflicts in a meaningful and important sense for somebody—and the somebody seems to be a man. On the basis of verse written by American women, we must wonder at the validity of these resolutions for a woman: Adam? Emerson's transcendental mysticism? Isolated individualism and egocentrism? A position largely opposed to a culture with a scientific and economic system that gave the woman poet time to write, freedom from unwanted children, and the prosperity to have a "room of her own"?

No, women's poetry has been both "popular" and vital because, from the very first, the American woman poet has been *communicative*. Her poetry has not been obscure, obviously or arrogantly erudite, or even written in a language which people must "learn." The conflicts are expressed, not resolved; the problems are universal, not simply American; and they are not necessarily the same conflicts expressed by the men. The women do not pretend to have final resolutions to such conflicts, because they recognize that many of them are unresolvable. Thus, for example, as Roy Harvey Pearce has pointed out, Whitman, Emerson, and Poe never do accept death as *"fact,"* while Emily Dickinson does. [5] Until recently, except for a "Threnody" or two for their dead children, the male poets have ignored the necessity for or the existence of children; but the women have always been aware of the conflicts and problems involved in bearing and raising children, conflicts more "cosmic," if you will, and certainly more universal than the male poet's concern for an American Adam. The women, in short, have not been so limited and parochial as the men in their approach to themselves, their environment, or their past.

As to "feminine realism," this term generally implies that women authors have not had cosmic vision, the kind of vision "heroes" have. It is true that women have not thought of themselves as "heroines," but this does not mean that they are without dignity or that they are "limited." A male "hero"—the actor who embodies the virtues of his race (and whom women serve and please)—is like a god or is at least allowed to communicate with God. In his righteousness, he confronts society and then is destroyed (as a martyr), or he escapes to the woods. He has, however, in some way, transcended. The majority of American women poets have not felt themselves to be godlike, nor could they hail God as a great Camerado. Most American women poets have been religious, although they have experienced a great gulf between God and woman, heaven and earth. Moreover, a surprising number of women who accepted religion at the same time expressed a deep pessimism concerning their lot in such a God-directed world; "cosmic pessimism" in women's poetry antedates the similar theme in the verse of men. Still other women have not transcended because they have been atheists or agnostics, or have ignored God in their verse.

For whatever reasons, the women have not expressed the essentially male image of the transcendent hero or American Adam. Perhaps they have been "realistic," because their children were tugging at their dresses. Or perhaps, because they have been treated as inferiors, they have realized the dangers inherent in Adamic superiority, in supermen, in transcendent godliness—all of which have, in the poetry of many major American male poets, amounted to the same thing. As I have said, "feminine realism" is a term used derogatorily to describe women's poetry. The American women have not created myths in any way comparable to those created by the American men.

When T. S. Eliot said in *The Waste Land* that the Fisher King (a variation of the American Adam) was languishing in a dry land and that the old myths were dead, the men agreed and mourned. For the women, there was poetic celebration in the verse of Edna St. Vincent Millay and Elinor Wylie in America. In Europe, Gertrude Stein and H. D. knew that Eliot's lamentation was premature, and continued their work to destroy the old myths. Only Sara Teasdale mourned. As Eliot described them, the women in the old myths are vessels of the male gods (the Sybil at Cumae), or sexual vessels and love objects for the men (Cleopatra and the hyacinth girl), or children (Marie). Eliot's implication is that the old myths must be reaffirmed.

Since the early 1800's, however, women poets in America had been rejecting the old myths and were busy formulating their own theories. (Their exploration is still continuing and has not, at least as of 1976, settled into any set of consistent myths.) Thus, when *The Waste Land* appeared, it was the men who were dismayed and in whose art the reverberations echoed. Occasionally, even today, a woman poet feels it necessary to remind the world that, as H. D. pointed out in *Helen in Egypt*, the "whole heroic sequence is over." Adrienne Rich wonders when "The Knight" will realize that the quest is over, and Gwendolyn Brooks believes that even the wives of these (white) knights must ultimately acknowledge that the old myths were never valid anyway, at least for the white mother and the black mother in "A Bronzeville Mother Loiters in Mississippi. Meanwhile, a Mississippi Mother Burns Bacon."

If the women have not been creating myths or expressing cosmic visions, what have they been doing? Some women have been writing of their relationships with other people—husbands, lovers, mothers, fathers, sisters, brothers, children, other women. Some have been writing directly of their inner world—an area more vast than those westward-spreading prairies the men used to symbolize their internal landscapes. Some have written of their minds, their ideas; some have written of their bodies, their senses. Some have written of their homes; some of the larger community. Some have written of conflicts; others of joys. Some are serious; some are humorous. All, however, are poets who have chosen a special way of expressing themselves. They saw in poetry a "possibility," a means of learning and of expressing what they had learned. All of them would undoubtedly agree with Emily Dickinson:

I dwell in Possibility—
A fairer House than Prose—
More numerous of Windows—
Superior—for Doors—

Of Chambers as the Cedars—
Impregnable of Eye—
And for an Everlasting Roof
The Gambrels of the Sky—

Of Visiters—the fairest—
For Occupation—This—
The spreading wide my narrow Hands
To gather Paradise—

Poetry, for the American women, has been an opening up, an extending.

Chapter One

1632-1758

Anne Dudley Bradstreet and the Other Puritan Poets

With the exception of a few scattered poems, poetry written by women in England first appeared during the Renaissance.[1] Against this background, the publication of Anne Bradstreet's *The Tenth Muse Lately sprung up in America* in London in 1650 is neither particularly surprising nor exceptional. In fact, several talented English women, such as Margaret Cavendish and Katherine Philips, published their own volumes of poetry shortly after *The Tenth Muse* appeared.[2] Anne Bradstreet, as a woman poet, had a tradition of nearly a century of female verse behind her (although her poetic forerunners were male, such as Guillaume Du Bartas and Sidney). Bradstreet (1612–1672) was born and educated in England and throughout her life considered herself a citizen of England.

On the other hand, Anne Bradstreet, a woman poet writing in Puritan America, has seemed remarkable to Americans, especially since her verse appeared in an era in America when very little good poetry was issuing from the pens of men. Too often, however, we have romanticized her image, as in John Berryman's "Homage to Mistress Bradstreet," or have distorted her poetry by forcing it into our conception of verse written by Puritan men. Nevertheless, especially in recent years, her poetry has received intelligent and fair treatment, better criticism than that for the verse of any other American woman poet before Emily Dickinson.[3] Her poetry is, as has been discussed by other critics, a blend of a variety of interests, forms, and tendencies. Not the least of these interests are particular aspects which point specifically to the later verse written by women in America—aspects which have not fully been discussed or perhaps understood by previous critics.

Her poetry is not vintage "American Puritan" because, as Roy Harvey Pearce has charged, she did not fix "once and for all the meaning of the event as that meaning is somehow bound up in a communal experience."⁴ The "communal experience" to which Pearce refers is the communal experience of male-dominated events in the political and religious life in the New World, which seems to him to form the foundation of the "continuity" of American poetry. Pearce's narrow charge that Bradstreet comments little on the American "communal" experience is correct. Her one true statement concerning such experience is "A Dialogue between Old England and New." Moreover, in "Contemplations," Bradstreet's images from nature are all borrowed from the flora and fauna of England— not America. When she does write poetically of history, as in "The Four Monarchies," it is certainly not the history of America or even of the historic thrust which brought the Puritans to the New World.

What has been overlooked in the past by many critics and literary historians dealing with Bradstreet's verse is that there is a whole other "communal" experience: the experience of a woman. It is this, in part, which has recently galvanized new interest in the poems of Bradstreet. Historically, Bradstreet's poetry is remarkable for its revelation of a woman's mind and interests, as well as for her celebration of women. Bradstreet, I believe, was the first woman poet who attempted to view women in some kind of historical perspective, as later American women poets were to do. Moreover, significantly, certain of her poems prefigure the mother-child poems later to be developed by other American women. Bradstreet found the domestic scene a perfectly respectable source of poetic images and topics. Her love poems to her husband are bold departures from standard Puritan poetry. Finally, in two more ways, Bradstreet's verse amazingly foreshadows thematic tendencies in later verse written by American women: her inability to experience God directly and her personal separation from nature.

Nearly every review of her verse comments specifically on certain passages which establish Bradstreet as an independent woman, proud of her sex and its accomplishments, at the same time often acutely aware of the limitations ascribed to women:

I am obnoxious to each carping tongue
Who says my hand a needle better fits,
A poet's pen all scorn I should thus wrong,
For such despite they cast on female wits:

If what I do prove well, it won't advance,
They'll say it's stol'n, or else it was by chance.

But sure the antique Greeks were far more mild
Else of our sex, why feigned they those nine
And poesy made Calliope's own child;
So 'mongst the rest they placed the arts divine:
But this weak knot they will full soon untie,
The Greeks did nought, but play the fools and lie.

Let Greeks be Greeks, and women what they are
Men have precedency and still excel,
It is but vain unjustly to wage war;
Men can do best, and women know it well.
Preeminence in all and each is yours;
Yet grant some small acknowledgement of ours.
                                        (from "The Prologue")

Now say, have women worth? or have they none?
Or had they some, but with our Queen, is't gone?
Nay masculines, you have thus taxed us long,
But she, though dead, will vindicate our wrong.
Let such as say our sex is void of reason,
Know 'tis a slander now but once was treason.
But happy England which had such a queen;
Yea happy, happy, had those years still been.

(from "In Honour of that High and Mighty
Princess Queen Elizabeth of Happy Memory")

However, women poets in England displayed much the same kind
of pride in their sex at approximately the same time. Although
Katherine Philips, "the matchless Orinda,"[5] did not speak so bluntly
and directly as Bradstreet, her celebration of other women and
their relationships indicates that her self-image and her opinion of
women's capabilities were high. In fact, a sense of pride and belief
in herself was absolutely essential for any woman to become a
poet, especially at this time. In the society of Western civilization,
the gap between the poetry of Sappho and that of the women
of the Renaissance is evidence of the lack of such a self-image
and of self-confidence. It is also important to note that poetry
written by women in England at this time was primarily the work
of women of the (educated) upper class, as that of Anne Bradstreet
must also be viewed in the context of American Puritan society.[6]

It was not really until the early nineteenth century, especially in America, that women from other classes published verse and thus created the broad and diverse basis for women's poetry today. On the other hand, Bradstreet's outspokenness is unique, even though her contemporary Margaret Cavendish offered a few such opinions. Poetry by women in England did not really exhibit Bradstreet's kind of bluntness until Anne Finch, Lady Winchilsea ("Ardelia," 1661–1720), published her verses in 1713 (*Miscellany Poems on Several Occasions, Written by a Lady*).

Thus Bradstreet's blunt poetic aggressiveness, her conscious defense of herself and her sex, is one difference between Bradstreet and her female contemporaries in England. Bradstreet's Puritan America was not necessarily the cause or condition of such bluntness, for, within only a few years, Lady Winchilsea would be saying more of the same thing in England. No, both Bradstreet and Lady Winchilsea were attacking a common and universal condition; Bradstreet, however, spoke first. Such poetic protest ultimately prepared the way for Mercy Otis Warren in America (to be discussed in Chapter 2) and in England for Mary Wollstonecraft's *Vindication of the Rights of Women*.

Bradstreet attempted to give a historical basis to her prefeminist ideas—and in this way she was truly an intellectual and poetic pioneer. In fact, in her two historical poems, her sympathies and interests are clear. Bradstreet's "The Four Monarchies" depicts the history of the world from the Assyrian Empire through the beginnings of the Roman Empire, at which point Bradstreet was unable to finish the poem (a situation which nobody mourns, since the poem itself is generally an adaptation of Sir Walter Raleigh's *History of the World* [1614]). "The Four Monarchies" is a history of war, intrigue, and human self-destruction in the world of men—a terrible tale which goes on and on. In such a world, Bradstreet noted, women are bargained for control of kingoms (l. 631), or are desired by cruel and lecherous men (ll. 756–765: "Oh, hellish husband, brother, uncle, sire,/Thy cruelty all ages will admire"), or are held for ransom in war (ll. 1775–1793), or can become depraved and cruel harpies when they have been treated unfairly (ll. 1168–1187). A few brave and effective women appear (Esther, ll. 1237–1240, or Semiramis, who "was both shame and glory of her sex," ll. 70–147). Some queens (ll. 1915–1918) are rightfully mourned by loving husbands, and a rare woman is simply evil (ll. 2946–3033).

Bradstreet does, in fact, pay more attention to the role of women throughout history than is typical of her sources, such as Raleigh's

History. She often enlarges the role of or more vividly depicts the women. "The Four Monarchies," however, remains primarily a history of the actions of men, with women playing minor and extremely unfortunate roles. It is a terrible world for the men, but it is worse for the women. No wonder Bradstreet could not finish "The Four Monarchies"! She had, I suspect, seen enough.

She found a much happier monarchy in more recent history—the reign of Elizabeth I, in "In Honour of that High and Mighty Princess Queen Elizabeth of Happy Memory." Ruling alone as queen and virgin (no woman in "The Four Monarchies" had been given such an opportunity),[7] Elizabeth is depicted as an Amazon and Minerva. Bradstreet carefully compares her accomplishments to those of former queens, Semiramis, Tomris, Dido, Cleopatra, and Zenobia (all of whom, except Dido and Zenobia, she also discusses in "The Four Monarchies"). Elizabeth proves superior, not only to ancient queens, but to the kings of her own day as well.

In short, in "The Four Monarchies," Bradstreet was searching long and hard, throughout history, to see, at least on one level, just what women had been doing all those years. She found a miserable story there, but one which seemed to be happier in the triumphs of Elizabeth I in "In Honour of . . . Queen Elizabeth." The brief comparison of Elizabeth to past queens (some of whom were also discussed in "The Four Monarchies") provides a link between these poems.[8] Bradstreet's interest in the historical role of women (and her disappointment at finding such limited and often disastrous examples) has continued in the verse of both English and American women. The task for the American women after 1776 was particularly difficult, however, because, being republicans, they were unable to accept the English queens as models, as Bradstreet, for example, was able to do: hence, in part, their interest in female mythological characters, an interest which became evident shortly after the Revolution and has continued until today (see Chapter 3).

We should also note that in neither "The Four Monarchies" nor "In Honour of . . . Queen Elizabeth" does Bradstreet trace woman's beginning to Eve. As Josephine K. Piercy has pointed out, such an omission in "The Four Monarchies" may be justified,[9] but Eve is even absent in "In Honour of . . . Queen Elizabeth." Only in "Contemplations" (ll. 79–85) is Bradstreet willing to claim Eve as the common mother of women, but even there Eve sinned "to be more wise" (i.e., the "Fortunate Fall," a doctrine certainly not part of American Puritanism). Her general rejection of Eve's traditional role, as well as her patent neglect of Eve, is especially notable when

we consider that the role and myth of Eve have not been accepted
by later American women.

Like all women poets of her day, Bradstreet thus had a consciousness of herself as a woman and as a person with something
valuable to say. Unlike other women poets of her day, however,
Bradstreet recognized that motherhood, at least for her, was a
major part of being a woman. Critics have always recognized the
"sincerity" and "feminine realism" of those passages, both in her
poetry and in her prose, which concern children. Real children, as
subjects for serious, adult poetry, have not been interesting to male
American (or English) poets or critics until the twentieth century
(the children of Shakespeare, Wordsworth, Emerson, and Whitman
are certainly not "real"). Thus the long tradition of poems concerning children by American women (more in number and much
earlier than similar poems by English women) has generally been
ignored.

Such poetic treatment of children is, in fact, first evident in the
kind of poem in which Anne Bradstreet first depicts children; that
is, as parts of poems which concern such topics as "Of the Four
Ages of Man."[10] Thus Bradstreet's "Childhood" is a description of
a child—cantankerous and spoiled, perhaps a reflection of one of
Anne's own children, but nevertheless a generalized portrait (linked,
however, to reality by the "realistic" details):

Ah me! conceived in sin and born with sorrow,
A nothing, here today and gone tomorrow,
Whose mean beginning blushing can't reveal,
But night and darkness must with shame conceal.
My mother's breeding sickness I will spare,
Her nine months weary burden not declare.

.   .   .   .

With tears into the world I did arrive;
My mother still did waste as I did thrive,
Who yet with love and all alacrity,
Spending, was willing to be spent for me.
With wayward cries I did disturb her rest,
Who sought still to appease me with the breast;
With weary arms she danced and "By By" sung,
When wretched I, ingrate, had done the wrong.
When infancy was past, my childishness
Did act all folly that it could express,
My silliness did only take delight
In that which riper age did scorn and slight.

In rattles, baubles, and such toyish stuff,
My then ambitious thoughts were low enough:

· · · · · · · · · · ·

Already, here, is some attempt to render not just the child, but
his relationship with the mother—a relationship which is not easy
for the mother. In fact, "Childhood" ends with the various sicknesses
(including the "tortures" of "breeding teeth") a child must suffer
(and through which the mother must nurse him).

After this early poem, Bradstreet became more personal in her
approach to children. The three elegies for grandchildren follow a
traditional elegiac form; however, unlike the majority of elegies
written by American Puritans, which concern men of civic or religious stature or their pure and religious wives, Bradstreet's elegies
concern babies. As Piercy has pointed out (*Anne Bradstreet*, p. 95),
poems elegizing children had already been written in England, but
they were to become standard in American literature, in one form
or another, for a long time. We should note, however, one particular
quality of Bradstreet's elegies: the parents are not mentioned. Bradstreet is using these elegies not as poems of comfort for the parents,
but rather as a means of justifying God's ways to herself. This justification is not easy, as in "On My Dear Grandchild Simon Bradstreet, Who Died on 16 November, 1669, Being But a Month, and
One Day Old":

No sooner came, but gone, and fall'n asleep,
Acquaintance short, yet parting caused us weep;
Three flowers, two scarcely blown, the last i' th' bud,
Cropt by th' Almighty's hand; yet is He good.
With dreadful awe before Him let's be mute,
Such was His will, but why, let's not dispute,
With humble hearts and mouths put in the dust,
Let's say He's merciful as well as just.
He will return and make up all our losses,
And smile again after our bitter crosses
Go pretty babe, go rest with sisters twain;
Among the blest in endless joys remain.

She may have had trouble accepting God's will, but she really had
no problem accepting death. For her, it was real and inevitable, as
Pearce (*The Continuity of American Poetry*, p. 24) has noted. Much
as for Emily Dickinson (and unlike, for example, the major Adamic
poets), for Bradstreet death is a *"fact."*

In another poem, "In Reference to Her Children, 23 June, 1659," she pictures herself as a mother hen: "I had eight birds hatched in one nest,/Four cocks there were, and hens the rest." The remainder of the poem describes the present circumstances of each child (one married, one at the "academy," and so on) and ends with a statement of their mother's real (and universal) concern for the future of each child.

These poems are the first of many such poems by American women—poems which eventually would be used to examine more fully the relationship of mother and child. Bradstreet did not, apparently, write any poems for her children to recite. Such verse, specifically for children, was written at this time only by adult "educators," as for example, the American Puritan John Wilson's *Song of Deliverance* (1626) [11] or the *New England Primer* (first published sometime between 1687 and 1690). Other than "In Reference to Her Children" (in which the "eight birds" are beyond infant years), she wrote no poems specifically to be read to her children. This kind of poem, which was written by nearly every woman poet in the nineteenth century and often published in volumes with "adult" verse, seems to have been a special means of communication between mother and child. All three kinds of poems, prominent especially in the verse of women in nineteenth-century America, were later to become vehicles for both the expression and examination of the relationship of mother and child, as in the verse of modern women such as Sylvia Plath and Anne Sexton.

Perhaps one of the most significant qualities of Bradstreet's poems concerning children is that the father is not mentioned or even suggested. The relationship is exclusively that of "dam" and children. We know from other poems that Anne and Simon's marriage seemed loving and happy, but neither in the poems concerning children nor even in the amatory verse is the husband's role as father mentioned. In "Before the Birth of One of Her Children," however, she asks Simon to "protect" the children, if she dies:

> And when thy loss shall be repaid with gains
> Look to my little babes, my dear remains.
> And if thou love thyself, or loved'st me,
> These O protect from step-dame's injury.[12]

Anne assumes that Simon will remarry if she dies, but she is extremely worried about the relationship of the children and their stepmother. It is an old theme—the Cinderella myth—and it lives well into the nineteenth century in the poems of American women.[13]

A fear of the "step-dame" is a legitimate concern for the mother for several reasons. First, obviously, there have been stepmothers who have favored their own children to the disadvantage of the step-children. Second, if fathers are as unimportant and insignificant in the raising of children as the poetry of American women suggests, a mother has even more solid reason for concern. That is, for what-ever reason (e.g., disinterest, or, in Simon's case, many trips on state business, or, beginning in the nineteenth century, long work hours away from home), if the father does not or cannot take a significant role in raising the children, then he will be unaware of and insen-sitive to the relationship of the children and their stepmother.[14] Finally, a mother might fear a stepmother because the role of woman in Western civilization has traditionally been that of mother, and, after all, quick and easy replacement by another woman suggests a loss of stature and importance for any mother.

The American women poets have believed for a long time that motherhood is simply not enough for a full and rich life—at least for them. In the seventeenth century, Anne Bradstreet turned to poetry but still worried about "step-dames." In the eighteenth cen-tury, Mercy Otis Warren announced that the mother acts only a "little part" and went on with her own particular blend of poetry and politics. In the nineteenth century, Lydia Huntley Sigourney's many dead mothers and children symbolized her distress. In June, 1852, Emily Dickinson wrote to the still single Susan Gilbert (her future sister-in-law) that "to the *wife*, Susie, sometimes the *wife for-gotten*, our lives perhaps seem dearer than all others in the world."[15] Dickinson then chose a life in which she would not have to worry about "step-dames."

Anne Bradstreet's amatory verse to her husband is charming and sincere, as everyone agrees, but it says very little about the actual relationship of Simon and Anne. It is exceptional in that it is ama-tory verse directed to a husband (and to the father of the poet's children)—something rare in the poetry of American women, at least until the 1920's. American women have written many fine poems expressing love, but only occasionally have such poems been directed specifically to the husband. The four poems which Anne wrote to Simon are the often anthologized "To My Dear and Loving Hus-band," "Another" ("Phoebus make haste"), "A Letter to Her Husband, Absent upon Public Employment," and "Another" ("As loving hind"). The poems all express a simple and direct quality and intensity of love. Two of the poems, "Phoebus make haste" and "As loving hind," are often examined because they appear to be attempts by Bradstreet to use metaphysical conceits.

As a group, however, they say very little about the Bradstreets as
people or about specifics of their relationship. Anne says only that
she loves Simon very much, that she misses him and "bemoans" his
absence, and that, at least from her point of view, they are a unified
pair ("If ever two were one, then surely we./If ever man were loved
by wife, then thee"—from "To My Dear and Loving Husband").
In two poems, Simon is the sun; in "As loving hind" he is the deer,
the turtledove's mate, and the male mullet. The source of the deer
and dove images is surely *The Song of Solomon*; the mullet is apparently her own addition. I would guess that both Simon and Anne
read this poem with *The Song of Solomon* in mind, and hence the
images would indicate more passion than we might otherwise perceive. Nevertheless, the love Anne expresses for Simon remains on
a rather theoretical level—honest statements, but incomplete. More
complete poetic statements concerning a love relationship would not
come from the pens of American women until the early nineteenth
century.

If Anne Bradstreet was secure in her husband's love, she was certainly not secure in God's love. However, if we examine the writing
of American Puritan men, we can understand that at least temporary
insecurity and uncertainty were common. Perhaps such feelings are
most obvious in Jonathan Edwards's *Personal Narrative* (written
1741), but they had been expressed by the earliest Puritans. It was
all part of the pilgrim's progress. On the other hand, such periods
of doubt and spiritual distress were followed by periods of often
mystic and ecstatic certainty. For Jonathan Edwards, it was a vision
of God: "Once, as I rode out into the woods for my health, in
1737, . . . I had a view that for me was extraordinary, of the glory
of the Son of God." Or, for Edward Taylor, who wrote his poems
shortly after Bradstreet, "When first thou on me, Lord, wrought'st
thy Sweet Print,/My heart was made thy tinder box" ("The Ebb
and Flow"). From Taylor and Edwards, it is a small step to the
"transparent eyeball" of Emerson, to that transcendence which has
been common among the male poets.[16]

Anne Bradstreet, however, could not transcend. As she wrote to
her children, "I never saw any miracles to confirm me."[17] Neither
did she see any miracles performed by others, nor did any miracles
(e.g., transcendency or mystical experiences or special "visions") occur for her. In fact, as has often been pointed out, this model
American Puritan wife and mother not only experienced no miracles
but also flirted with atheism ("Many times hath Satan troubled me
concerning the verity of the Scriptures, many times by atheism how
I could know whether there was a God") and with the Roman

Catholic Church ("why may not the Popish religion be the right?").
As she says in her letter, her only recourse was self-examination: "I
have argued thus with myself." Her conclusion is that there must be
a God and that, "If ever this God hath revealed himself, it must
be in His word" (not, obviously, in a transcendent experience or
miracle). Thus she formed a belief in a God whose presence she
never experienced. At least He offered a better world hereafter.

Many American women poets would later follow just such a
course—a belief in a God who refused to make any personal appear-
ances, so to speak. Atheism, as in Bradstreet's case, or agnosticism
has often been an option. Emily Dickinson, the wavering and rebel-
lious "Atheist," was not unique, nor was Edna St. Vincent Millay's
later agnosticism. On the other hand, such limited theism has not
kept the women from writing a number of superior religious poems.
In Bradstreet's work, the affirmation of a God comes in sickness in
a number of poems, including her earliest extant poem, "Upon a
Fit of Sickness, Anno 1632 *Aetatis Suae*, 19"; in the woods, as in
"Contemplations"; in Biblical elaboration, as in "The Vanity of All
Worldly Things"; or in traditional morality pieces, such as "The
Flesh and the Spirit."

In the verse of later American women, limited theism appears in
lyrics, elegies, and other forms, but perhaps their religious beliefs
have found most successful expression in hymns, such as Julia Ward
Howe's "The Battle Hymn of the Republic" (1861), Katharine Lee
Bates's "O beautiful for spacious skies" (1904), or Julia Bulkley
Cady Cory's "We praise thee, O God, our Redeemer, Creator" (first
sung in 1902). Even there, however, there is a separation between
woman and God (as opposed to the hymns by English women, such
as Sarah Flowers Adams's "Nearer, My God, to Thee" [1841]).

Bradstreet had difficulty getting "nearer" to God, but, as she
wandered in the woods, she could at least reason a God from nature.
"Contemplations" has often been called "pre-Romantic,"[18] but it
seems to me rather a curious blend of two elements—Puritan natural
typology (especially stanzas 4–7) and natural theology (reasoning the
existence of God from nature, or empirically), a movement which
later led to English Deism.[19] In "Contemplations," there is none of
the sense of unity or sympathy with nature so typical of the verse
of both English and American Romantics. Although "every little
pine needle expanded and swelled with sympathy and befriended"
Thoreau (*Walden*, V), they certainly did not even nod to Anne Bradstreet. In fact, there were few American woman poets, even in the
nineteenth century, whom the pine needles befriended. The robins
and bees about whom Emily Dickinson wrote did not respond to

her, even though she may have learned from or even sympathized with them.

Anne Bradstreet, who always thought of herself as English, thus foreshadows the development of poetry by American women in a variety of ways. In this sense, she stands apart from her sister poets in England, who were busy establishing their own tradition. However, after Bradstreet's death in 1672 and for the next approximately eighty years, poetry by American women nearly disappeared as the Puritan oligarchy became firmly established. When the dark and silent days for the poetry of American women finally ended, it was to some extent with the help of the women poets in England.

The Puritan Poets

The years between the second and third editions (first and second American editions) of Bradstreet's poetry (1678–1758) represent the only interval since the settlement of Massachusetts Bay Colony in 1630 until today that American women have not written poetry which is assertive and original in some way or another. We should note, however, that no really original verse by men was tolerated by the Puritan fathers either. Yet the men did write much more poetry at this time, and it was published. I can find only seven women (including one uncertain case) whom we can specifically identify as poets in all these eighty years. Six of these can be classified as "Puritan poets." Because they are so exceptional, I list them here:

1. Anne Yale Hopkins (?–1698): perhaps a poet. No work survives. We know of her interests only from a note in John Winthrop's *History of New England*:

> [April 13, 1645.] Mr. Hopkins, the governor of Hartford upon Connecticut, came to Boston, and brought his wife with him, (a godly young woman, of special parts,) who was fallen into a sad infirmity, the loss of her understanding and reason, which had been growing upon her divers years, by occasion of her giving herself wholly to reading and writing, and had written many books. Her husband, being very loving and tender of her, was loath to grieve her; but he saw his error, when it was too late. For if she had attended her household affairs, and such things as belong to women, and not gone out of her way and calling to meddle in such things as are proper for men, whose minds are stronger, etc., she had kept her wits, and might have improved them usefully and honorably in the place God had set her. He brought her to Boston, and left her with her brother, one Mr. Yale, a merchant,

to try what means might be had here for her. But no help could be had.[20]

2. Mercy Dudley Woodbridge, Anne Bradstreet's sister (dates unknown): one poem, which was last mentioned in 1829, now lost.[21]

3. Sarah Kemble Knight (1661–1727): five doggerel verses which survive in her *Journal*.[22]

4. Anna Tompson Hayden (or Haiden) (1648?–after 1714): two elegiac poems.[23]

5. Martha Brewster (dates unknown): *Poems on Divers Subjects*, seventeen poems and two acrostics in her own volume of poetry! This book was published in 1757 in New London, Connecticut, and then in 1759 in Boston.

6. Esther Hayden (?–1758): one sixty-seven-line poem in *A Short Account of the Life, Death, and Character of Esther Hayden, the Wife of Samuel Hayden of Braintree*, published in Boston in 1759.

The seventh woman who wrote during this period was Jane Colman Turell, whose poetic remains were picked over and published by her father and husband in 1735. However, her verse represents the interests and talents of women in the later eighteenth century. She was not a Puritan poet, as will be discussed in Chapter 2. For her, the "dark days" were at least partially illuminated.

The women I have listed were all from New England; women in the middle Atlantic states did not publish until the later eighteenth century, and, with a few exceptions, women in the South did not publish verse until the early nineteenth century. Altogether it is a miserable and tragic record, especially after the vigorous beginning of Anne Bradstreet. The women in England were actively versifying at the time, and, in France, women translators, such as Anne Lefèvre Dacier (1654–1720), were gaining prestige. Something was wrong in the New World, and it is worth our while to examine the various hindrances to women's verse at this time.

First, no intellectual freedom existed in Massachusetts Bay Colony, even for the men. However, the image of Anne Hutchinson must have haunted many women, and most of those killed at Salem for witchcraft in the 1690's were women. On the other hand, one must wonder why women did not publish verse in the other colonies either. In fact, the only poetry by women came from Massachusetts Bay, so the lack of intellectual freedom cannot be the only factor.

Another hindrance was most certainly the Puritan marriage. As John Winthrop explained in 1645, "civil" or "federal" liberty places man in "subjection" to the theocratic state, just as woman is in subjection to her husband: "The liberty is maintained and exercised in a way of subjection to authority; it is of the same kind of liberty wherewith Christ hath made us free. The woman's own choice makes such a man her husband; yet being so chosen, he is her lord, and she is to be subject to him, yet in a way of liberty, not of bondage; and a true wife accounts her subjection her honor and freedom, and would not think her condition safe and free, but in her subjection to her husband's authority."[24] Wife is to husband as husband is to Christ. On the other hand, the Puritans believed that everyone (male or female) is equal before God: a saint is a saint. Even a female saint, however, must live in the "liberty" of "subjection" to her husband. It is no coincidence that one of the last of the Puritan women poets, Martha Brewster, warned her soon-to-be married sister-in-law that she must not "love" her husband too much for fear of provoking God. Ironically, the "liberty" of "subjection" could, at least for these Puritan women, be broken only by the greater love for God.

A third hindrance to women's verse is the general illiteracy of women in the New World. In a land in which literacy was not very high to begin with, the literacy of women was particularly low.[25] The Puritans did allow girls to attend the primary schools, where they learned only to read, not to write.[26] However, in the late seventeenth century, there was a decline even in this tentative educational situation.[27] In short, the girls had to depend on fathers, brothers, or husbands to teach them to read and write. Again, Martha Brewster's poems indicate the end of the dark and silent days, as she urges her daughter to "Increase in Learning" and "delight in Reading." Anne Bradstreet and, presumably, Anne Yale Hopkins had been educated by their families in England.

A final reason, perhaps, for the almost total lack of women's verse at this time is the physical conditions of pioneer life. For the women, even more than for the men, such conditions were crucial. It is sufficient to mention the baby-a-year policy, or the one-room cottages and cabins in which most families lived.[28] Only the wealthy could afford multiple-room homes; thus only the wives of governors, such as Bradstreet and Hopkins, could have "a room of their own." Even in the less affluent homes, the male writers could escape to their offices, whether commercial, legal, or clerical, or to the woods, while the women were left with the many children in small cottages or cabins.

The women who did manage to write verse and who did have it published are therefore noteworthy. Clearly, it took a special kind of woman to write in those dark and silent days.

Sarah Kemble Knight was a diarist, a poet, and a businesswoman. She lived most of her life in Boston and married Richard Knight sometime before 1689. Before he died (sometime before 1706), they had a daughter. Madame Knight (where she got the Madame no one knows) kept a shop in Boston for some time and owned land in Connecticut, where her daughter lived after her marriage. Her *Journal* records her journey in 1704 from Boston to New Haven and then to New York. *The Journal of Madame Knight* was first published in 1825.

Her five brief verses appear mixed with the prose narrative early in the *Journal*. Knight has no real sense of herself as a poet, but her verse is not devotional nor even remotely religious. It is honest, funny, and outspoken:

I ask thy Aid, O Potent Rum!
To Charm these wrangling Topers Dum.
Thou hast their Giddy Brains possest—
The man confounded wth the Beast—
And I, poor I, can get no rest.
Intoxicate them with thy fumes:
O still their Tongues till morning comes!

Of an inn whose facilities she finds despicable, she writes:

May all that dread the cruel feind of night
Keep on, and not at this curs't Mansion light.
'Tis Hell; 'tis Hell! and Devills do here dwell:
Here dwells the Devill—surely this's Hell.
Nothing but Wants: a drop to cool yo'r Tongue
Cant be procur'd these cruel Feinds among.
Plenty of horrid Grins and looks sevear,
Hunger and thirst, But pitty's bannish'd here—
The Right hand keep, if Hell on Earth you fear!

Her spirit was unusual for a Puritan woman, as was her career.

Anna Tompson Hayden was the half-sister of the Puritan poet Benjamin Tompson, who is considered the first native-born poet of America. We know very little about her, except that she came from a cultured family, married Ebenezer Hayden of Boston and Braintree sometime before 1679, and had a child in 1679.[29] Her two poems which survive are "Upon the Death of yt desireable young uirgin, Elizabeth Tompson, Daughter of Joseph & Mary Tompson of Bileri-ka, who Deseased in Boston out of the hous of Mr legg, 24 August, 1712, aged 22 years" and "Verses on Benjamin Tompson, by his sister, Anna Hayden."[30] The better of the two elegies concerns her niece, the "desireable young uirgin":

> A louely flower Cropt in its prime
>   By Deaths Cold fatall hand;
> A warning hear is left for all
>   Ready prepard to stand.
> For none Can tell who shall be next,
>   Yet all may it expect;
> Then surely it Concerneth all,
>   Their time not to neglect.
> How many awfull warnings that
>   Before us oft are sett,
> That as a flameing sword to mind
>   Our youth hath often mett,
> To stop them in their Cours
>   & mind them of their end,
> To make them to Concider
>   Whither their ways to tend.
> We se one suddainly taken hence
>   That might haue liud as long
> For the few years sheed liued hear
>   As any she liued among.
> Her harmles blameless life
>   Will stand for her defence,
> And be an honour to her name
>   Now she is gone from hence.
>   *a supliment*
> Charity bids us hope that sheel among those uirgins be,
>   When Christ shall Com to rain,
> Whome he will own a mong the wise,
>   & for his entertain.

The moral lesson of the event and the eulogy for the pure dead woman mark this poem as typical of the elegies of the American Puritans. Hayden's longer elegy for her brother is similar, except for one important detail. Hayden notes that she and her brother were good friends—a fact which apparently surprised some people:

Many a time we walk't together
& with discorce haue pleasd each other.
(Sum yt haue wondred how i could find
Discours with you to pleas your mind.)

The implication is that a woman could not "Discours" intelligently
enough to "pleas" a man's mind.

We know even less of Esther Hayden; perhaps she was a relative
of Anna Hayden. She was married to Samuel Hayden of Braintree,
had eight children (one of whom preceded her in death), and died
in 1758. *A Short Account of the Life, Death, and Character of Esther
Hayden* contains a brief biographical sketch, a long poem by Hayden, and some "verses" concerning her by a "near relative" who
claims to have known her for over twenty years. The "near relative"
tells us that she was "A meek and quiet Spirit" who was "saving,
diligent, and neat" and who "well adorned her Place."
   Her poem was "composed about Six Weeks before her Death,
when under distressing Circumstances, . . . —She lay Sick, in this
melancholy and sorrowful Case, above one Year." Faced with death,
she urges friends to draw near to hear her and also begs Jesus to
"bow" his "Ear." Although she hopes to go to heaven, she feels
great uncertainty as to her status with God:

I'm sore distress'd, and greatly 'press'd
   With filthy Nature, Sin;
I cannot rise to view the Prize
   Of happiness within.
The Vale above, where Jesus loves:
   He loves unto the End;
O that I'd a sense hereof
   When these few Lines I penn'd!

Like Anne Bradstreet, Mrs. Hayden has not seen "miracles" either
—even on her deathbed. The poem ends in advice to her children
to fear God and to pray daily and in a warning to her friends to
turn to God. Her choice of meter—the fourteener or iambic heptam-
eter—is that used by Michael Wigglesworth in *Day of Doom*
(1662), that great best-seller among the Puritans until the mid-
eighteenth century.

While Esther Hayden lay dying, Martha Brewster of Lebanon,

Connecticut, was writing more ambitious and interesting verse. She
had some sense of herself as a poet, but her references, allusions,
and influences are still limited to the Bible and the general culture
of American Puritanism. Apparently, a number of people doubted
whether or not she had actually written her poems, and thus she was
forced to paraphrase a Psalm extemporaneously in the presence of
a number of witnesses—clearly, a humiliating circumstance. She was
proud of being a woman poet, as she tells us in her verse introduction to *Poems on Divers Subjects*:

> Pardon her bold Attempt who has reveal'd
> Her thoughts to View, more fit to be Conceal'd
> Since thus to do was urged Vehemently,
> Yet most no doubt will call it Vanity;
> Condemn the Stile you may without Offence,
> Call it Insipid, wanting Eloquence.
>
> .   .   .   .
>
> For why my Muse had but a single Aim,
> My self and nearest Friends to Entertain;
> But since some have a gust for Novelty,
> I here presume upon your Clemency,
> For rare it is to see a *Female Bard,*
> Or that my sex in print have e're appeared:
> Let me improve my Talent tho' but small,
> And thus it humbly wait upon you shall.

This is the first example of heroic couplets written by an American
woman since Bradstreet's verse. We must wonder with what other
"Female Bards" Brewster was familiar; her poetry reflects Bradstreet
only vaguely at most, and there seems to be no influence at all of
the English women poets.

Her poems are generally standard Puritan fare: "On the last
Judgment," a shorter and less legalistic version in fourteeners of
Day of Doom; "A Prayer"; an elegy (for the Reverend Isaac Watts,
known to the Puritans for his hymns and piety); paraphrases of
Psalms; "God's Judgments are our Monitors" ("Prepare, prepare
to meet an Angry God"); and "On the Four Ages of Man," which
we are told, resemble "the four Seasons of the Year." It is possible
that, in this poem in heroic couplets, she joined together Brad-
street's "Of the Four Ages of Man" and "The Four Seasons of the
Year," but the topic was not uncommon among the Puritans.[31] In
"To the Subjects of the Special Grace of God and it's Oppressors.
Compos'd Aug. 1741," she seems to reflect the first surge of New

England's Great Awakening. In these several poems, Brewster exhibits a metaphoric flow which is paralleled in Puritan sermons of the time—a flow which is certainly not inimical to poetic expression.

In other poems, however, Brewster's verse indicates that the dark and silent days for the Puritan women were coming to an end. I have already mentioned her poems to her sister-in-law and to her daughter. Two poems deal with events normally reserved for male verse: "Braddock's Defeat, July 9, 1755" and "To the Memory of that worthy Man Liet. NATHANAEL Burt of *Springfield*" who died "in the Battle of Lake-George in the Retreat, September 8th, 1753." The first line of the elegy for Burt suggests Brewster's desire to do something different (even if unsuccessful) in verse: "Oh! - - - - - - - - - he - - - - - - - - - is - - - - - - - - - gone." "The Noble Man" is not, as might be expected for a Puritan, a minister or a civil officer, but is rather Anyman with Wisdom, Prudence, and Virtue. Brewster also wrote an acrostic for her "Only Son," a prayer for her "Only Daughter" (who was married but had no children), and a poem for her two grandsons (the children of her daughter: Brewster's prayer was answered). Her acrostic for her husband is a love poem which approaches the quality of Anne Bradstreet's amatory verse:

Oh, may propitious Heaven still extend,
Lasting Delights, to Solace thee my Friend;
Injoying ev'ry lawful Sweet below;
Viewing by Faith, the Fountain whence they Flow,
Erected be his Throne, within thy Heart,
Rule and Replenish there, thy ev'ry Part

Blest with a Vine, whose Love and Loyalty,
Richest than choicest Wine her Progeny,
Each like an Olive Branch adorn thy House,
With the Fair Transcript of thy loving Spouse:
Soft are the Charms inviolable Bands,
Twine round the Lovers Heart, Raptur'd he stands:
Eternal King that hath these Powers giv'n,
Renew our Love to Thee, and Love us up to Heaven.

Chapter Two

1735-1804

Another Kind of Independence

Literary historians have spent a great deal of time searching for something good to say of the mid- and late eighteenth century in American cultural history. Alas, the literary output of these years is a national embarrassment, as any man will admit:

> . . . poetasters abounded in mid-eighteenth-century America. We remember their names—Mather Bales, William Livingston, Thomas Godfrey, Benjamin Church, among them—not because of the poems they wrote, but just because they wrote poems. Their work was painfully derivative, seizing upon the best English models, now Pope, now Milton, in order to get guaranteed effects. . . . For they wrote imitations of imitations of imitations. There was no pressing need for a poetry, as Franklin, like many others writing in the same vein, testified, and have been testifying ever since.[1]

Only two poets seem to be worth anybody's serious attention: Philip Freneau, whose poetry is generally treated only as a precursor to American nineteenth-century Romanticism, and Joel Barlow, whose *Columbiad* (1807) is the first American democratic "epic" (if such a thing can exist). Our critics long ago concluded that the period produced many poetasters, but no real poets as such and very little poetry worth reading (although some is worth "examining").

If it was, however, a nonproductive period for the men, it was an extremely important time for the women. It begins with the censored verse of Jane Turell and ends with Susanna Rowson's artistically self-conscious and gentle verse of *Miscellaneous Poems* (1804). In those years alone, at least twelve different women published a significant number of poems, either in journals, such as *The Columbian Magazine*, or in book form. Six other women published a limited number of poems in the journals. These women are only the ones who are clearly identifiable, either because they wrote under their own names or because they published obviously feminine verse under feminine pseudonyms. The dam was to burst after 1800, but the trickle had begun.

What is even more important, however, is the quality of verse written by these American women. It is surprising that the women of this period wrote such clever, intelligent, and, at times, profound verse: that they had something original to say in a time of "imitation." Like the men, they did continue to imitate English verse forms and poetic conventions, but, within the prescribed structure, they presented new modes of expression and new angles of vision. We should not, I think, be embarrassed by the verse written by Americans from 1735 to 1800.

Jane Colman Turell (1708–1735)

By her dates, her ancestry, and her marriage, Jane Turell should have been a Puritan poet and should have been discussed in the preceding chapter. She represents, however, a new generation of women who were approaching cultural sophistication, who searched for other women as models, and whose ideas were not limited to the Puritan's two "Books" (the Bible and nature). Her poems and prose survive only in truncated form in an elegiac volume, some sections of which were written by her father, the prominent Puritan minister and president of Harvard College Benjamin Colman, and other sections by her husband, the Reverend Mr. Ebenezer Turell, M.A.: *Reliquiae Turellae et Lacrymae Paternae. Two Sermons Preach'd at Medford, April 6, 1735 . . . To Which are added some long memoirs of her life and death* (1735).

Jane was educated by her father, who was quite justly proud of her and with whom she exchanged poems when she was only eleven years old. Benjamin Colman states that, between ages five and ten, "she lov'd the *School* and the Exercises of it and made a laudable Progress in the various kinds of learning proper to her Age and Sex." What exactly he taught her in his school is not clear, but, like the boys in her day, she was well grounded in the classics and the Bible, as is evident from references in her poems. Later, before she was eighteen, "she had read and (in some measure) digested all the English *Poetry*, and polite pieces in *Prose*, printed and Manuscripts in her Father's well furnish'd Library, and much she borrow'd of her Friends and Acquaintance."

She married Ebenezer Turell in 1726 and continued to write a prose or verse "essay" once a month, but, as her husband is careful to point out, "she made the writing of Poetry a Recreation and not a Business." Despite all the evidence Colman had already given in the preceding pages of this volume, Turell himself wanted credit for having educated Jane: "what greatly contributed to increase her knowledge in *Divinity, History, Physick, Controversy*, as well as *Poetry*, was her attentive hearing most that I read upon those Heads thro' the long Evenings of the Winters as we sat together." Turell favored the poetry of Sir Richard Blackmore and Edmund Waller, and the poems he chose to cite from Jane's marital years are terrible: stiff, full of clichés, imitations of Horace, a panegyric to Waller ("Hail Chaste Urania"), these poems resemble those written by the male poetasters of her day, now so justly condemned by literary historians. And yet she must have written other kinds of poems, for, as Ebenezer Turell points out, "I might add to these some Pieces of Wit and Humour, which if published would give a brighter Idea of her to some sort of Readers; but as her Heart was set upon graver and better Subjects, and her Pen much oftener employ'd about them, so I chuse to omit them, tho' innocent enough."

The little volume concludes with Jane's father getting the final word. In a postscript, Colman briefly outlines his methods for educating his daughter and urges other parents to follow his example. The conflict between Colman and Turell over Jane's mind and over the body of her writing is obvious and frightening. As literary executor, neither Colman nor Turell is honest or complete, but Colman is more thorough, and clearly his influence upon Jane's poetry was more favorable. Colman gave her a certain freedom to explore in her verse, but her husband set out to mold her to his tastes; thus, at least so far as we can judge from what verse has survived, he ruined her mind and her art. The pattern of the free daughter for whom marriage is a restriction could not be better exemplified. It is just this pattern which Page Smith has found to exist throughout American society,[2] and just such domination on the part of the husband which ultimately caused the traditional Puritan concept of marriage to collapse. Most later American women poets have not suffered from such domination, although it is true that many began their careers only after their husbands' deaths and that others remained single.

One of the more interesting undercurrents in this volume is Jane's interest in improving "her Sex." Her father, not threatened by an intelligent and talented daughter, approvingly states, "I find she was sometimes fir'd with a laudable Ambition of raising the honour of her Sex, who are therefore under Obligation to her." However, the introduction to the book is a long epistolary poem by the Reverend John Adams, addressed to Ebenezer Turell (not Colman), in which it is clearly pointed out that "Nor was She vain, nor stain'd with those Neglects,/In which too learned Females lose their Sex."

Among the slight quantity of verse left, Jane Turell's best poems are those written before her marriage in 1726, all therefore composed before she was eighteen. They are the productions of a young woman, somewhat immature. Many of the poems which her father chose to reproduce are paraphrases of the Psalms, a traditional Puritan genre. In one poem labeled as a paraphrase, however, her verse runs beyond the Biblical passage. Based on "the *Fifth Chapter of Canticles* paraphras'd from the *8th.* verse," this poem was written in 1725, shortly before her marriage:

You beauteous *Dames*, if that my *Love* you see,
With eager Steps conduct him here to me,
Tell him no Joy to me you can impart,
And that no Pain is like a bleeding Heart.
Say I am *sick of Love*, and moaningly,
Whilst the sad *Eccho* to my Groan's reply,
   Who is thy Love? the scornful *Maids* reply,
And for what *Form* waste you your Bloom in sighs?
Let's know the *Man*, if he be worth your Care,
Or does deserve the Tender Love you bear.
   Whilst your Request with Pleasure I obey,
Your strict Attention give to what I say.
My *Love* excells all that's on Earth call'd Fair,
As the bright *Sun* excells the meanest Star.
His Head is Wisdoms spacious Theatre,
Riches of Grace and Beauty there appear.
A down his Shoulders with becoming Pride
Falls his fine Hair in beauteous Ringletts ty'd.
His sparkling Eyes in splendent Lustre vie,
With the Twin Stars that grace the azure Sky.
His cheeks excel the fragrant blushing Rose
Which in the fruitful Vale of *Sharon* grows.
His lips like *Lillies* in their flowry Bloom

Yield a sweet Odour and a rich Perfume.
His Ivory Arms more charming to behold
Than orient Pearls, incas'd in shining Gold.
His well turn'd Legs like stately Pillars stand
Of Marble, polish'd by a curious Hand.
His Mien is noble and august his Air,
His Countenance as *Lebanon* doth appear.

Like Bradstreet, Turell turned to *The Song of Solomon* (*Canticles*) for appropriate images to express love. Turell's "paraphrase" and Bradstreet's "As loving hind," however, exhibit several important differences: First, Turell is interested in expressing the physical beauty of the man, while Bradstreet uses conceits to express the quality of her love for her husband (in "To My Dear and Loving Husband," it is again the quality of love which is described). Second, Bradstreet's poem is apparently part of a letter to her husband, personal and intimate; Turell's poem is in the form of a dialogue in a social setting. The poet is declaiming before a group of women ("Dames" and "Maids") the physical beauty of a man. Neither poem mentions God, although Bradstreet does refer to herself as "wife," a religiously sacred position in Puritan society. If, by chance, Turell's "Love" is meant to be Jesus, he is an extremely physical and sexually desirable Jesus.

Turell's "paraphrase" is the first amatory poem by an American woman to center upon the sensual nature of love. The poet is "sick of Love" and "moaning." Such a convention is not at all new for male poets, but it certainly is for women poets in America. Moreover, such sensual awareness is not something to be confided only to one's husband, but is to be told to other women. Finally, the man is not seen as a "husband," but as a lover (not, however, in an adulterous sense, but rather as a suitor). It is clear that Turell's images, derived in large part from *The Song of Solomon*, and even her attitude toward love are derivative from male verse. However, this poem marks a beginning of imaginative freedom in the amatory verse of American women.

Turell's consciousness of herself as a woman, as noted by her father, is evident in a brief poem, "On reading the Warning by Mrs. Singer." Elizabeth Singer Rowe, "Philomela," was English, a popular and pious writer of hymns, pastorals, and scriptural paraphrases. Although she published a number of poems before 1710 (the year of her marriage to Rowe), I have not found any one which is specifically a "Warning." However, several poems contain traditional warnings of hell and eternal damnation. One such poem, "An Ode on Virtue," traces historical examples of both sinful and virtuous men, but concludes with two extremely virtuous women (Eulalia and Nicetas, both of whom bravely confront stern and sinful men). Perhaps it is this poem which so stirred Jane Turell:

> Surpriz'd I view, wrote by a *Female* Pen,
> Such a grave Warning to the Sons of Men.
> Bold was the attempt and worthy of your Lays,
> To strike at Vice, and sinking Virtue raise.
> Each noble Line a pleasing Terror gives,
> A secret Force in every Sentence lives.
> Inspir'd by Virtue you could safely stand
> The *fair Reprover* of a guilty land.
> You vie with the fam'd Prophetess of old,
> Burn with her Fire, in the Cause grow bold.
> Dauntless you undertake th' unequal strife,
> And raise dead Virtue by your verse to life.
> A *Woman's* Pen strikes the curs'd *Serpents* Head,
> And lays the Monster gasping, if not dead.

Evidently, at this point in her life, Turell had read no other poetry by women, not even Bradstreet's verse (it is not evident that she ever did read Bradstreet's verse). What seems to have amazed Turell is Rowe's courageous aggressiveness in warning men of their sins, as well as the quality of a "Woman's Pen." The prophetess to whom Rowe is compared is Huldah, as the reader is told in a footnote. Huldah (2 Kings 22: 14–20) was a kind of Hebrew Sibyl of Cumae, a vessel for the Lord's words, who lived "in the college" in Jerusalem. Other than her Biblical paraphrases, however, the only "warning" or "reforming" spirit in Turell's verse is contained in a short (16-line) poem, "Imitation of 133 *Psalm*," intended as a plea for peace during "Some unhappy Affairs of *Medford* in the Years 1729 & 30," as her husband tells us.

Her interest in women is further evident in an early poem which is a welcome to a female friend who has returned from a journey (only eight lines are preserved), and in 1725 she addressed a poem "To My Muse." Her poetic models are all women:

> Come Gentle Muse, and once more lend thine aid,
> O bring thy Succour to a humble Maid!
> How often dost thou liberally dispense

To our dull Breast thy quick'ning Influence!
By thee inspir'd, I'll cheerful tune my Voice,
And Love and sacred Friendship make my Choice.
In my pleas'd Bosom you can freely pour,
A greater Treasure than *Joves Golden Shower.*
Come now, *fair Muse,* and fill my empty Mind,
With rich Idea's, great and unconfin'd.
Instruct me in those secret arts that lie
Unseen to all but to a *Poet's* Eye.
O let me burn with *Sappho's* noble Fire,
But not like her for faithless Man expire.
And let me rival great *Orinda's* Fame,
Or like sweet Philomela's be my Name.
Go lead the way, my Muse, nor must you stop,
'Till we have gain'd *Parnassus* shady Top:
'Till I have viewed those fragrant soft Retreats,
Those Fields of Bliss, the Muses sacred Seats.
I'll then devote thee to fair *Virtues* Fame,
And so be worthy of a Poet's Name.

This poem was apparently inspired by Sappho, by the pious poems of "Philomela" (Rowe), and by the "neo-Platonic" poetry of "the great Orinda," Katherine Philips. Artistic self-consciousness; the sense of continuity with other women; the realization of being a person who has something to offer, something better even than "Joves Golden Shower"; the growing awareness of a culture outside of Puritan America—each of these qualities was important in the development of poetry by women in America. Shortly after she wrote this poem, Jane Colman married the Reverend Mr. Turell.

Phillis Wheatley Peters (1753?–1784)

Phillis Wheatley was brought as a slave to America from Africa when she was five or six years old. Fortunately, she was owned in Boston by John Wheatley, who quickly recognized that she was a bright and precocious child. The Wheatley family saw that she was educated not just in reading and writing, but also, in the New England tradition, in the classics and the Bible. She began writing poetry as early as 1768 and continued until the end of her short life. Never a healthy woman, Wheatley was sent, while still a slave, for medical attention in 1772 to London, where she was received in London society and met Benjamin Franklin. By 1778, Wheatley was a free woman and the wife of John Peters.

A number of satisfactory modern editions and treatments of
Wheatley's poetry already exist.[3] Her verse has been both condemned and defended by black and white critics: condemned, on
one hand, because she did not use her verse to declaim against the
enslavement of her people and, on the other hand, because her
poems are "imitations of imitations"; defended because, within mid-
eighteenth-century Boston society, she had little choice in the kind
of poetry she was exposed to or was allowed to write and because
she seems no worse than the "poetasters" of her day. Her one volume
of poetry is *Poems on Various Subjects, Religious and Moral* (1773).

Two aspects of her life, which have been noted by others but
which need further emphasis, are the humiliating circumstances
preceding the publication of her book and her limited production of
poetry after her marriage to a free black, John Peters. The first pages
of the 1773 edition of her poems include a letter written by John
Wheatley, her owner, giving a brief biographical account of Phillis,
and a statement "To the Publick" attesting that the young slave
girl was truly the author of the following poems—a statement
signed by the governor and lieutenant governor of Massachusetts
and by sixteen other prominent men. A public display of talent had
also been necessary, as we have seen, before the publication of Martha Brewster's verse. The talents of women, whether black or white,
were still seriously doubted in mid-century.

After she herself became free and married Peters, Phillis wrote
very few poems. The reason for her lack of productivity is generally
recognized as the plight of the free black in Boston in the 1770's
and 1780's. Without doubt, the economic insecurity and poor living
conditions of the Peterses could only have lessened whatever poetic
inspiration she had had. Another consideration, however, should
be the births and quick deaths of three children in six years. Furthermore, as has been recently pointed out,[4] the adverse influence
of John Peters was probably as disastrous for Phillis as was the
influence of Ebenezer Turell upon Jane. Phillis, who had never been
healthy under any circumstances, died only six years after she became free.

The representative anthology pieces of Wheatley are "On Imagination," "An Hymn to the Evening," "On Being Brought from
Africa to America," and "To His Excellency, General Washington"
—all poems no better and no worse than those written by her fellow
poetasters. Full of exclamatory phrases and neoclassical abstractions,
most of her poems are "imitations of imitations." On the other
hand, there are four significant tendencies in her poems which
have not been previously noted.

Wheatley is the first American woman poet in 120 years to speak poetically of politics or other such "men's work." From Anne Bradstreet ("Dialogue between Old England and New") to Wheatley, the women had expressed pious sentiments and domestic concerns. Only Martha Brewster's two poems concerning Braddock's campaign and Turell's biblical "Imitation" which obliquely treats "Some unhappy Affairs of *Medford*" are in any way comparable. Wheatley wrote a number of such poems: for example, "To His Excellency, General Washington," "Liberty and Peace," and "To the Right Honorable William, Earl of Dartmouth." Her most bold piece in this manner was never published in her lifetime and has just recently come to light. "America,"[5] is, in fact, her most vigorous poem and indicates that her bland sweetness in the published poems was perhaps only a public face. Although not so graceful and fluid as her published verse, "America" has a metaphoric flow and honesty unique in her poetry. Moreover, it is now clear, the manuscript version of "To the King's Most Excellent Majesty, 1768" was also weakened in the published version. These poems are the first of many by women which comment on political situations in this time of revolution.

Second, a number of poems treat the death of babies and children and are generally addressed to both parents. The elegy for a child was not unusual in her day, although elegies for adults (men and women) were more prevalent. Over one hundred years before, Bradstreet had written three elegies concerning infant grandchildren. What, then, is unusual in finding these poems among Wheatley's verse? There is a comparatively large number of them, almost as many as elegies memorializing adults. Moreover, the value of infants is strongly affirmed, not only in the earthly realm, but also in the heavenly. (The dead infants are, of course, all going to heaven.) Finally, the mourning of both father and mother is noted equally. Sorrow for the dead child is not primarily the mother's, as in the poetry of women in the next century, nor are the child's parents simply omitted, as in Bradstreet's verse.

Furthermore, apparent throughout her poems is a celebration of liberty. One of her final poems, "Liberty and Peace" (1784) expresses what was for that time a common enough theme, praise of Columbia and her "blessed" freedom. It is this kind of poem for which black critics, especially, condemn her,[6] because, of course, there was no freedom for her own people in 1784. We should not forget that the optimism and belief in an ultimate "freedom for all" was a powerful hope at this time. Moreover, her opposition to "tyrannic sway" is also evident in certain prewar poems, such as "To the Right Honorable William, Earl of Dartmouth," which reads in part:

>   Should you, my lord, while you peruse my song,
> Wonder from whence my love of *Freedom* sprung,
> Whence flow these wishes for the common good,
> By feeling hearts alone best understood,
> I, young in life, by seeming cruel fate
> Was snatch'd from *Afric's* fancy'd happy seat:
> What pangs excruciating must molest,
> What sorrows labour in my parent's breast?
> Steel'd was that soul and by no misery mov'd
> That from a father seiz'd his babe belov'd:
> Such, such my case. And can I then but pray
> Others may never feel tyrannic sway?

Freedom and liberty, as themes in the poetry of Americans, began with the Puritans who came to the New World to seek freedom of worship. In the eighteenth century, the freedom sought was national freedom, but also, for Wheatley, freedom from bondage and "tyrannic sway." For her, the desire for freedom was personal, and, by extension, for her people. She spoke, I feel, as boldly as she could.

Finally, it is important to examine a poem which has been totally ignored. Wheatley's longest poem (over two hundred lines) is "Niobe in Distress for Her Children Slain by Apollo, from Ovid's Metamorphoses, Book VI, and from a View of the Painting of Mr. Richard Wilson." The poem concerns Niobe, a woman from classical mythology, the proud and boastful mother of seven daughters and seven sons, whose children were brutally murdered by Apollo and his sister Artemis, after Niobe had urged the Thebans to cease their worship of Leto (the mother of Apollo and Artemis). As poetry, it reads much like other "imitations" in the eighteenth century, written by either men or women. Its subject matter is notable, however, because of Wheatley's interest in a mythological woman (an interest to be intensified in the poetry of women in the next century), because Wheatley chose to devote her longest poem to a woman, and because she has not followed Ovid's interpretation of Niobe. Ovid treats Niobe much more harshly: he feels that Niobe has truly sinned and deserves her fate. However, Wheatley depicts Niobe as a proud and beautiful woman who has dared to challenge the gods (as her grandfather Tantalus had). Although Wheatley calls Niobe "haughty," she omits Ovid's assertion (*Metamorphoses* 6.169–172) that Niobe had asked to be worshipped by the Thebans. In Wheatley's poem, Niobe asks the Thebans only to cease worshipping Leto. In Wheatley's (perhaps unfinished) poem, Niobe seems to be an unfortunate rebel against an established order.

Mercy Otis Warren (1728–1814)

Certainly one of the most intelligent and best educated women of her day, Mercy Otis Warren produced a variety of poetry and prose. Her farce *The Group* (1776) was the hit of revolutionary Boston; a collection of two plays and poems appeared in 1790; and her three-volume *History of the Rise, Progress, and Termination of the American Revolution, Interspersed with Biographical and Moral Observations* appeared in 1805. She wrote other farces, as well as an anti-Federalist pamphlet, *Observations on the New Constitution, and on the Federal and State Conventions* (1788). There is no modern edition of her works, but there are two twentieth-century biographies, one facsimile edition of *The Group*, and a generous discussion of her farces and plays in Arthur Hobson Quinn's *A History of the American Drama from the Beginning to the Civil War*, pp. 33–64. Of her nondramatic poetry, critics rarely speak.[7]

Mercy Otis was born into a prominent family in Barnstable, Massachusetts. When her older brother, James (who later became the celebrated "Patriot"), was being tutored by a local minister for entrance to Harvard, his sister was allowed to listen. James himself apparently completed Mercy's education during his vacations from Harvard. Fortunately, in 1754, she married a man who enjoyed intelligent women, James Warren, a Harvard friend of James Otis and John Adams. James Warren was to become a member of the Massachusetts legislature just before the war and a financial aide to Washington during the war (with the rank of major general). The friendship of the Warrens and Adamses was lifelong and close;[8] Abigail Adams was one of Mercy's few close friends. Following the war, James Warren re-entered politics to oppose the Constitution because he feared that it did not adequately provide for protection of individual rights. Mercy again joined her husband in political battle, but the passage of the Bill of Rights marked the end of their long period of political agitation. The Warrens had five sons, born between 1757 and 1766.

In whatever literary form Warren wrote, she had but one theme —liberty. In her farces and history, it was national and political freedom. In her poems, it was intellectual freedom. In her anti-Federalist pamphlet, it was individual freedom. Throughout all of these works, moreover, runs the thread of freedom (equal treatment) for women. Not "militant," she nevertheless urged men to educate their daughters and to treat their wives as equals. Her ideas concerning women were formed and had already been distributed to America long before Mary Wollstonecraft's *Vindication of the*

Rights of Women (1792) appeared.[9] In the midst of the male poet-asters' abstract and personified panegyrics to Freedom and Liberty, Warren particularized freedom and, at the same time, gave it a scope and intellectual foundation simply not evident in the poetry of the men in her day.

Two of her farces are short, in blank verse, and were never acted (nor is it clear that they were meant to be acted, because the theaters were closed during the Revolution). *The Adulateur* and *The Group* are directed against the Tories, who, the colonists felt, had betrayed them. Thomas Hutchinson, who appears as Rapatio in both farces, is depicted as a true villain, vain and cruel. Warren's pen is certainly not gentle, but as sharp and quick as that of any man in her day. The farces themselves are no longer funny to us, partially because of the now obscure topical references and partially because the historical figures on whom the fictional characters are based are now shadowy to us. The farces have little action and much conversation, and the satire is built upon exaggeration.

Warren accuses the Tories of every kind of sin and corruption, but in *The Group* she adds one evil which does not appear in other political satires of the time: the Tory men are cruel to women. In act 2, scene 3, Hateall, who has married "nut brown Kate" for her dower, speaks:

> I broke her spirits when I'd won her purse;
> For which I'll give a recipe most sure
> To ev'ry hen peck'd husband round the board;
> If crabbed words or surly looks won't tame
> The haughty shrew, nor bend the stubborn mind,
> Then the green Hick'ry, or the willow twig,
> Will prove a curse for each rebellious dame
> Who dare oppose her lord's superior will.

Simple Sappling is equally cruel to Silvia, who, Publican admits, "descended to become thy wife." The colloquialism and direct dialogue of the farces are amazingly realistic. The high rhetoric, invocations, and neoclassical abstractions which abound in the verse of most of Warren's contemporaries are remarkably absent.

Warren apparently hoped that her two tragedies, *The Sack of Rome* and *The Ladies of Castile* (both published in the 1790 edition of her *Poems*), would surpass Shakespeare. They cannot rival Shakespeare, but they are better than most of the bombast created by her contemporaries. In five acts of blank verse, the plays feature noble women acting decisively in times of national crisis. *The Sack of Rome* is the better of the two tragedies and establishes the kind of woman ("Roman matron") Warren hoped would develop in America. The ideal woman for her is Edoxia, the empress of Rome. The mother of two adolescent girls and a loyal wife to her depraved husband, Edoxia spends most of the play trying to outwit Genseric, the King of the Vandals, whose troops are now at Rome's gate. Ardelia, another one of "th' illustrious matrons" and the wife of an honest but weak Roman nobleman, has been deceived and raped by Edoxia's husband, Emperor Valentinian (who appropriately dies before act 3).

The plays are, as Quinn says, "carefully constructed" and are by no means dull. Written as moral pieces, as Warren points out in a prefatory statement, they nevertheless contain some true poetry. Strangely enough, the best lines are spoken by men (most of whom are lecherous, selfish, and brutal). For example, in *The Sack of Rome*, Traulista, a barbarian prince, questions a young man in love:

Why does my friend wear that soft April eye?

.　.　.　.　.　.　.　.　.　.

Come, be thyself again; nor longer bask
Upon the silken, downy lap of hope;
Leave her to sigh, and whisper to the winds—
Else snatch by force, and bear her o'er the wilds,
Through growling forests—hideous, broken cliffs,
And frozen seas—to Scythia's icy banks,
Where rugged winds pour from the brindled north
Adown the mountain's brow—a blast may cool
The transports of thy love.

(act 4, scene 5)

The young lover, Gaudentius, is a Roman noble in love with one of Edoxia's daughters. He is the model young Roman for whom only honorable marriage can provide relief from the "transports" of love. No double standard for Warren! I should note, however, that Warren provided more complexity in character motivation than my summary suggests. Indeed, Edoxia seeks God's help in solving such "complicated guilt."

The same general theme is repeated in *The Ladies of Castile*. The heroine is again a mother, Maria. She states to her condemned husband during their final interview:

Maternal softness weakens my resolve,
And wakes new fears—thou dearest, best of men,
Torn from thy side, I'm levell'd with my sex.
The wife—the mother—made me less than woman.

(act 4, scene 5)

Nevertheless, Maria is soon leading the troops, upon "the prancing steed."

Warren's high and optimistic estimation of woman's possibilities is undoubtedly based on her own capabilities and her own propagandistic accomplishments during the war. Warren's women can be as influential as men and are, in fact, wiser. They are capable of murder (justifiable, of course), trickery, and all kinds of male heroics. Her Roman matrons (under some influence from Joan of Arc) are Minervas, but Minervas who suckle the babe with one arm while wielding the sword with the other. This kind of woman will survive throughout the poetry of American women, but she will not, for the most part, emulate male heroics, nor will she be so active in the larger social or political scene. Warren's matrons represent an attempt to create a model for the American women of her day—a model who is by no means an Eve, nor a mystic, nor any kind of ideal woman espoused by the American men in the late eighteenth century. Warren, however, was not naïve; she was aware of the limited possibilities of success for this kind of woman: Edoxia's Rome and Maria's Castile fall to the forces of the barbarous Genseric and the vicious Charles V.

Warren's best poetry appears in her farces and plays, but her poems, generally occasional verse, reveal an analytic and educated mind attempting to solve the moral and social crises of her day. As such, her poetry is no less poetically interesting than the later, discursive verse of T. S. Eliot, or W. H. Auden's political verse of the 1930's. Indeed, in terms of reason and logical analysis, her poems are more interesting. They are imitations of English Augustan discursive verse, written in heroic couplets, but are intellectually independent.

In a 124-line poem, "To Torrismond" ("a young Gentleman educated in Europe"), Warren argues against both "superstitious" religion and Hobbesian materialism:

Then the grey druid's grave, majestic air,
The frantic priestess, with dishevell'd hair
And flaming torch, spoke superstition's reign;
While elfin damsels dancing o'er the plain,

Allur'd the vulgar by the mystic scene,
To keep long vigils on the sacred green.

. . . .

. . . artful politicians saw the jest,
And laugh'd at virtue as a state machine,
An engine fit the multitude to rein;
With more facility to rule mankind,
They lent their efforts to obscure the mind.

Her intellectual heroes are Boyle and Locke and, especially, Newton, whose authority she used to refute English Deism. We should remember that Franklin's *Autobiography*, which also refutes English Deism, was not published at this time, nor had Thomas Paine's Deistic *The Age of Reason* appeared. Warren understood the metaphysical side of Newton's work, although she appreciated his scientific discoveries and analytical methods as well. She is a traditional "Christian Deist," not a "Deist" or even a "methodical Deist" like Benjamin Franklin (if such distinctions can clearly be made).[10] The Deists, she tells Torrismond, have "The depths of erudition just skim'd o'er;/Nurs'd in refinements of a skeptic age." Their out-of-hand rejection of "revelation" is condemned. For Warren, "revelation" can be found in the Bible and in writers such as Newton.

The Deistic theories, she saw, had two weaknesses. The first is that man is not wise enough to pursue the intellectually independent course suggested by the Deist. Ironically she comments, "They all things doubt but their superiour sense." Man's reason is too weak, and he must "grope his way." Her villains are Hobbes, Hume, Shaftesbury, and Voltaire. Perhaps most interesting is her objection to Voltaire (also an intellectual follower of Locke and Newton). I suspect that she was reacting against his consistent stand against organized religion (and perhaps, considering Warren's feminist tendencies, against his brutal burlesque of Joan of Arc in *La Pucelle*, which appeared in 1755 and, in final form, in 1762).

Dependence on "frail reason," Warren felt, had forced the Deists to two positions: The first is a moral vacuum, in which no firm standards exist. For Warren, the standards are evident in the Bible and in the works of the more traditionally religious philosophers, such as Newton. The Deists, however, based their ethical considerations on individual reason and individual conscience and thus, as far as Warren could see, justified any kind of vice or any kind of "unreasonable action." The Deist had an "oscillating brain." For Warren, the various liberties she espoused could exist only in a society based on firm moral principles. (As we can see in Warren's later prose works, such moral principles were embodied at least in part in the Bill of Rights.)

Absolute dependence on "frail reason" also led the Deists, she felt, to a personal isolation and alienation from any ideas beyond their limited, individual minds and consciences. In short, Deism led to a vain and dangerous self-centeredness, an egocentrism: "They spurn . . . /The wish of man to be to God ally'd." Warren did not suggest a transcendence (no Emersonian "transparent eyeball" for her) but rather argued the necessity for man to find values outside of himself, to take history, "revelation," and religion into consideration.

She thus rejected what she saw as a morally dangerous and potentially self-destructive path. It is clear that she was not advocating Calvinism or simply "orthodox religion." She remained a Christian Deist throughout her life. In other poems, such as "To Mr. ————," she rejects a system of fatalism and Hobbesian self-love; and in "The Genius of America weeping the absurd follies of the Day," Warren's criticism of the Deists, one of whom she calls "a smooth romantic bard," produces some of her best verse:

> An *ignis fatuus* floats from lake to bog,
> The vapor plays in pestilential fogs,
> Sparkes and sinks in the dark marshy tomb,
> As modern wits in metaphysic fume.

Her poems are also political and social; "The Squabble of the Sea-Nymphs; or the Sacrifice of the Tuscararoes" concerns the Boston Tea Party. In the epilogue to a long poem, "Simplicity," she mentions "The narrow bounds, prescribed to female life." And, although the "mother" is "kind," she acts a "little part."[11] Another poem, "To the Hon. J. Winthrop, Esq.," satirizes women who devote their lives to luxury and adornment, but the men who court such ladies are gently chastised too.

Warren was not without intelligence and humor. Her poetry is certainly not so weak as the current critical neglect suggests. Moreover, in light of the social and political history of America, her poems, farces, and plays are certainly more valuable and interesting than the poetry of the Connecticut Wits. She was a woman who refused to allow herself to be limited to woman's prescribed "narrow bounds" and, in her refusal, found an intellectual and artistic independence.

Ann Eliza Bleecker (1752–1783)

The best lyric poet of her day was Ann Eliza Bleecker, whose verse appeared only posthumously, in 1793.[12] What we have of her verse is only a small portion of what she wrote. She destroyed all the poetry she wrote before her marriage in 1769; and much of her poetry written after 1769 (described as "satires, songs, and burlesques") was given to friends and has since disappeared. Despite the fact that her literary remains are meager and that some of these surviving poems are imitations of imitations, Bleecker has a true lyric voice, an intimate and personal style (many of her poems are actually letters in verse, and this personal quality carried over into her other poems), a teasing and sophisticated wit, and, at the same time, a profound sense of personal limitation in the face of the infinite universe.

Bleecker was born in New York City into a prosperous family. She read early, but did not like "school." What this school was or what was taught is not recorded. She apparently wrote a great deal of verse at an early age, and it is not clear why she destroyed this early work. Her husband, John Bleecker, seems to have at least tolerated her poetry and obviously allowed her to buy whatever books she chose. (After her marriage, as her poems and letters indicate, she read Shakespeare and such classics as Homer, Virgil, Tasso, and Donne, among many others.) The only explanation given for the destruction of her verse is her daughter's (Faugères's) belief that her father was slow "to cherish her [mother's] genius."

The Bleeckers lived most of their lives on inherited lands in the then wilderness area near Tomhanick, in upstate New York. Their home was large and comfortable, a garden in the wilderness, where Mrs. Bleecker played with her children, wrote her poems, and fed the wild birds, which she allowed no one to kill and which nested in the porch of the house. But her home was not an Eden: in 1777, at the approach of Burgoyne's forces, she and her two small daughters fled to Albany, where Mr. Bleecker, unaware of Burgoyne's proximity, had gone to arrange for lodgings for his family. It was a difficult journey, and one of the little girls died. In 1783, while John Bleecker and his men were harvesting the fall crops, he was captured by Loyalist raiders but was rescued after six days. Shortly after, Ann Bleecker died.

Included in the 1793 volume are two prose works, both short stories, "founded on facts." "The History of Maria Kittle" tells of a vicious Indian attack upon a wilderness home during the French and Indian War. "The Story of Henry and Anne" concerns the immigration of a young German and his childhood sweetheart to America. They are biographical sketches, written with honesty and surprising boldness. More interesting, however, are Bleecker's prose letters to friends which provide a description of her life and the wilderness perils, as well as some of Bleecker's personal observations and beliefs. For example, she reports that when women she knows discuss politics there is "nonsensical controversy." And she defends Jeffersonian agrarianism: "There is a great gulph between the vulgar aspects of nature, and the artificial, mechanical sons of ceremony."

Most significant, however, is her poetry, which obviously was simply a part of her usual means of communication with others. (Like that of Dickinson, her poetry was conceived as her "letter to the World.") Many poems, as I have said, are actually letters. Concerning others, Faugères tells us: "As most of these pieces were intended for the amusement of herself and particular friends, and not for the public eye, they appeared as they flowed extempore from her pen. Frequently she wrote while with company, at the desire of someone present, without premeditation, and at the same time bearing a part of the conversation." Thus her poems often need revision; she is not quite aware of herself as an artist; and many of her poems are for a specific occasion.

One such poem, "To Mr. L****," concerns a crowd of her husband's friends rather drunkenly celebrating New Year's Day in the Bleecker home. The "elegant" rhetoric of the first stanzas is a conscious parody of the pastoral tradition, as the rest of the poem reveals:

> The sun that gilds the western sky
>   And makes the orient red,
> Whose gladsome rays delight the eye
>   And cheer the lonely shade,
>
> Withdraws his vegetative heat,
>   To southern climes retires;
> While absent, we supply his seat
>   With gross, material fires.
>
> 'Tis new year's morn; each rustic swain
>   Ambrosial cordials take;
> And round the fire the festive train
>   A semi-circle make:

While clouds ascend, of sable smoke,
From pipes of ebon hue,
With inharmonick song and joke
They pass the morning through.

You tell me this is solitude,
This Contemplation's seat;
Ah, no! the most impervious wood
Affords me no retreat.

But let me recollect: 'tis said
When *Orpheus* tun'd his lyre
The Fauns and Satyrs left the shade,
Warm'd by celestial fire.

His vocal lays and lyra made
Inanimated marble weep,
Swift-footed Time then paus'd, 'tis said,
And sea-born monsters left the deep:

Impatient trees, to hear his strain
Rent from the ground their roots:—
Such is my fate, as his was then
Surrounded here—by brutes.[13]

In a series of two poems to the same "Mr. L.," she writes a mock-heroic sequence concerning the death of a gander and the widow goose's search for a new husband. Light and clever, the lines move easily. It is possible that the goose and gander are actually acquaintances of the poet and Mr. L. Contained in the prologue of the first poem is one of Bleecker's only extant critical judgments concerning poetry. Apparently, Bleecker and Mr. L. had previously agreed to write each other in verse:

You've broke th'agreement, Sir, I find;
(Excuse me, I must speak my mind)
It seems in your poetic fit,
You mind not jingling, where there's wit;
And so to write like *Donne* you chose,
Whose prose was verse, and verse was prose:
From common tracts of rhyming stray,
And versify another way.
Indeed, it suits, I must aver,
A *genius* to be singular.

In her own singular and nonmetaphysical way, Bleecker attacked both man and God. Many of her social satires are directed against men, who are, as in the poem to Mr. L., "brutes," egocentric and rough. Generally, however, Bleecker's touch is very light, not harsh or bitter, as in "On a great *Coxcomb* recovering from an Indisposition":

> Narcissus (as *Ovid* informs us) expir'd,
> Consum'd by the flames his own beauty had fir'd;
> But N——o (who like him is charm'd with his face,
> And sighs for his other fair-self in the glass)
> Loves to greater excess than *Narcissus*—for why?
> He loves himself *too much* to let himself die.

There is a series of such brief poems which indicate that Bleecker's plan was to "reform" by laughter.

With God, however, she is more serious. Like Emily Dickinson, she yearns to make contact, but finds herself a rebel, as in these two concluding stanzas from "An Hymn":

> Oh! was I but some plant or star,
>   I might obey him too;
> No longer with the Being war,
>   From whom my breath I drew.
>
> Change me, oh God! with ardent cries
>   I'll venture to thy seat;
> And if I perish, *hell* must rise
>   And tear me from thy feet.

But, ultimately, Bleecker, like Dickinson, could not find God, and for her man is only a tiny creature uncertain of heaven. Her poetry is clearly opposed to the simple religious principles of Freneau's "On the Uniformity and Perfection of Nature," as well as to the bright optimism of many of her contemporary poets. Neither Franklin's "Ephemera" nor Freneau's "The Wild Honeysuckle"[14] approaches the sense of cosmic despair in Bleecker's "On the Immensity of Creation":

> Oh! could I borrow some celestial plume,
> This narrow globe should not confine me long
> In its contracted sphere—the vast expanse,
> Beyond where thought can reach, or eye can glance,
> My curious spirit, charm'd should traverse o'er,

New worlds to find, new systems to explore:
When these appear'd, again I'd urge my flight
Till all creation open'd to my sight.
   Ah! unavailing wish, absurd and vain,
Fancy return and drop thy wing again;
Could'st thou more swift than light move steady on
Thy sight as broad, and piercing as the sun,
And *Gabriel's* years too added to thy own;
Nor *Gabriel's* sight, nor thoughts nor rapid wing,
Can pass the immense domains of th'eternal King;
The greatest seraph in his bright abode
Can't comprehend the labours of a God.
Proud reason fails, and is confounded here;
—Man, how contemptible thou dost appear!
What are thou in this scene?—Alas! no more
Than a small atom to the sandy shore,
A drop of water to a boundless sea,
A single moment to eternity.

Bleecker, however, was not continually on the attack, nor was she always in despair. She was the first American woman poet to write poems expressly for her children, such as "A Short Pastoral Dialogue (Designed for the use of Her daughter and niece when very young.)" Moreover, she finds the activities of children worthy of adult poetic consideration. The children she describes are not dead, nor is she concerned with them because they are her children:

The village children, rambling o'er yon hill
With berries all their painted baskets fill,
They rob the squirrels little walnut store,
And climb the half exhausted tree for more;
Or else to fields of maize nocturnal hie,
Sportive, they make incisions in the rind,
The riper from the immature to find;
Then load their tender shoulders with the prey,
And laughing bear the bulky fruit away.
      (from "Return to Tomhanick")

She also wrote several poems concerning the death of her daughter during the flight from Burgoyne. In fact, "Written in the Retreat from Burgoyne" was widely anthologized in the nineteenth century. It is, however, one of her least "singular" poems.

Not surprisingly, the only "muse" Bleecker claimed is Minerva.

Like certain modern poets (e.g., Sylvia Plath in "The Disquieting Muses"), Bleecker had difficulty associating with any of the traditional symbols of poetic inspiration. In an era bursting with elaborate poetic invocations, she generally did not invoke anything at all. When she did, however, her invocation was to Minerva. In a short epistolary poem, "To Mr. Bleecker," she approaches this serious question with humor and double rhyme and explains her original and personal resolution of this problem:

> Yes, I invok'd the Muses' aid
> To help me write, for 'tis their trade;
> But only think, ungrateful Muses,
> They sent Dame *Iris* with excuses,
> They'd other business for to follow,
> Beg'd I'd apply to God *Apollo*.
>   The God said, as heav'n's charioteer,
> He had no time to mind us here;
> Said if we rac'd the earth like *Phoebus*
> One day, it sadly would fatigue us;
> Yet we expect, when tir'd at night,
> He'd stay from bed to help us write:
> Nor need we ask his Sister *Phoebe*,
> For turning round had made her giddy;
> Her inspiration would confuse us,
> So counsell'd us to coax the Muses.
> Quite disappointed at this lecture
> I left his worship sipping nectar;
> But, pettishly as I left his dome,
> It chanc'd I met the Goddess *Wisdom*.
> No wonder she is wise, 'tis said
> She was the product of Jove's head.
>   'Bright Queen,' said I 'in these abodes
> 'I beg'd a favour of the Gods:
> 'They wish'd the poets at the devil,
> 'And the nine ladies were uncivil:
> '*Apollo* told me he was lazy,
> 'And call'd his sister *Phoebe* crazy
> 'Permit me then your kind protection,
> 'From you I cannot fear rejection.'

Like Turell, Bleecker was searching for a different muse from the ones the men were following. She had, of course, already found it. Bleecker is unknown today; her verse is not mentioned in critical studies, nor has any poem of hers appeared in any modern anthology.

The Magazine Poets

With the rise of journals and magazines in the mid-eighteenth century, a new group of poets emerged. These poets, at first only men, contributed a number of different kinds of poems, most, however, imitations of imitations. After the Revolutionary War, many magazines opened their poetry columns more widely to women. Margaretta Bleecker Faugères, in fact, first published her mother's prose and poetry in *New-York Magazine,* and her own works first appeared in the journals. Judith Sargent Murray, whose prose essays were first published in journals and who gained some fame as "the Gleaner," also wrote poems, as "Constantia," for *Massachusetts Magazine* and other journals.[15] In fact, two of her poems were the only ones by women in *The Columbian Muse: A Selection of American Poetry, from Various Authors of Established Reputation,* published in New York in 1794, one of the earliest American anthologies. The journals provided an outlet for a large number of men and women who wished to publish their verses, nearly all of whom used pseudonyms. For the women especially, they offered not only a chance for publication but also a chance to read poetry written by other women (and by men too). Of the women poets we can identify, all were from the upper and middle classes.

The *Columbian Magazine, or Monthly Magazine*[16] seems to have published the most poems by women and to have accepted poems by the largest number of women. It began publication in 1786 in Philadelphia and continued, under various names, until 1792. Many contributors (both men and women) remain unidentified, although such women as Ann Young Smith ("Sylvia") and Elizabeth Graeme Fergusson ("Laura") have been recognized. Besides a wide selection of poetry by women, *The Columbian Magazine* also carried many articles of special interest to women: for instance, several essays concerning education for women and other educational reforms (April 1790 and August 1790); several poems praising women's boarding schools (October 1786 and February 1787); and an article by "Philokoinoneas" entitled "On the HAPPY INFLUENCE of the FEMALE SEX in Society, and the ABSURD practice of separating the SEXES immediately after DINNER" (March 1791). *The Columbian Magazine* was clearly making a bid for women readers—a fact which indicates a large enough number of literate women for economic consideration.

The best of the magazine writers are Faugères and Sarah Wentworth Morton. Margaretta Bleecker Faugères (1771–1801) married a French physician who squandered most of her inheritance from her father. When Mr. Faugères died in 1798, she taught school in New Jersey and New York to support herself and her daughter. She wrote both prose essays and poems and was even asked to write public odes, such as, for example, her "Ode" for a July 4, 1798, celebration in New York City.[17]

She wrote a five-act tragedy, *Belisarius* (1795), which appears to some extent to be an artistic rebuttal to Warren's Roman matrons. Theodora (roughly parallel to Edoxia, the empress in *The Sack of Rome*) is a villain, a "manly" woman who destroys kind and noble old men like Belisarius. Faugères describes Theodora's heart as "Black as the caverns where her victims suffer . . . /Devil incarnate, scourge of this wide empire." Faugères's ideal women are Julia, who loves Belisarius (a widower) and vainly attempts to overthrow Theodora, and Eudoxa, Belisarius's pure and lovely daughter. One of the most interesting elements of *Belisarius* is the preface, which Faugères herself undoubtedly wrote and which reflects a new American taste in drama: "She has endeavored to avoid all that unmeaning *rant* which forms so conspicuous a part in most productions of this kind, together with the awful *asservations* and *maledictions*.—— What their effect upon the stage may be, she knows not, but to a mere reader they are ever tiresome, and frequently disgusting; for which reason, as *Belisarius* was from its commencement intended for the closet, she has attempted, in their stead, to substitute concise narrative and plain sense." Although her intentions were correct, Faugères unfortunately replaced bombast with syrupy sentiment. Nevertheless, Faugères clearly had a sense of herself as a poet and, like her mother and Warren, was willing to strike out independently at social abuses. In *The Ghost of John Young, the Homicide Who was Executed the 17th of August last For the MURDER of Robert Barwick, a Sherif's Officer*, she uses the case of Young to argue poetically against capital punishment and the inconsistency of "sanguinary Laws . . . in a country which boasts of her Freedom and Happiness."[18]

Much of her poetry in the 1793 volume of her own and her mother's works is derivative and dull, but several poems prefigure Poe in an astonishing way. Her mother had written two fine poetical accounts of thunderstorms (e.g., "The Storm"), which stand as competent passages of description. Faugères also describes storms, but they have become internal and spiritualized storms, as, for example, in this passage from "Winter":

Or, where some ragged cliff, with low'ring brow,
    Blackens the surface of the swelling deep,
Where bellows dash, and howling tempests blow,
    Where *wizard shapes* their mighty revels keep;

Or on the shelly shore, where *spirits* roam
    Sounding their sorrows to the midnight gale,
While round their steps the restless waters foam,
    And hollow caves respond the dismal wail.

There (as upon the flood float the moon's rays,
    And rolling planets shed their silv'ry light;)
There, wrapt in musings deep, and steadfast gaze,
    In solemn rapture hath she past the night.

The dead poet in "To Aribert" speaks from the grave to loved ones, as in Poe's "To Annie."[19] In this passage from "Night," which bears a striking resemblance to Poe's "Dream-Land," Faugères explores the land of the dead:

Ah, the dread *King* of Terrors e'en they call
To hurl with speed the long expected dart!
Perhaps he strikes! perhaps just now the soul
Sprung from its bands into eternity!
Dark seems the passage—all the lights are clos'd,
And the dim eyes of my affected soul
Open upon the doleful scene, in vain:
How feels the soul just stepping from its barque,
Upon those boundless shores, dreary and dark,
Where ends all space and time, a stranger there?

.   .   .   .

There finds the weary traveller a rest,
And *there* the child of Poverty a home;
The bosom that with sharp affliction throbb'd,
And the sad heart that swell'd with many a sigh,
There rest in silence . . .

Other poems also suggest Poe's poetry (e.g., Faugères's "Arria's Tomb" and Poe's "Ulalume").

Faugères was wandering into the poetic and imaginative realms usually, as we have thought, occupied only by Poe (and, in one instance, by Freneau). Although Poe was a better poet, certainly Faugères succeeded in occasional lines and images. Moreover, with this knowledge of Faugères's poetry, we should no longer consider Poe such a strange and isolated phenomenon.

In another poem, Faugères cleverly satirizes male taste in women and, at the same time, predicts the "light" and "dark" heroines of nineteenth-century prose fiction:

> The following Lines were occasioned by Mr. Robertson's refusing to paint for one Lady, and immediately after taking another lady's likeness   1793

> When Laura appear'd, poor APPELLES complain'd,
> That his sight was bedim'd, and his optics much pain'd
> So his pallet and pencil the artist resign'd,
> Lest the blaze of her *beauty* should make him quite blind.
> But when fair ANNA enter'd the prospect was chang'd,
> The paints and the brushes in order were rang'd;
> The artist resum'd his employment again,
> Forgetful of labour, and blindness and pain;
> And the strokes were so lively that all were assur'd
> What the *brunette* had injur'd the *fair one* had cur'd.

> Let the candid decide which the chaplet should wear,
> The *charms* which *destroy*, or the *charms* which *repair*.

Finally, in "Elegy to Miss Anna Dundass," the speaker (Ella) recalls her mother's death and her final words:

> "When I am gone—ah! who will care for thee?
> "What tender friend will guide thy infant thought
> "When cares shall call thy father far away?
> "By whom wilt thou to act aright be taught?
> "Ah, who, my ELLA, who will care for thee?"

The mother's concern for her child is real and natural, although expressed with sentimentality. What is significant is the mention of the father as advisor to the child, a role which can be played only by the mother in the poetry of the women in the next century.

Sarah Wentworth Morton ("Philenia, a Lady of Boston," 1759–1846),[20] is notable, if only because she is the one woman poet whose work is contained in what seems to be the first post–Revolutionary War anthology of American verse, *American Poems, Selected and Original*, compiled by Elihu H. Smith.[21] Smith himself, in fact, should also receive special notice for being the first of a long line of American editors, compilers, and anthologists who have chosen poetry most imitative of the poems of men to represent women's verse. With the work of women like Warren, Bleecker, and Faugères to publish, Smith chose the nationalistic odes and derivative Augustan amatory verse of Morton, a poetaster whose poems in this anthology exhibit less originality than the verse of Wheatley. Typically, the most recent evaluation of her is that "she was the foremost woman poet of her own generation."[22]

A member of the "Boston aristocracy" and a friend of the Adamses and Warrens, Sarah Morton seems to have had a certain amount of poetic talent and was willing to try (just a step or two behind the men) various verse forms. She was the first American woman and one of the first Americans to attempt the sonnet ("To Major Lincoln") and even published the first part of what was planned to be a national epic, *Beacon Hill: A Local Poem, Historic and Descriptive* (1797). Apparently discouraged by its critical reception, she never completed it. Morton stood firmly against slavery in "The African Chief" and against the French Revolution in "Batavia." However, Morton's poetry is as full of invocations, personifications, and clichés as that of her fellow poetasters.

Her verse remained at a public and impersonal level, except for two poems contained only in her book *My Mind and Its Thoughts, in Sketches, Fragments, and Essays.* These two poems apparently reflect a reconciliation with her husband ("ONE . . . with soul-illumined eyes") who was the lover of her sister Fanny. The scandal, which quickly became public after a daughter was born to Fanny and Perez Morton, caused Fanny to commit suicide. Sarah and Perez's marriage survived, and Perez went on to important political positions in Massachusetts state government.

Morton's women are pure, noble, and passive. In several essays, she viciously attacked Mary Wollstonecraft (*My Mind and Its Thoughts*, pp. 155–160) and, although admitting that woman's role in life was nearly negligible (pp. 219–221), claimed that woman must submit to the "*dictatorship* of *men.*" Morton pointed out, however, that American women suffered less than women from pagan countries; thus, by her reasoning, woman's only hope was Christianity.

Morton did write one notable poem, *Ouâbi, or The Virtues of Nature: An Indian Tale in Four Cantoes* (1790).[23] As imitative as her later verse became, *Ouâbi* is comparatively original. Morton, who intended her poem to be "wholly American," based the plot on several sources, which she cites, such as William Penn and Thomas Jefferson. The story itself is based on "*Azâkia*: A Canadian Story" from *American Museum* 6 (1789). The poem (primarily in quatrains of heroic couplets, with the dialogue an uneven tetrameter) concerns Celario, "Europe's finest boast," who finds "truth and godlike justice" on the plains of Illinois. The poem is strongly anti-European: Celario describes the evils of civilized Europe in a string of personifications, extending even beyond the Seven Deadly Sins. The "noble savages" are Ouâbi, an Illinois chief, and Azâkia, his wife. As in the nineteenth-century Leatherstocking Tales of James Fenimore Cooper, there are also evil Indians, and, moreover, as in *The Last of the Mohicans*, the evil Indians are Hurons. Unlike the ever virgin Natty Bumppo, however, Celario is allowed to marry Azâkia, after Ouâbi heroically dies. The "noble aborigine" was not, of course, a new theme (Aphra Behn's *Oroonoko* had appeared in England over one hundred years earlier), but Morton's poem is an important early statement of what was to become a major theme for American men and women.

Finally, Morton's verse reflects the schizophrenic nature of male poetry in the new American republic. With the establishment of the new nation, everyone hoped for a national culture and literature. On the one hand, American poets sought to compete with poets of other nations in traditional verse forms with traditional poetic topics (Morton's poems in Smith's anthology); on the other hand, others hoped that the new nation would produce native verse with native topics (*Ouâbi* and *Beacon Hill*). The argument culminated in the nineteenth century—and thus will be discussed more fully in the next chapter.

Morton was neither an intelligent nor an original poet, but she is the best of those who competed with the men on their terms. In that sense, her verse should be read with that of the Connecticut Wits. Even juxtaposed to their verse, however, her poems appear advantageously: they are shorter.

Susanna Haswell Rowson (1762–1824)

Although the daughter of a British military officer, Susanna Rowson spent her formative years in America (1769–1778) and eventually (1793) returned to America for a career in the theater (as both actress and playwright) and as a poet and educator. A friend of the Warrens and James Otis, she chose as her major theme freedom in its various modes (including equality for women too). Her novel *Charlotte Temple*, published in England in 1791, was the first American best-selling novel, and her American plays were quite popular. Rowson was apparently the first American woman to be editor of a journal, *The Boston Weekly Magazine* (1802–1805). As an editor, she was soon followed in her profession by Sarah Josepha Hale and Caroline Gilman—a line continued throughout the nineteenth and twentieth centuries by such women as Harriet Monroe. Except for *Charlotte Temple*, her work is today critically neglected, although Quinn has briefly discussed her contribution to the American stage.[24]

By whom Susanna Rowson was educated, no one is certain, but she was able to read and write quite early. When she was twenty-four, her first novel, *Victoria*, was published in England. The next year she married William Rowson, whose young sister and illegitimate son she raised (she had no children of her own, but adopted a daughter). *Charlotte Temple*, the story of (masculine) dangers in the world for an innocent girl, was published the year before William Rowson's business failed. Both Rowsons became actors, and, after a brief career in England, joined an American company in 1793. They soon settled in Boston, where she wrote four plays, four more novels, several school textbooks, and a book of poems. Her school in Boston is credited with being one of the first in America to offer girls some education beyond the elementary level.

Rowson's one surviving play, *Slaves in Algiers; or, A Struggle for Freedom* (performed in Boston in 1794), can only make us sorry that her other plays were not preserved. Those lost plays are *The Volunteers* (1795), which concerned the Whiskey Rebellion; *The Female Patriot* (1795), apparently with a "feminist" theme; and *Americans in England* (1797). *Slaves in Algiers*, as Quinn observes, employs methods generally used in comic opera and is still very funny. The story concerns Americans who have been captured and are being held for ransom by pirates in the Mediterranean—a topic of interest to her contemporaries.

The play is in prose, but scattered throughout are songs, and the epilogue, a poem "Written and Spoken by Mrs. Rowson," is perhaps a clue as to just what her lost *The Female Patriot* concerned. The best songs are given to the men. One song, "Ven I vas a mighty little boy," is sung by Ben Hassam, a Jew masquerading as an Arab, and has a "riches to rags" theme. In dialect and using underworld jargon, it records how Ben Hassam "cheated the Gentiles, as Moses commanded." Sebastian's "Song" depicts, with humorous exaggeration, a battle of the sexes—with Sebastian triumphant in a Walter Mitty fashion.

The plot itself is complicated, but, throughout the confusion, it is clear that English and American women are "free" (the young American Rebecca has a soul "secure in its own integrity") and that even Ben Hassam's daughter Fetnah can, under the influence of Rebecca, claim that "Nature made us [women] equal to them, and gave

us the power to render ourselves superior." The same theme is continued in the epilogue, which reads in part:

> "Well, Ladies tell me—how d'ye like my play?
> "The creature has some sense," methinks you say;
> "She says that we should have supreme dominion,
> "And in good truth, we're all of her opinion.
> "Women were born for universal sway,
> "Men to adore, be silent, and obey."
>
> True, Ladies—bounteous nature made us fair,
> To strew sweet roses round the bed of care.
> A parent's heart, of sorrows to beguile,
> Cheer an afflicted husband by a smile.
> To bind the truant, that's inclined to roam,
>
> .   .   .   .
>
> To raise the fall'n—to pity and forgive,
> This is our noblest, best prerogative.
> By these, pursuing nature's gentle plan,
> We hold—in silken chains—the lordly tyrant man.

She continues with an argument against "slavery" and "bondage,"
which refers directly to the "slaves" of Algiers, but also indirectly
to the slavery of the American Negro (Quinn, p. 122) and, perhaps,
the "slavery" of women demanded throughout the play by such men
as Sebastian and Dey Muley Moloc.

Rowson is not, however, a feminist as compared, for example, to
Warren or to the women soon to follow in the nineteenth century.
Her *Miscellaneous Poems* (1804) continues a theme of limited femi-
nism, as in "Rights of Women," which begins this way:

> While Patriots on wide philosophic plan,
> Declaim upon the wondrous rights of man,
> May I presume to speak? and though uncommon,
> Stand forth the champion of the rights of woman?
> Nay, start not, gentle sirs; indeed, 'tis true,
> Poor woman has her rights as well as you;
> And if she's wise, she will assert them too.

These rights are pride and self-respect, authority in domestic matters, a share in men's interests, and the freedom to help one's own
parents as well as in-laws and to nurse the sick. Rowson does not
want women "To interfere/With politics, divinity, or law." It should

be noted that the domestic duties of Rowson's ideal woman are those of a preindustrial age and that she does not feel a woman is limited to childbearing, as in the poems of nineteenth-century women who were beginning to write even before her death.

In another poem, "Women As They Are," Rowson chastises parents who cause their daughters to grow up as idle-brained beauties, or as domestic experts ("what is she fit for, but an upper servant"), or as teasing temptresses who walk "with a more than manly swagger," or as overly emotional readers of novels, or as angry termagants. An avowed social environmentalist in this poem, Rowson urges men to help women to be properly educated. The poem may owe a slight debt to John Trumbull's *The Progress of Dulness* (especially Part 3, "The Adventures of Miss Harriet Simper"), but Rowson's poem is far more clever and more generally applicable.

The rest of the poems are standard neoclassical imitations—except for one important quality in several of them. As is evident from most of her poems, Rowson could jingle along in verse with the best jinglers in her day, but in several poems she struck out alone in a new prosodic direction, which she called "Irregular Verse." Warned by this term, the reader is soon aware that there are two experimental irregularities. The first is the use of a variety of stanzaic structures in no regular sequence and often in no traditional form throughout a single poem. A similar method had been used in America for some time for odes, but generally the stanzas were more regular and the topic was public (e.g., Faugères's ode for a July 4 celebration). Rowson attempts to use such variety of stanzaic structure in narrative and lyrical verse. It should be noted that, at about the same time Rowson was trying to experiment with her "Irregular Verse" (which seems to have derived from odes), the English Romantic poets were working out the problems which would lead to their odes.

The second irregularity is that Rowson is not regularly "jingling." She has created very uneven metrical lines, carefully balanced by more regular lines. The irregular stanzaic forms tend to emphasize further the metrical irregularities. Her prosodic explorations point to the verse of later experimenters in the nineteenth century. Several poems could be chosen to demonstrate her "Irregular Verse," but perhaps these two stanzas from a long poem, "The Birth of Genius," best demonstrate her methods:

> Beside a spring, whose clear translucent wave
> O'er variegated pebbles softly crept,
> O'er which the lovelorn willows wept,

Deep in a coral rock, was form'd a cave.
There Nature still in sportive mood
  Had deck'd the grot with spar's, and gems, and ore;
    The flaming ruby there was seen,
    The modest amethyst's unchanging blue,
    Pure rocks of diamond, the emerald green;
And tho' the hand that deck'd it thus was rude,
  The more 'twas gaz'd upon it pleas'd the more,
    Forever various and forever new.

    He spoke, and swift ascending,
      Cut th' etherial way;
    While clouds, with lightning blending,
      Shot a pale doubtful ray;
  GENIUS beheld him rise
    And eager would pursue,
  But clouds enwrap'd the skies,
    And shut him from his view.
Low on the earth bending, his hands rais'd in air,
To his parent ascending, he offer'd this prayer.

There are three notable qualities in these stanzas. First, her conscious construction of different stanzaic form[25] indicates that the poet is thinking in terms of line and stanza shape—an insistence upon the importance of the visual quality of poetry. Moreover, almost every stanza in this poem consists of a single sentence, extended by parallel grammatical phrases and, often, by contrasting images or ideas. In fact, each stanza is so self-contained and so internally varied that the poem itself is difficult to follow. Finally, she carefully groups lines of quite different metrical form. In the last couplet quoted above, a couplet which has been typographically set off from the rest of the stanza, the first line ("Low on the earth . . .") has eleven syllables, with six stresses; the next line has twelve syllables, with four stresses (actually, a regular line of anapestic tetrameter). In the first stanza, lines 1, 4, 5, and 10 are typographically parallel but metrically different. In short, there is a jarring between the eye and ear.

Rowson's experiments did not continue; they never got beyond the experimental stage. Perhaps she was discouraged by her early efforts (they obviously were not successful). Nevertheless, she is the first of a number of American women to experiment with original prosodic methods, both in metrical variations and stanzaic forms. In the later nineteenth century, only Emily Dickinson was as bold as

Rowson; her experiments (or, perhaps, metrical adjustments) were successful. In the twentieth century, a number of women, such as H. D. and Moore, have been recognized as major contributors to new prosodic techniques.

Chapter Three

1800–1850

The Rise of Female Poetry

At the beginning of the nineteenth century, the journals reflected a concern for a national "culture" and, consequently, a national literature—a concern which Ralph Waldo Emerson eventually summarized in "The American Scholar" (1837). Thus, for example, in the April 1826 number of the prestigious *North American Review*, a writer reviewing *Miscellaneous Poems Selected from the United States Literary Gazette* insisted that American poets should be "strictly American; their productions should retain a flavor of the soil in which they were formed. The feelings they express, and the outward forms they portray, should partake of something of the air of the place." On the other hand, the same writer insisted that the American poet must "aspire to rival the richest strains, which have been breathed from the country of Shakespeare and Milton." Still, no one knew just what a national literature might be.[1] In 1841, William Gilmore Simms asserted that there were two "types" of national literature: "It is that which distinguishes and illustrates, especially, the fortunes, tempers and peculiar characteristics of the people with whom it originates; or, it is that which is produced by native writers, from the common stock of human knowledge, in a fair competition with the reflective minds of other nations."[2] This poetic split personality was developing at the end of the eighteenth century in the poetry of the men, especially, but also in the verse of women like Morton, as we have seen.

In a general overview of nineteenth-century American poetry, it is clear that most writers who now appear to be our major poets fall into the first of Simms's categories: poets who say something about or reflect the American experience. As R. W. B. Lewis and Roy Harvey Pearce have shown us, it was, more specifically, the Adamic experience. The women poets, who in the first half of the nineteenth century grew greatly in numbers, continued on their own way and, at least generally, fall into the second of Simms's categories: poets who draw from the "common stock of [female] human knowledge." And yet, because they were American women, they too were saying something about America—not the same things, however, that the men were saying.

Two themes commonly treated by the women of the late eighteenth century are quite noticeably lacking in the poems of women in the early nineteenth century. The first is a nationalistic or patriotic consciousness, a belief in the possibilities of freedom for all in America, as had been expressed in the earlier verse of women like Warren and Rowson. While the men turned their attention to utopian and "cosmic" concerns (i.e., the creation of that masculine, nationalistic image, the American Adam), the women looked at themselves and their situations and found many other things to say. In part, the reason for a lack of nationalistic consciousness in the poetry of the women at this time is that the country was generally at peace. The poetry of American men and women seems to converge primarily in times of national crisis. Another reason for the lack of national consciousness is that the women were in large part excluded from national concerns. The men no longer needed the strong helpmate to fight for liberty, as in the eighteenth century. Furthermore, the women had no vote, and no professions were open to them, although girls were allowed to work in the factories of Lowell, Massachusetts. When Rowson wrote that women should not become involved in medicine, law, or divinity, she was simply reaffirming the social circumstances.

The women thus began to develop other kinds of poems—poems which, however, had been a part of the verse of American women since Bradstreet's time. The women concentrated upon themes which concern women, children, their homes, and their local communities—each of which they examined in a variety of new ways. Their poems became even more intentionally communicative to other women. Indeed, it is understandable why their verse emphasized more universal or human aspects and just how such poetry ultimately led to an Emily Dickinson.

Another element which had appeared in the verse of eighteenth-century women but which nearly disappeared in the verse of women in the early nineteenth century was an outspoken plea for feminine equality. The feminist movement in America, which built upon the foundation established by such women as Warren and Bleecker, was active and vigorous at this time, but few women poets directly advocated it. The poetry produced by avowed feminists, such as Margaret Fuller, is simply second rate.[3] This is not to say, however, that feminism is absent from the verse of the better women poets. In fact, the images and themes of the poems clearly support certain principles advocated by the more active women. However, the best poems extend beyond feminism to woman herself and thus to more universal concerns.

Two of the most significant factors contributing to the creation of verse by American women at this time were the sudden appearance of large numbers of women poets and the diversity of their backgrounds. Of the women writing from 1800 to 1850, not including any of those discussed in the last chapter, such as Rowson and Morton, who were still working in the early years of the nineteenth century, I count over eighty who published at least one volume of verse or whose verse was regularly published in the anthologies. The number of women who published only in journals (most with a wide distribution) is at least twice that number. Moreover, no longer were the poets exclusively from upper or upper-middle-class homes; many were from poor backgrounds. A majority were from the eastern seaboard communities, but a growing number of women on the frontier were beginning to write.

In fact, one of the most disappointing aspects of this period is that the women on the frontier, who might have continued the independent and original poetic strain of an earlier writer like Bleecker, seem to have fallen prey to the styles and clichés of the Atlantic coast magazines, which largely continued the traditions of a poet like Morton and which found their way even to the edges of civilization. It is disappointing that the best that writers such as Lydia Jane Peirson, who lived in Liberty, Tioga County, Pennsylvania, could produce is this kind of generalization:

> There are sumptuous mansions with marble walls,
>   Surmounted by glittering towers,
> Where fountains play in perfumed halls
>   Amongst exotic flowers.
> They are a suitable home for the haughty in mind,
>   Yet a wildwood home for me,
> Where the pure bright streams, and the mountains wind,
>   And the bounding heart are free.
>   (from "The Wildwood Home," in *Forest Leaves*)[4]

And Amélia Welby, upon visiting Mammoth Cave in her native
Kentucky, could only rhetorize:

> Oh silent cave! amid the elevation
> Of lofty thought could I abide with thee,
> My soul's sad shrine, my heart's lone habitation,
> Forever and ever thou shouldst be!
> (from "Mammoth Cave")[5]

Peirson and Welby do derivatively reflect two strains of American
male writing of the time: Peirson, the "freedom" associated with
the American wilderness; and Welby, the reflective attitude inspired
by the wilderness—both of which were first and better expressed by
William Cullen Bryant.[6] Such poems, however, are not really common among the better women poets of the time.

This is not to say that the women poets ignored all concerns
which, today, we would term "native" and which they shared with
many male poets at this time. Almost every woman poet showed a
participation in the American community in certain types of poems:[7]

1. Those which express a traveler's yearning for "home." These
poems, however, are so generalized, except for a specific place name,
that any other place name might be substituted.

2. Those which praise George Washington in idealized terms: an
inherited type from the eighteenth century. Perhaps only five or six
exist among poems written by women in the years 1800–1850.

3. Those which explore local or regional stories or legends. These
almost exclusively concern men and are comparable to poems by the
male poets, such as Whittier's "Abraham Davenport" and "Skipper
Ireson's Ride."[8] One notable exception of this type is Caroline Gilman's "Mary Anna Gibbes, the Young Heroine of Stono, S.C."[9]
Written in 1837, "Mary Anna Gibbes" is the narrative of a thirteen-
year-old girl who bravely crosses enemy lines to retrieve her little
brother whom her family has inadvertently left sleeping in his crib
as they flee before the approaching British soldiers during the
Revolution. She is the only white or black American woman who is
at all comparable to the "active" women of, for example, Mercy
Warren, that I have found in all the poems I have read of this
period written by American women.

4. Those which concern Indians. Most of these are the noble
savages of Sarah Morton's *Ouâbi*. A number of poems concern the
heroism of Pocahontas, the one consistent American heroine at this
time. Lydia Huntley Sigourney attempted in the 1850's to write an

epic concerning Pocahontas, modeled upon Longfellow's "Hiawatha," but could not finish it. Sigourney's partial poem represents the one attempt at the epic by the women at the same time that Longfellow, Melville, and Whitman were all writing national epics. The epic demands a sense of national consciousness—and the women clearly were not thinking of the American community, of "progress," of the vague realization westward, of the outspreading democratic soul, or of any of the similar "national" themes which so interested the men.[10]

5. Finally, those poems which concern social problems. In this area, there is a broad concern: from abolition of slavery to the establishment of local schools for the deaf and dumb, from missionary funds for the Indians to feminism. These were never, however, major poetic concerns. Such a peripheral, though nevertheless sincere, interest in social issues has been a constant concern among the American women poets. In fact, the women poets of the early nineteenth century wrote more of this kind of poem than the men did.[11]

Despite this variety of poems identifiably "American," it should be emphasized that these poems represent only a comparatively minor thread among the women writers. Moreover, their themes are limited to very specific topics and do not really reflect the more broad philosophical and social "American" concerns of the men. Clearly, the women stood outside the "main currents of American thought."[12]

The poems which are "American" are buried in the mass of verse written by women in the early nineteenth century. Nearly all of these women were writing for the widely spreading magazine trade, and their poems were addressed to the broad interests of their primarily female readers. It was actually easier and more "respectable" for women to publish poetry at this time than it was for men. The magazines, published primarily in the eastern centers, such as New York, Boston, and Philadelphia, largely appealed to the new middle-class women readers. For this reason, the first American poet who could actually be called a poet by profession, who actually made enough money to support herself and her family was probably Lydia Huntley Sigourney.

The male poets suffered from two problems: the attitude of other American males to male poets and the popularity of the women poets. Benjamin T. Spencer has pointed out, in postrevolutionary America, "the man of letters was neither honored nor respected by the majority of his compatriots. Hence belletristic writing faltered because it lacked motivating power of social approval."[13] In an 1832 article in the *North American Review*, Longfellow proclaimed that the public (here, presumably the male public) thought poetry to be "effeminate nonsense."[14]

Moreover, the popularity of the women poets caused nothing but unhappiness for the men.[15] Hawthorne detested the "d——d mob of scribbling women" and their "trash."[16] Feminine poetry has, in fact, never been more popular than it was at this time. Lydia Sigourney was soon followed by many others who either made their living by writing or supplemented their family's income by verse.[17] Moreover, there were a number of powerful women editors, such as Sarah Josepha Hale (*Ladies American Magazine* and *Godey's Lady's Book*) —powerful, of course, because they selected just what was to be published.

When Ralph Waldo Emerson declared in "The Poet" that "the people fancy they hate poetry," he was, by implication, asserting that the people hated *his* kind of poetry. That he would so arrogantly exclude from his definition of poetry the poems written by women (and by the men, such as Poe, who contributed to the popular journals) indicates the nature of his attack upon the taste of the "intellectual middle class," which was composed primarily of women readers. Emerson's exclusiveness thus involves a judgment against the middle-class readers as well as against the women poets.[18] The attacks of both Emerson and Hawthorne upon women poets and their readers are paralleled by their scorn of Margaret Fuller.[19]

Moreover, the magazines of the (principally New England) intellectual aristocracy, *North American Review*, *Knickerbocker's*, and *Atlantic Monthly*, did not publish many poems by women. These were the magazines whose editors were establishing "the standardization of American authors—the creation of the canon of Great Names in our literature," as Howard Mumford Jones has observed.[20] In effect, from this time, the poetry of women has not even been considered part of the canon, unless, of course, like Morton, the poet created verse imitative of male poetry.

"Female poetry," in fact, took its beginnings from this time, in part as a result of male reactions to the popularity of women's poetry and in part as an expression of the then current sociological and psychological estimation of women. The women were proving that they could write poems which were popular, and they were serving ably as editors. For the first time in the history of Western civilization, women were writing poetry in comparatively vast numbers on a variety of concerns. In the first half of the century, nearly all of the women poets were married or had at least been married at one time.[21] And, although some husbands still demanded that their poet-wives use pseudonyms, most women refused such restrictions and published their poems under their own names. The bitterness of writers such as Longfellow, Hawthorne, and Emerson, as well as of other literary males,[22] in conjunction with the dominant psychology of the day, thus produced the potentially restrictive and condescending concept of "female poetry."

One of the earliest American attempts to classify poetry as "female" was written by an unidentified reviewer in the April 1827 number of *North American Review* in a discussion of two books of poems by Felicia Hemans. An Englishwoman, Hemans was extremely popular in both England and America and was widely imitated by women (and men) on both sides of the Atlantic. A voluminous writer, she is remembered today as a minor Romantic, famous for her "Stately Homes of England" and "Casabianca."[23] Hemans, the reviewer contends, is the model of a female writer: "In her pursuits of literary renown she never forgets what is due to feminine reserve. . . . She sets before herself a clear and exalted idea of what a female writer should be." Indeed, the reviewer continues, "It is high praise of Mrs. Hemans' poetry, that it is feminine. The sex may be well pleased with her productions, for they could hardly have a better representative in the career of letters. All her works seem to come from the heart, to be natural and true." The significant words in this early description of female poetry are "reserve": modesty, nonassertiveness; "should be": clearly, there is an idea of what a female writer should not be; and "heart": female poetry must express the "affections," not the intellect or the logical and erudite faculty.

By 1840, critics could confidently assert that there was a "school of poetry, essentially feminine," as Sigourney declared in her introductory essay to an edition of Hemans's poems (*The Works of Mrs. Hemans*, 1:vii–xxiii). Sigourney's definition of "female poetry" emphasizes "woman's self-sacrificing virtues," piety, and "domestic affections." Hemans's freedom from "bigotry," as well as her sense of professionalism, is also praised.

While Emerson was seeking "The Poet" of the intellect, who must be a "beholder of ideas and an utterer of the necessary and causal," the "affections" continued to be the essential ingredient in subsequent recipes for female poetry. In 1848–1849, three major anthologies of female poetry appeared. Thomas Buchanan Read's *The Female Poets of America* contained no definition of female poetry, but, in *The American Female Poets*, Caroline May assertively associated female poetry with the affections:

It must be borne in mind that not many ladies in this country are
permitted sufficient leisure from the cares and duties of home to
devote themselves, either from choice, or as a means of living, to
literary pursuits. Hence, the themes which have suggested the
greater part of the following poems have been derived from the
incidents and associations of every-day life. And home, with its
quiet joys, its deep pure sympathies, and its secret sorrows, with
which a stranger must not intermeddle, is a sphere by no means
limited for woman, whose inspiration lies more in her heart than
her head. Deep emotions make a good foundation for lofty and
pure thoughts. The deeper the foundation, the more elevated
may be the superstructure. . . . And where should women lavish
most unreservedly and receive most largely, the warmest, purest,
and most changeless, affection, but in the sacred retirement of
home. (p. vi)

It should be no surprise that the majority of poems which May
selected for her anthology concern happy homes, pure and noble
motherhood, protestant Christian morality, and the nation. So far
as I can tell, May is the first editor of an American anthology to include selections from the poetry of Phillis Wheatley, whom she calls
a "literary curiosity." On the other hand, May admits that she includes several poems by Amanda M. Edmond because Edmond's
verses "are all dictated by a truly religious spirit; and, therefore,
claim respect for the author as a Christian, whatever may be thought
of her abilities as a poet." Needless to say, May's anthology is a
parade of undistinguished poems, nearly monolithic in tone, form,
diction, and theme.

Rufus Griswold's anthology, *The Female Poets of America*, has
proved as treacherous to women poets as his "Memoir" in volume 3
of *The Works of the Late Edgar Allan Poe* (1853–1856) was to Poe's
reputation. Although his poetic selections parallel and generally
repeat those of May, Griswold divides the poetry of men and women
more severely than May did:

The conditions of aesthetic ability in the two sexes are probably
distinct, or even opposite. Among men, we recognise his nature as
the most thoroughly artist-like, whose most abstract thoughts still
retain a sensuous cast, whose mind is the most completely trans-
fused and incorporated into his feelings. Perhaps the reverse
should be considered the test of true art in woman, and we should
deem her the truest poet, whose emotions are most refined by
reason, whose force of passion is most expanded and controlled

into lofty and impersonal forms of imagination. (*Female Poets of America*, p. 7).

Griswold's definition is the first to assert that women are probably incapable of "intellectual" poetry. The prescriptive tone of his last sentence was fortunately unheeded by most women, whose work was becoming more personal and less involved in "lofty . . . forms."

Because it is through the anthologies of Read, May, and Griswold or through anthologies of later editors who largely depended upon them, such as E. C. Stedman,[24] that Americans have read these women poets, we have believed their poems to be derivative, dull, sentimental, limited, and humorless. It is therefore with justification that one of the few modern critics who seems honestly to have studied at least the anthologies, Louise Bogan, condemns the nineteenth-century women poets' "often completely ridiculous record of sentimental female attitudinizing."[25] For the same reason, Fred Lewis Pattee could generalize and thus condemn the writers and readers in the "Feminine Fifties" (the decade following immediately after the anthologies of May, Read, and Griswold): "The great mass of American readers, for the most part women, did not think at all."[26]

The concept of female poetry was clearly based on the nineteenth-century concept of femininity, although the critics did not admit (or perhaps realize) this right away. Griswold's statement for his anthology does suggest that the dichotomy between male and female poetry is psychologically or biologically based, and in 1850 Griswold became even more explicit. It is important to quote a large section from Griswold's statement not only because of its artistic and psychological implications, but also because of the nature of its indirect attack on woman's poetry which does not conform to the "female tradition" and because of its direct attack on feminism:

It is Longfellow who says,
　　——"What we admire in woman,
　Is her affection, not her intellect."
The sentiment is unworthy a poet, the mind as well as the heart claims sympathy, and there is no sympathy but in equality; we need in woman the completion of our own natures; that her finer, clearer, and purer vision should pierce for us the mysteries that are hidden from our senses, strengthened, but dulled, in the rude shocks of the out-door world, from which she is screened, by her pursuits, to be the minister of God to us: to win us by the beautiful to whatever in the present life or the immortal is deserving a great ambition. We care little for any of the mathematicians,

metaphysicians, or politicians, who, as shamelessly as Helen, quit
their sphere. Intellect in woman so directed we do not admire,
and of affection such women are incapable. There is something
divine in woman, and she whose true vocation it is to write, has
some sort of inspiration, which relieves her from the processes
and accidents of knowledge, to display only wisdom, in all the
range of gentleness, and all the forms of grace. The equality of
the sexes is one of the absurb [*sic*] questions which have arisen
from a denial of the *distinctions* of their faculties and duties . . .
The ruder sort of women cannot apprehend that there is a distinction, not of dignity, but of kind; and so, casting aside their
own eminence, for which they are too base, and seeking after ours,
for which they are too weak, they are hermaphroditish disturbers
of the peace of both. In the main our American women are free
from this reproach; they have known their mission . . .[27]

Such definitions of female poetry have done much, undoubtedly,
to create not only the critical division of male and female poetry
today, but also the atmosphere in which women must still write in
the twentieth century. When Robert Lowell comments in his introduction to *Ariel* that Sylvia Plath is "certainly not another 'poetess,'" he is complimenting her. Obviously, such critical criteria for
female poetry are inextricably intertwined with the psychological
and biological definition of woman herself. When John Crowe
Ransom speaks of the "poet as woman," he describes a psychological
and biological state:

[Edna St. Vincent Millay] is an artist. She is also a woman. No
poet ever registered herself more deliberately in that light. She
therefore fascinates the male reviewer but at the same time horri-
fies him a little too. He will probably swing between attachment
and antipathy, which may be the very attitudes provoked in him
by generic woman in the flesh, as well as by the literary remains
of Emily Dickinson, Elizabeth Barrett, Christina Rossetti, and
doubtless, if we only had enough of her, Sappho herself. I shall
simulate perfect assurance in speaking to that point. A woman
lives for love, if we will but project that term to cover all her
tender fixations upon natural objects of sense, some of them more
innocent and far less reciprocal than men. . . . Less pliant, safer
as a biological organism, she remains fixed in her famous attitudes, and indifferent to intellectuality. I mean, of course, comparatively indifferent; more so than a man.[28]

Only the twentieth-century jargon separates Ransom from Griswold.

It is true, of course, that, in the early nineteenth century, many women wrote of marital love, their homes and children, as well as emotional or affective situations. It is equally true that a vast majority of the men, such as the now forgotten Nathaniel P. Willis and George H. Boker, did too. For the journalism trade, most poetry by men often seems to be indistinguishable from much of the poetry of the women, as Pattee has observed. That such a woman as Emily Dickinson could have written poetry immediately following and in the face of such examples and manifestations and definitions of female poetry has always seemed amazing and grand. That one of the best (if not the best) of the American poets could have been writing against the background of such "female sentiment" has caused critics to scurry for sources and reasons. One critic explains Dickinson's work by reasoning that she "remained unaffected by this prevailing literary climate."[29] Others can explain her poetry only in terms of Emerson.[30] Pearce honestly admits that she is the "noble exception" to his continuity of American poetry.[31] No one has seriously suggested that her roots lay close to her sister poets of America who preceded her in the nineteenth century.

The poems which Griswold, Read, May, and others chose for their anthologies are not necessarily the best poems of the women writing at this time (or in the centuries before). These poems were chosen with reference to traditional morality and values, as well as in accordance with the accepted definitions and evaluations of female poetry. The anthologists omitted, of course, a large number of poems from their collections. These rejected poems, however, were probably read almost as widely in their own day as were the poems selected by the anthologists. Both men and women poets in the early nineteenth century made their poems serve double or even triple duty; a poem generally appeared first in a journal, then in a collection of the author's poems, and then in an anthology or yearbook. Thus a nineteenth-century poem was often available in a variety of publications at varying times. The lack of a copyright law also allowed newspapers and journals, often on the opening frontier, to reprint freely poems from the eastern-based publications.

Thus a strange and ambivalent atmosphere existed for the woman poet at this time. Women were still expected to imitate male verse; anyone who wished to echo Bryant or repeat the themes of Longfellow could find a spot in some journal. Moreover, any woman could be published who conformed to the strictures of "female poetry," who would, that is, write sentimental, moral, and "affective" verse. Ironically, a number of men, such as Willis, saw the commercial advantages of writing such verse, and rivaled the women in this kind of poetry. It is for this reason that Pattee could with justification observe in *The Feminine Fifties* that, with few exceptions, the verse of the men sounded just like that of the women.

There was, however, another group of women who wished to write verse more truly expressive of their own beliefs, values, and interests. For these women, paradoxically, that potentially (and eventually) restrictive critical categorization of "female poetry" provided not only a shelter for experimentation, but even a galvanizing element in the development of poetry by women in America. Actually, contrary to what might be expected, the conditions for women's poetry in the early nineteenth century were nearly ideal for experimentation with poetic themes and for the emergence of a new and original kind of poetry. As a rule, poetry by women had to be "moral," but, as we will see, the rule of "morality" could be circumvented in several ways. Moreover, the better poets quickly discovered that the concept of "female poetry" offered freedom of expression, albeit within a certain area. For example, as long as the setting was "home," nearly any topic was acceptable, except the open advocacy of adultery. Thus the women explored and probed their own relationships with their children and, in effect, created a new poetic genre (although the women at this time had inherited at least the first explorations of such a theme from their sisters in the eighteenth and seventeenth centuries). Or, in another facet of "home," they could express dissatisfaction with their husbands specifically or with marriage in general, and not necessarily limit their protest to "feminism."

Moreover, the categorization of female poets made it only too easy for male critics and editors to skim or not even read their work, as long as the poems seemed to be "female." And because these poets were women, writing "female poetry," most critics applied less stringent standards than those used for male poets. On the one hand, such conditions gave women freedom to experiment and explore. On the other hand, however, it is clear that much weak and redundant verse was published for the same reasons. Nevertheless, it is fortunate that few male editors and critics, at this time, paid serious attention (except economically) to the development of the woman poet. And develop, of course, she did, in ways quite contrary to those of the male poets in the early nineteenth century.

One way in which the women, as a group, circumvented the prescribed poetic limitations of "female poetry" was in the use of female figures from classical mythology and history as major, personal poetic images. The use of female mythological characters was, in part, a logical and natural extension of the abundant classical references in an eighteenth-century poet like Bleecker, but it was also, I suspect, a response to the appearance of male mythological heroes in the poems of the English Romantic poets, whose works were carefully read by the American women. I can find little trace of a corresponding interest in the poetry of American men at this time. Indeed, it was not until the early twentieth century that Pound and the Imagists were to incorporate classical mythology into their verse, and the mythological characters were then predominantly male and their use was different.

In the first half of the nineteenth century, the American men (even the minor male poets) were generally busy with native male heroes and were creating an American mythology of innocent Adams. The men did write a few poems dealing generally with classical mythology, such as Emerson's "Bacchus." Only Poe, however, centered poems on mythological women: Helen, in "To Helen," who is, however, merely Beauty, a Psyche; and, in "Ulalume," Astarte and Diana, who represent lovers, not the poet himself. The American women had no national models, except for Mary Anna Gibbes and, later in the century, Barbara Frietschie (whom Whittier immortalized), and, in fact, found in neither American nor English history supportive evidence for a dignified femininity. The bravery of Anne Hutchinson, who might have been an appropriate subject, had unfortunately been darkened by her "traitorous" descendant, the ex–Royal Governor of Massachusetts Thomas Hutchinson, who was remembered even at this time with bitterness.[32]

The women did write an occasional verse concerning Mary, Queen of Scots, and the women who had visited Europe wrote of Queen Victoria, but the American women were republicans, not royalists. Pocahontas was a topic for nearly all the poets, and, although she has continued to be significant for the male writers, she ultimately was an unsatisfactory model for the women, perhaps because the women poets have simply not as a rule conceived of themselves "heroically," or as being able to alter a decision of state, so to speak. Even this early, the American women conceived of classical and mythological women as middle-class housewives, not as queens or otherwise powerful figures. Felicia Hemans had written a few poems concerning classical or mythological women, but, in her poetic treatment, Hemans is only "telling a story," with no identification of poet and mythological figure. In her one poem concerning Sappho, Sappho is ("alas!") alone and despairing after her lifetime of passion.

The association of mythological figures with their own roles and situations is indicative of the American women's general treatment of myth. That is, they have not interpreted or understood myth as a positive affirmation of societal values or as the positive expression of a cohesive structure within a culture. That is, unlike T. S. Eliot, who used mythological and archetypal characters to represent the societal values and structure of past civilizations, the women looked upon the female figures as "sisters" who had experienced and suffered much as they themselves were experiencing and suffering. When the American women searched history for models, they found only women of the French or English aristocracy, Biblical women, and the female characters from classical history and mythology. In the early nineteenth century, some women still identified with Biblical figures (a trend which began with the Puritans and continues to a limited extent today); however, the "mother" of the Biblical women is always Eve, an unsatisfactory model for nearly all American women poets. Thus they turned to the mythological women, who gave them a sense of continuity as well as further justification for their protests.

Moreover, it is clear that Sappho has always had a special significance for American women. In the eighteenth century, Jane Turell, in "To My Muse," hoped to "burn with Sappho's noble Fire,/But not like her for faithless Man expire." The better American women poets in the early nineteenth century agreed, but, unlike Turell, they did not want to "burn" for God or Puritan virtue either. They wanted to "burn" in a variety of other ways. Sappho was important because she was the most celebrated woman poet in Western civilization. Like Sappho, the American women considered themselves self-conscious artists, struggling with both their environment and their art.

Finally, the American women in the early nineteenth century quickly realized that, by the use of mythological tales or by labeling poems "An Imitation of Sappho," they could circumvent the moral strictures and censorship of their own day which affected men as well as women. As we will see, poems which center on mythological characters are more sensuous and, in some ways, more explorative than other kinds of verse. As Wheatley saw in the eighteenth century, by discussing Niobe, she could also write of herself.

Female mythological characters, as central, personal images in poems, actually appeared first in the early nineteenth century, but such figures had been invoked on a personal basis in a few poems in the late eighteenth century. The earliest example I can find is "To Delia," by "Matilda," a poem which appeared in the December

1786 issue of *The Columbian Magazine* and which indicates that
"Matilda" had read the poems of Ben Jonson:

> Woulds't thou, my Delia, bliss obtain?
> Unfetter'd range the peaceful plain,
> Let not the soothing tale of love
> Your better resolutions move;
> But read for once his annals o'er;
> Nor heed the gay deceiver more.
> Believing nymphs, and perjur'd swains,
> Repentant sighs, and plaintive strains,
> Appear in crowds on ev'ry page:
> The records these of ev'ry age.
> See sad Oenone there too late,
> Lament her undeserved fate;
> And ev'ry vale, and ev'ry grove,
> Repeat her ill-requited love.
> See hapless Sappho there deplore;
> See Ariadne's desert shore;
> And stern Medea's crimson stain;
> And Thisbe love, but love in vain.
> Can e'en a mutual flame bestow
> The bliss we roving damsels know?
> But blooming Strephon dies for you:
> Ah! think Dorinda thought so too.
> Now see her mourn, unhappy fair,
> A never ending state of care!
> How pleas'd you dwell on ev'ry grace,
> His charming voice, his matchless face;
> And when you call his eyes divine,
> How their soft langour speaks in thine!
> Each nobler grace his soul informs;
> The patriot firm his bosom warms;
> With ease and dignity he moves——
> Ah! 'tis too plain, my Delia loves.

Three elements of this little poem prefigure the later use of female
mythological figures in the poetry of American women: first, the
identity of the ancient women and their experiences with American
women and their experiences. In this poem, the poet, however, has
not drawn a parallel with her own situation, but with the situation
of her friend, Delia. Second, Sappho, who is of course a historical,

rather than mythological, figure, is listed among the mythological women. Until the twentieth century, Sappho seems to have been classified as "myth," in large part because so little of her poetry was recognized or collected in the eighteenth and nineteenth centuries. Finally, the witch Medea is not given a negative connotation. Juxtaposed in this list with "wronged" women, her "stern" qualities seem justified.

In the first half of the nineteenth century, a number of women wrote one or two poems each concerning female mythological figures. Despite the fact that higher or advanced education was not easily available to women, many had read Ovid, Horace, and other classical poets, a few in the original, others in French or English translations. Maria Gowen Brooks, who apparently learned of Sappho from French sources, seems to have been the first of many American women to associate herself with the ancient poetess. The poem itself, entitled "Written after passing an evening with E.W.R.A.*****, Esq., who has the finest person I ever saw" and published in 1820,[33] is also notable for its comparatively unembarrassed sensuality:

Who that has seen the breathing stone,
　　Or loved the Rhodian art,
Or heard the bard's enraptured tone
　　With pleasure-quickened heart,
Or who that ever felt that fire
　　Which prompts the minstrel's lays
Can sink to rest, nor strike the lyre
　　One moment to the praise?—
Thus ere his guilt, sweet Paris strayed
　　Through wandering grots and groves,
Ere yet his fair Idalian maid
　　Weeps him untrue—but loves.
Thus from the bath young Phaon came,
　　With that divine infusion
All glowing to the Lesbian dame,
　　Like a bright dream's illusion.
Like thine around his yellow hair
　　The fond light loved to play,
Like thine his lip allured the air
　　More fresh than breathed away.
Like thee he towered, his blue eye beamed
　　Like thine; a matchless grace
So o'er his form soft floating, seemed
　　To veil its powerfulness.

> And yet not so—had Phaon shone
>   So fair, Apollo's pride
> Had never such a rival borne
>   And Sapho had not died.

Harriette Fanning Read's verse drama *Medea* was published with
her two other plays (*Ermina; A Tale of Florence* and *The New
World*) in 1848.[34] *Ermina* and *The New World* are bathetic rendi-
tions of love lost or endangered or won, but *Medea* follows the traditional myth, with Medea the witch favorably interpreted as an
independent and noble woman. The blank verse is reasonably
effective, and at times Medea speaks like a nineteenth-century feminist:

JASON: Medea, list!
            Not grateful is it to a warrior's ear,
            That even a wife should boast her benefits:
            Remembrance is his part, and silence hers.

MEDEA: Thou know'st that mine is not the ignoble soul
            Which prompts a boaster's tongue. I boast of naught
            Save of thy love, which made me what I am,
            Thy equal partner, not thy household slave,—
            As Grecian dames to Grecian lords must be,—
            But worthy deemed by thee to aid thy councils,
            To share thy wanderings, and assuage thy woes.

In this passage, the mythological figure has been associated with a
problem contemporary with the poet. Whether or not Read herself
was intimately concerned with feminism cannot finally be ascer-
tained. Read was an actress, but I can find no mention of her or her
plays in any works dealing with nineteenth-century American drama.
Nevertheless, Read's obvious use of a female mythological figure as a
symbol for a contemporary (and perhaps personal) situation has
continued throughout the poetry of American women, as in H. D.'s
"Persephone" and Plath's "Medusa."

Mary E. Hewitt was a popular poet in the 1840's and 1850's, part
of the New York journalistic literati. The majority of her poems are
undistinguished, but she wrote a comparatively large number of
poems based on classical mythology and historical figures. Some,
such as "Narcissus," concern men, but most concern women. Perhaps originally inspired by Hemans's little poem concerning Sappho
and having read a life of Sappho,[35] Hewitt wrote three poems concerning the only prominent historical woman poet known to these

American women. In "Imitation of Sappho," Hewitt is able to capture the sexual passion of Sappho's poems in a way then unknown among American writers:

> If to repeat thy name when none may hear me,
>   To find thy thought with all my thoughts inwove;
> To languish where thou'rt not—to sigh when near thee—
>   Oh! if this be to love thee, I do love!
>
> If when thou utterest low words of greetings,
>   To feel through every vein the torrent pour;
> Then back again the hot tide swift retreating,
>   Leave me all powerless, silent as before—
>
> If to list breathless to thine accents falling,
>   Almost to pain, upon my eager ear;
> And fondly when alone to be recalling
>   The words that I would die again to hear—
>
> If at thy glance my heart all strength forsaking,
>   Pant in my breast as pants the frighted dove;
> If to think on thee ever, sleeping—waking—
>   Oh, if this be to love thee, I do love!

Except for the poems of Frances Sargent Osgood, whose verse is discussed in the next chapter, there is no other poet at this time, male or female, who dared to approach woman's sexuality this explicitly. Moreover, the poem is not simply a translation of Sappho, but a true "imitation." In the original poem (preserved for us in Longinus's *On the Sublime* and also imitated by Catullus), the poem is addressed by Sappho to another woman. Moreover, Hewitt has rearranged and altered certain of Sappho's images. She has, for example, substituted the "frighted dove" in the last stanza for the original "drying grasses" in order to emphasize "love," as opposed to Sappho's conclusion of suffering love-death.[36] Hewitt's poem also illustrates that the poetic association of the poet with the mythological figure allowed the nineteenth-century woman poet more freedom in the treatment of sensuality than she might otherwise have been willing (or perhaps allowed) to assume.

In "The Child of Fame," the poet begins by rejecting a lover in order to dedicate herself to poetry:

> Nay—call me not thy rose—thine own fair flower
>   For oh, my soul to thy wild woods is mute—

Leave me my gift of song—my glorious dower—
    My hand unchained, and free to sweep the lute.

By the end of the poem, however, the poet is sorry that she vainly
chose the "laurel crown" ("Alas! alas!") and that she could not have
found "one true heart." The poem itself, whose epigram is from
Anne Lefèvre Dacier's *La Vie de Sapho*, is obviously conceived in the
spirit of Hemans's treatment of Sappho. On the other hand, the use
of the image of "wild woods" to indicate marriage (or sexual en-
tanglement) is striking in the context of early nineteenth-century
American poetry, in which the "wild woods" generally represent
freedom, purity, and Eden.

    The third poem, "Sappho to the Sibyl," seems to be a combination
of the other two. A graceful poem, it develops the ironic situation of
a popular poet whose lover has perhaps never listened to her song:

Beyond the hills, where flows the Egean wave,
    I sweep the lyre amid the applauding throng—
Tell me, dread sibyl of this mountain cave,
    Has he I lov'd e'er listened to my song?

He is more glorious than the sculptured God
    Of sacred Delos—and, with step elate,
He moves as though his airy feet had trod
    Adown the clouds from Morning's amber gate.

I saw him borne in triumph—he had gained
    The olive chaplet in the chariot race,
When I, whose heart a mortal's love disdained,
    Gazed with wild rapture first upon his face.

Then, as the dew exhaleth to the dawn,
    To him that hour my life exhaleth away;
And now my heart and lyre fore'er unite
    With love's bewildering madness in my lay.

And now, dread sibyl of this mountain wild,
    I joy no longer in the applauding throng—
Oh, say! if ever Venus on thee smiled,
    Has he I love e'er thrilled beneath my song?

Hewitt wrote other poems concerning mythological women, such
as Clytia, who is changed into a flower after being deserted by her
lover, Apollo. Clytia is a helpless and forever sorrowing victim of
love, rendered passive by her love much as Elizabeth Barrett Brown-

ing was at the same time revealing herself to be. In another poem, Ariadne is deserted by Theseus, but only Theseus speaks while Ariadne sleeps. In two sonnets ("Cameo I" and "Cameo II"), the licentious and sensual pleasures of mythological pairs are condemned —but condemned only in the final couplet. "Cameo I," subtitled "A Centaur and Bride of the Lapithae," is amazingly evocative of W. B. Yeats's "Leda and the Swan" in several lines:

> With springing hoof that would the earth disdain,
>   Broad, swelling chest, and limb with motion rife,
>   From Lapithaean banquet and the strife,
> Fleetly he bounds along Thessalia's plain.
> And on his back, in rude embrace entwined,
>   A captive bride he bears. Her traitorous veil
>   Reveals her brow, as Juno's roses pale,
> And floats, like a scarf of Iris, on the wind.
> All vainly struggling 'gainst that bold caress,
>   Her outstretched arms essay the air to grasp;
>   But firm the captor holds his iron clasp,
> And strives with ruthless lips to press.
> Thus vice has power to sway the feeble soul,
> And bear it on in measureless control.

Despite the moral tag, the sensual nature of the rape and the theme of beauty and the beast are uncommon among American poets, both men and women, at this time. Hewitt's poems, in fact, look to the passionate and sensual nature of later nineteenth-century poems written by men, such as Whitman, and Melville in "After the Pleasure Party."[37] Moreover, in the context of this trend in women's poetry, Emily Dickinson's "Wild Nights" should not be such a surprise. We must remember that, although most of us have never heard of Hewitt, her poetry was widely read and valued in her own day. Hewitt's mythological poems featuring female figures and her Sapphic poems prefigure the continuing interest of American women in these themes and associations.

Chapter Four

1800–1850
Sigourney, Smith, and Osgood

Of the many women poets writing in America at this time, the three most important are Lydia Huntley Sigourney, Elizabeth Oakes Smith, and Frances Sargent Osgood. They are however, significant for quite different reasons. Sigourney set the pattern for women's poetry for many years and was an innovator in a number of ways. Smith is a poet who was sensitive to the "main currents" of early nineteenth-century male poetry but at the same time was involved in the feminist movement. Osgood is simply the best poet of all the women who wrote during these years.

Lydia Huntley Sigourney (1797–1865)

Two years before William Cullen Bryant's "Thanatopsis" was published,[1] Sigourney's first book of poems appeared in 1815. Sigourney was more popular as a poet than was Bryant in their own day. She was hailed as "the American Hemans," the "Sweet Singer of Hartford," and a "female Milton." If she is mentioned today, the judgment is harsh. Pearce, for example, writes her off quickly: "Below [the Fireside poets] were other poets, Mrs. Sigourney and her kind, who, lacking the intelligence to assume their proper responsibilities, catered to and exploited the general (or generalized) reader."[2] Jay Hubbell believes that, with Hemans, Sigourney "helped greatly to popularize a kind of debased Romanticism among readers who did not care for the far greater poems of Wordsworth, Shelley, and Keats."[3] Only Louise Bogan has a kind word for her: "She was fluent, industrious, and rather pushing; but she managed to put feminine verse writing on a paying basis, and give it prestige; even Poe did not quite dare to handle her work too roughly."[4] No one reads the poetry of Sigourney today, at least not as poetry.[5]

Lydia Howard Huntley, like many of the women poets in the early nineteenth century, came from a poor home; her father was a gardener. Nevertheless, the wife of her father's employer saw that she was educated and introduced her to poetry. For eight years, 1811–1819, Huntley and a friend operated a school for young women in Norwich and Hartford, Connecticut. When she married a widower, Charles Sigourney, in 1819, she became the mother of his three young children and, in 1827 and 1831, she had her own two children. Her first book, *Moral Pieces, in Prose and Verse* (1815), was published under her own name, but after her marriage, until 1833, she published anonymously because her husband objected. Mr. Sigourney, a hardware merchant, bank president, and college trustee, felt that his position might be injured by having it known that his wife was a poet.[6] His fortunes failed in the early 1830's, however, and it became imperative for his wife to help support the family. Lydia Sigourney attached her name to her next book, and her popular and prosperous years began. However, during her earlier years, her public anonymity had allowed her great personal freedom in themes and topics for her poems.

It is true that Sigourney wrote too much too fast. Her poems need much cutting and reworking. She ran out of topics and tended to repeat herself. Especially when her family's meals depended on her pen (after 1832), her poems were padded, pedantic, and prudish. Her most satisfying poems were written before 1832; the little collection entitled *Poems* (1834) represents her best poetry and is the volume from which I quote throughout this chapter, except as otherwise noted.

Her own preface to this edition acknowledged a debt to Coleridge; and Poe, in an 1836 review in *Southern Literary Messenger*, accused her of being overly imitative of Hemans. Other authors from whom she "borrowed" include Cowper, Hannah More, Wordsworth, and Byron.[7] She "imitated," but that is all anyone can really assert. Her "imitation" was that of an independent poet, who may have drawn thematic inspiration from the other poets, who did in fact learn prosodic techniques from the other poets, but whose thematic and image development was clearly her own.

Like nearly all poets in the nineteenth century, Sigourney wrote many poems about death. In the 1834 edition, the dead are mostly children and their mothers. We have seen that elegies for children had been a common genre in America since Bradstreet's poetry, and dead wives and mothers had been mourned in verse so often in the eighteenth century that Benjamin Franklin's "Silence Do-Good" could even offer a "receipt" for such elegies (no. 7). With the infant and maternal death rate still high, however, it is not surprising that nineteenth-century poets, both men and women, continued to write many elegies.

And yet, if we compare the elegies of Sigourney with similar poems written by American men or by an Englishwoman like Hemans, there is a great deal of difference in concept and theme. Springing from the graveyard poetry of late-eighteenth-century England, the death poems of the American men were generally the reflective meditation established by Bryant's "Thanatopsis." Or, for Poe and others, the dead were lovely young women lost to their male lovers. Later, Whitman would write the death song of "Out of the Cradle Endlessly Rocking."[8] Longfellow did carry "The Cross of Snow" for his wife, but, as a group, the American male poets (major and minor) since 1800 have not been interested poetically in dead children or even their dead mothers,[9] until the twentieth century when John Crowe Ransom was astonished by the "brown study" of John Whiteside's daughter and Robert Frost examined the very different reactions of a mother and father to their child's death in "Home Burial."

Hemans wrote many poems of death, but they seldom concern dead children and mothers. Many poems deal with strange burial rituals, as in "The Sword of the Tomb," or death customs, as in "The Stranger in Louisiana." Many women do die in the section of her works called "Records of Women" (some are mothers), but they are generally famous or brave women who die for some noble cause or reason, such as "Joan of Arc" or "The Switzer's Wife." In other poems, such as "The Siege of Valencia," women do not die, but their cowardly husbands do, after the wife has acted heroically and bravely to "save the kingdom." There are only a few poems which deal in a more specific and personal sense with death, such as "The Invocation: Written After the Death of a Sister-in-Law," "The Child's First Grief," and "The Dying Girl and Flowers."

Sigourney and her followers are, in fact, legitimate heirs of the seventeenth- and eighteenth-century "native" American elegies. It is, of course, clear why the nineteenth-century male poets wished to do something quite different with the elegy, since the genre had become overworked and thus, however sincere a poem of this kind might be or however clever the poet, the genre had been fossilized by the end of the eighteenth century. Sigourney, however, reiterated this form time and again. It is too easy to explain her elegies by saying that she knew her audience, that she "catered to" her reader. If we read her poems closely, we see that she was using this form as a vehicle for several different kinds of poetic investigations.

On the most simple level, Sigourney was attempting to deal honestly and in fairly real terms with the emotions, frustrations, and tragedies of the deaths of real children and their real mothers. Unlike her contemporary Bryant, she was simply not satisfied with the general thought that we all die. Nor would she have accepted Whitman's later solution ("the low and delicious word death") because such a resolution did not really affect the problems of the survivors. Long before Whitman finally approached the problems of survivors, as in "Come Up from the Fields Father," or Dickinson asked us to "Endow the Living—with the Tears," Sigourney had declared in "Hebrew Dirge":

> I saw an infant, marble cold,
>   Borne from the pillowing breast,
> And in the shroud's embracing fold
>   Laid down to dreamless rest;
> And moved with bitterness I sighed,
>   Not for the babe that slept,
> But for the mother at its side,
>   Whose soul in anguish wept.
>
> .   .   .   .
>
> We live to meet a thousand foes,
>   We shrink with bleeding breast,
> Why shall we weakly mourn for those
>   Who dwell in perfect rest?
> Bound for a few sad, fleeting years
>   A thorn-clad path to tread,
> Oh! for the *living* spare those tears
>   Ye lavish on the *dead*.

Of course, in Whitman's poem, the mourning mother simply dies from grief. For Sigourney and Dickinson, however, life, even if unpleasant, must continue.

In another poem, "Lochleven Castle," Sigourney satisfied herself as to just why queens die; and she realized that biblical children were sometimes raised from the dead, as in "The Widow of Zarephath." Her elegies for fathers and ministers were celebrations of these good and righteous men, as in "On the Death of Dr. Adam Clarke" and "Thoughts at the Funeral of a Respected Friend."

The majority of dead children and mothers in Sigourney's poetry may be identical (just as the poems tend to follow a certain pattern), but they are identical because they are American women and children—not queens or heroines or children of nobility. If there is anything really American in the more broad philosophical sense in her poetry, it is this democratic tendency: her realization that the death of those who have "achieved" nothing or who are part of the mass (not even the humble beggar of Wordsworth's poems) is as important as the death of ministers, queens, civic leaders, heroes, or even fathers.[10] Thus, on one level, her realization of the equalizing of death is developed parallel to Bryant's. On another and more important level, however, her concentration upon dead mothers and children is indicative of other interests for which Sigourney was poetically a pioneer.

First, Sigourney's elegies display a profound concern for the family, with each member, even the tiniest baby, as important as another, as in " 'Twas But a Babe." Although we have seen that concern with infants and children was already evident in the poetry of Bradstreet and Wheatley, it was Sigourney who repeated again and again the significance of the family—and she was one of the very first poets to insist upon the importance of the family as we know it and upon each of its individual members.

In the poetry of most American women after 1800, men as fathers are almost totally absent,[11] but in Sigourney's elegies the father is nearly always present.[12] His voice is muted, or he feels the "poverty of speech" (" 'Twas But a Babe"), but he is at least a presence. It is clear, however, that the father was less important to Sigourney than the mothers and children. Naturally, in a society in which woman's chief role was to bear and raise children, Sigourney tried to understand just why there were so many "failures." In early nineteenth-century middle-class American society (of which Sigourney is representative), women took little or no part in business or government; thus woman's role, her identity, was dependent upon her success as a mother. The death, therefore, of mother or child represents a kind of failure. The many dead mothers and children in Sigourney's poems are not simply reflective of historical fact, but are images of woman's limited social role. In fact, already evident in her poetry written before 1832 is Robert J. Lifton's *total nurturing ethos: . . . a despairing effort to achieve self-esteem and power through a mother-child relationship.*"[13]

Time and again, Sigourney insisted that a mother's death would seriously cripple and deprive the children:

> I wandered to a new-made grave,
>   And there a matron lay,
> The love of Him who died to save,
>   Had been her spirit's stay,
> Yet sobs burst forth of torturing pain;
>   Wail ye for her who died?
> No, for that timid, infant train
>   Who roam without a guide.
>   (from "Hebrew Dirge")

> A father's hand your course may guide
>   Amid the thorns of life,
> His care protect those shrinking plants
>   That dread the storms of strife;
> But who, upon your infant hearts
>   Shall like that mother write?
> Who touch the strings that rule the soul?
>   Dear, smitten flock, good night!
>   (spoken by the newly widowed father in
>   "A Father to His Motherless Children")

The mother as the child's spiritual guide and comforter suggests a "soul-relationship" for mother and child which the father cannot achieve. The "soul-relationship" is, in fact, the only "achievement" noted in Sigourney's poems for the dead mother. Such a situation is evidence of the disintegration of the role of woman in the early nineteenth century. Even in the late eighteenth century, as we have seen in the poetry of Margaretta Faugères, the "soul-relationship" could still be shared to some extent by the father.

Sigourney's "soul-relationship" of mother and child is extended in other poems which do not deal with death. For example, in a poem which is typical of much nineteenth-century verse in its division of city and country ("Sad I came/From weary commerce with the heartless world,/But when I felt upon my withered cheek/My mother Nature's breath"), it is not so much nature itself that salves the weary heart, but rather:

> ... a cradle at a cottage door,
> Where the fair mother with her cheerful wheel
> Carolled so sweet a song, that the young bird,

Which timid near the threshold sought for seeds,
Paused on his lifted foot, and raised his head,
As if to listen . . .

(from "A Cottage Scene")

The innocent mother with her innocent babe thus inspires a response from both nature and the weary poet.

Woman's role, in Sigourney's view, is properly that of her own youth, that of a pre–industrial revolution, rural housewife—of a time before the machine replaced woman's own "domestic" industry and thus, at the same time, limited her role and excluded her from the economic world. In one of Sigourney's most anthologized poems, "Connecticut River," the woman's role in the new Eden, the land of "Freedom," is idyllically described:

His thrifty mate, solicitous to bear
An equal burden in the yoke of care,
With vigorous arm the flying shuttle heaves,
Or from the press the golden cheese receives;
Her pastime when the daily task is o'er,
With apron clean, to seek her neighbour's door,
Partake the friendly feast, with social glow,
Exchange the news, and make the stocking grow;
Then hale and cheerful to her home repair,
When Sol's slant ray renews her evening care,
Press the full udder for her children's meal,
Rock the tired babe—or wake the tuneful wheel.

The role of woman in this, Sigourney's most patriotic and nationalistic poem written before 1832,[14] is as an "equal" bearer of burdens in a rural, preindustrial society. The machine had not yet entered the garden.[15]

Correspondingly, Sigourney's poems which center on dead babes and their mothers emphasize their "innocent" natures. In "Death of an Infant," the innocent babe dies, but defeats death and flies to heaven:

Death found strange beauty on that polished brow
And dashed it out.—
There was a tint of rose
On cheek and lip.—He touched the veins with ice,
And the rose faded.—
Forth from those blue eyes

> There spake a wishful tenderness, a doubt
> Whether to grieve or sleep, which innocence
> Alone may wear.—With ruthless haste he bound
> The silken fringes of those curtaining lids
> Forever.—
>   There had been a murmuring sound,
> With which the babe would claim its mother's ear,
> Charming her even to tears.—The Spoiler set
> His seal of silence.—
>   But there beamed a smile
> So fixed, so holy, from that cherub brow,
> Death gazed—and left it there.—
>   *He dared not steal*
> *The signet ring of Heaven.*[16]

The invariably innocent children and mothers go to a heaven which is infinitely better than earth. For Sigourney, there is a vast difference between heaven and earth, God and humanity; and, although God may be present at all times ("Solitude"), there is no sense at all of mystical experience, of transcending the body or the earth in any way. Neither Sigourney nor the other woman poets of her time could have become a "transparent eyeball," nor could they have hailed God as a "Camerado." Religion is traditional and ritualistic, as in "The Sabbath Bell." On the other hand, the sense of innocence is incompatible with the traditional concept of Eve. It is possible to see Sigourney's innocent mothers and babes as a parallel to the innocent Adam of the New World. And yet these mothers and babes die much too early. Something was wrong in Eden. Thus what appears to us as morbidity and what becomes, in fact, a dull repetition of poetic genre developed into an attempt not only to justify the limited role of women in a quickly industrializing society, but also at the same time to acknowledge the existence of woman's "failure" and the resulting problems for the children. Sigourney's resolution of a heavenly destination may seem limited and "nonintellectual," but, except for the high maternal and infant mortality rate, the conflicts which she suggested in her elegies are still present.

Sigourney, who was our first professional woman poet, was also the first woman actually to understand and express her realization that her role as a poet was in conflict with that of a housewife. In "To a Shred of Linen,"[17] Sigourney uses an eighteenth-century form as a vehicle for rather revolutionary thoughts. Other women before Sigourney had shown a conscious sense of self as poets and had, further, denigrated the role of housewife. Even in Sigourney's own day, many women pleaded "loneliness" or a desire to "teach friends" as excuses for their poetry. Sigourney, however, asserted that, in fact, a role conflict does exist and, at the same time, indicated her sensitivity to the changing role of women in the early nineteenth century. I quote the entire poem:

> Would they had swept cleaner!—
> Here's a littering shred
> Of linen left behind—a vile reproach
> To all good housewifery. Right glad am I
> That no neat lady, train'd in ancient times
> Of pudding-making, and of sampler-work,
> And speckless sanctity of household care,
> Hath happened here to spy thee. She, no doubt,
> Keen looking through her spectacles, would say,
> "*This comes of reading books*:["]—or some spruce beau,
> Essenc'd and lily-handed, had he chanc'd
> To scan thy slight superfices, 'twould be
> "*This comes of writing poetry.*"—Well—well—
> Come forth—offender!—hast thou aught to say?
> Canst thou by merry thought, or quaint conceit,
> Repay this risk, that I have run for thee?
> —Begin at alpha, and resolve thyself
> Into thine elements. I see the stalk
> And bright, blue flower of flax, which erst o'erspread
> That fertile land, where mighty Moses stretch'd
> His rod miraculous. I see thy bloom
> Tinging, too scantly, these New England vales.
> But, lo! the sturdy farmer lifts his flail,
> To crush thy bones unpitying, and his wife
> With 'kerchief'd head, and eyes brimful of dust,
> Thy fibrous nerves, with hatchet-tooth divides.
> —I hear a voice of music—and behold!
> The ruddy damsel singeth at her wheel,
> While by her side the rustic lover sits.
> Perchance, his shrewd eye secretly doth count
> The mass of skeins, which, hanging on the wall,
> Increaseth day by day. Perchance his thought,
> (For men have deeper minds than women—sure!)
> Is calculating what a thrifty wife
> The maid will make; and how his dairy shelves
> Shall groan beneath the weight of golden cheese,
> Made by her dextrous hand, while many a keg

And pot of butter, to the market borne,
May, transmigrated, on his back appear,
In new thanksgiving coats.
                                    Fain would I ask,
Mine own New England, for thy once loved wheel,
By sofa and piano quite displac'd.
Why dost thou banish from thy parlor-hearth
That old Hygeian harp, whose magic rul'd
Dyspepsia, as the minstrel-shepherd's skill
Exorcis'd Saul's ennui? There was no need,
In those good times, of calisthenics, sure,
And there was far less of gadding, and far more
Of home-born, heart-felt comfort, rooted strong
In industry, and bearing such rare fruit,
As wealth might never purchase.
                                    But come back,
Thou shred of linen. I did let thee drop,
In my harangue, as wiser ones have lost
The thread of discourse. What was thy lot
When the rough battery of the loom had stretch'd
And knit thy sinews, and the chemist sun
Thy brown complexion bleach'd?
                                    Methinks I scan
Some idiosyncrasy, that marks thee out
A defunct pillow-case.—Did the trim guest,
To the best chamber usher'd, e'er admire
The snowy whiteness of thy freshen'd youth
Feeding thy vanity? or some sweet babe
Pour its pure dream of innocence on thee?
Say, hast thou listen'd to the sick one's moan,
When there was none to comfort?—or shrunk back
From the dire tossings of the proud man's brow?
Or gather'd from young beauty's restless sigh
A tale of untold love?
                                    Still, close and mute!—
Wilt tell no secrets, ha?—Well, then, go down,
With all thy churl-kept hoard of curious lore,
In majesty and mystery, go down
Into the paper-mill, and from its jaws,
Stainless and smooth, emerge.—Happy shall be
The renovation, if on thy fair page
Wisdom and truth, their hallow'd lineaments

Trace for posterity. So shall thine end
Be better than thy birth, and worthier bard
Thine apotheosis immortalise.

Moreover, not all of Sigourney's poems feature dead women or children. She takes delight in the child for himself and yet, much like a twentieth-century mother, Sylvia Plath in "Mary's Song," fears for his future:

Thou dost not dream, my little one,
　　How great the change must be,
These two years, since the morning sun
　　First shed his beams on thee;
Thy little hands did helpless fall,
　　As with a stranger's fear,
And a faint, wailing cry, was all
　　That met thy mother's ear.

But now, the dictates of thy will
　　Thine active feet obey,
And pleased thy busy fingers still
　　Among thy playthings stray,
And thy full eyes delighted rove
　　The pictured page along

.　　.　　.　　.　　.　　.　　.

Fair boy! the wanderings of thy way,
　　It is not mine to trace,
Through buoyant youth's exulting day,
　　Or manhood's bolder race,
What discipline thy heart may need,
　　What clouds may veil thy sun,
The Eye of God, alone can read,
　　And let his will be done.
　　　　　(from "The Second Birth-Day")

The anxiety of the mother for the child who must grow up and yet the mother's acceptance of the "buoyant youth's exulting day" indicate another facet of Sigourney, which is not morbid or death-centered. Furthermore, it is significant that a living child is considered a perfectly legitimate subject for serious, adult poetry. Only Ann Eliza Bleecker, in the late eighteenth century, preceded Sigourney in this type of verse.

Two poems, apparently written for Sigourney's children, are the happiest and, in some ways, the most successful poetically in the 1834 edition. Although we have seen that American women were writing poems for children at the end of the eighteenth century, it was not until the beginning of the nineteenth century that both men and women viewed such poems as a respectable genre. Two of the most popular of all American poems for children date from this time—Sarah Josepha Hale's "Mary Had a Little Lamb" and Clement Moore's "The Night before Christmas." Nearly every woman poet tried her pen at children's poems, a genre which affected women's "adult" poetry in a variety of ways. First, it encouraged the women (more than the men) to examine their own relationships with their children. Thus, in large part, from the "children's poems" developed the modern poetry written by such women as Plath and Sexton, who were deeply interested in the mother-child relationship. Second, it is obvious that writers of children's poems (both men and women) did not, at least at this time, employ the nineteenth-century "poetic diction" in this genre. Critics have tended to cite Robert Browning as influential in shifting use of the heightened and affected "poetic diction" to more colloquial diction in American poetry. But children's poems had employed common and simple diction for many years before Browning's poems reached America. Finally, for the women, their poetry for children was more informal, more personal, and more free in diction and meter than their other works. Often, the women made observations in poems for their children that they would not possibly have made in their poems for adults. In fact, some of the most startling and original poetry written in the second half of the nineteenth century was written by women purportedly for their children. (One must wonder whether or not the "nursery-rhyme" quality of Dickinson's poems can be traced to this situation.) Thus, by the 1870's, an otherwise "nonliberated" mother could tell her children:

> If I had made the world—ah me!
>   I might have left some things undone!
> But as to *him*—my boy, you see,
> A pretty world this would be,
>   I'd say, without George Washington!
>
>   .   .   .   .
>
> I'd *not* have made the wind, because
>   It's made of—nothing. Never mind,

Nor any white bears—they have claws;
(Nor "Science," no, nor "Nature's Laws!")
   Nor made the North Pole hard to find!

I'd *not* have made the monkeys—(then
   No one could ever prove to me
There ever was a season when
All these fine creatures we call men
   Hung chattering in some tropic tree!)

Once more, Good Night. This time you hear?
   Please hear as well my morning call.
—Yes, first I'll tell you something queer:
If *I* had made the world, I fear—
   I'd not have made the world at all![18]

Lydia Sigourney's poems for children established such an independence of spirit and diction. In "Flora's Party," she not only satirizes in a light and ironic manner nineteenth-century society, but
also parodies the sentimental "flower morality" so common in wom-
en's (and Poe's) poetry at this time (for example, Hale's *Flora's Interpreter; or, The American Book of Flowers and Sentiments*).
Sigourney depicts a tea party to which Lady Flora extends "cards"
to personified flowers, buds, and blossoms. Both males and females
are gently nudged: "prudish Miss Lily" (who in the solemn moralizing of the floral anthologies is usually associated with purity or
friendship) leaves the party in a huff because the Soldiers in Green
"stared at her *so*"; Madame Damask complains of household chores;
Ragged Ladies and Marigolds gossip; and Mr. Snowball, in a discussion of painting with Fleur de Lis, proclaims that *"all Nature's
Colouring was bad."* The stilted diction, the "gemmy" words are
gone. The conversational tone, the looser poetic line, the common
diction dominate. Some of Sigourney's most successful lines appear
in this poem as, with anapests swinging, she describes the dance of
Lady-slippers, Aspens, and Sweet-briars: "And sweet 'twas to see their
light footsteps advance/Like the wing of the breeze through the
maze of the dance." However, the dance quickly ends:

But the Monk's hood scowled dark, and in utterance low,
Declared " 'twas high time for good Christians to go;
He'd heard from his parson a sermon sublime,
Where he proved from the Vulgate—*to dance was a crime.*"

So folding a cowl round his cynical head,
He took from the side-board a bumper and fled.

The poem ends with Flora confessing that she " 'was never so glad
in her life' " that the guests had left.

"The Ark and Dove" begins with the poet's daughter asking
" '*Tell me a story—please.*" The mother's story of Noah is inter-
rupted once "to see if her young thought/Wearied with following
mine. But her blue eye/Was a glad listener." The story itself is told
in diction and phrasing appropriate to a child:

[I] told her how it rained, and rained, and rained,
Till all the flowers were covered; and the trees
Hid their tall heads, and where the houses stood,
And people dwelt, a fearful deluge rolled.

Sigourney did not always write about mothers and children and
home. She herself was active in a variety of charitable and other social concerns and used her poetry to encourage such causes. She considered the plight of the Indians (who she hoped would be converted
to Christianity), slaves, temperance, and blind and deaf children. All
of these topics, however, are treated in a passive sense; that is, the
reader never feels that the poet can do much about the situation,
except, as in "Intellectual Wants of Greece," sending Christian
books to Greece (itself, as she realized, an ironic situation).

Sigourney's prosody is as confined to eighteenth-century verse
forms as was that of most of her contemporaries; in her "adult"
poems, she was careless and euphemistic in diction. Her resolution
of problems and many of her sentiments are traditional ones, but
she opened new areas for poetic exploration and she showed a sensitivity to the roles of women in the quickly industrializing society
of her time. I do not agree that she was unintelligent or that she
failed to "assume her responsibilities" (as Pearce would have it). She
was not a man-hater, as were some of her feminist contemporaries;
she supported the family (father, mother, and each child, as individ-
uals) but at the same time realized that something had happened to
the role of women, to their identity in nineteenth-century society.
As a professional herself and as a housewife/mother, she sensed that
something was wrong and expressed her knowledge through the images of dead mothers and children. We find her dull because she
never developed and, later in her career, simply repeated her earlier
poems. We find her poetically unsatisfying because she was sloppy

and too often unaware of her craft. And yet she was a unique voice in American poetry at her time.

Elizabeth Oakes Smith (1806–1893)

Lydia Sigourney's innocent babe and mother, the sinless Eve in the new Eden, the proper mate for the new Adam, quickly reached an imaginative dead end in Elizabeth Oakes Smith's "The Sinless Child," a best seller of seven cantos in the 1840's. Never again were the more thoughtful American women poets to suggest that an Eve (alive or dead) could exist in the new Eden of America. Clearly, the women understood the fallacies of both the image and the situation long before the men did.

When only sixteen, Elizabeth Oakes married Seba Smith, at that time a well-known humorist and editor of the Portland *Eastern Argus*. Greatly resenting the marriage forced upon her by her parents, she considered it "an annihilation."[19] She had been able to read by the age of two and had hoped somehow to attain a college-level education. For the next few years, she raised a family of five boys and helped her husband with the newspaper. In the early 1830's, Seba Smith lost his money in poor investments, and eventually the family moved to New York City, where both husband and wife attempted to make a living by their pens. Elizabeth Smith quickly became one of the most popular writers (both socially and "artistically") in the New York literary scene, praised by both men and women.[20] Her poems and essays appeared in nearly every major journal, and she was friendly with Poe, Bryant, Emerson, and the other great names of American literature at this time.

Except for "The Sinless Child" and one short poem, her verse is generally undistinguished. It is highly derivative ("Love Dead" is a poor "The Raven") and highly impersonal. The bulk of Elizabeth Oakes Smith's poetry was written hastily for publication and, in order to sell more poems, she adopted a number of pseudonyms. At first, she published as Mrs. Seba Smith, then as Elizabeth Oakes Smith and (at the same time) Ernest Helfenstein, and finally as Oakes Smith, a name she liked so well that she arranged for her sons to use it as a surname. In the 1842–1845 issues of *Graham's Magazine*, poems, sketches, and essays by Elizabeth Oakes Smith and Ernest Helfenstein appeared side by side; they are generally similar in tone, sentiment, theme, and prosody.

Her one notable short poem, "The Drowned Mariner" (in *The Poetical Writings* [1845]), is listed by Melville at the beginning of *Moby Dick* among the "Extracts." Melville quotes only the first five lines, but the comparative situations of Smith's "Mariner" and Melville's "watergazer" on "The Masthead" (Chapter 35) can be understood only by a reading of the entire poem:

A Mariner sat on the shrouds one night,
    The wind was piping free,
Now bright, now dimmed was the moonlight pale,
And the phosphor gleamed in the wake of the whale
    As he floundered in the sea;
The scud was flying athwart the sky,
The gathering winds were whistling by,
And the wave as it towered, then fell in spray
Looked an emerald wall in the moonlight ray.

The mariner swayed and rocked on the mast,
    But the tumult pleased him well,
Down the yawning wave his eye he cast,
And the monsters watched as they hurried past,
    Or lightly rose and fell;
For their broad, damp fins were under the tide,
And they lashed as they passed the vessel's side,
And their filmy eyes, all huge and grim,
Glared fiercely up, and they glared at him.

Now freshens the gale, and the brave ship goes
    Like an uncurbed steed along,
A sheet of flame is the spray she throws,
As the gallant prow the water plows—
    But the ship is fleet and strong:
The topsails are reefed and the sails furled,
And onward she sweeps o'er the watery world.
And dippeth her spars in the surging flood;
But there came no chill to the mariner's blood.

Wildly she rocks, but he swingeth at ease,
    And holds him by the shroud;
And as she careens to the crowding breeze
The gaping deep the mariner sees,
    And the surging hearest loud.
Was that a face looking up at him,
With its paled cheek and its cold eyes dim?
Did it beckon him down? did it call his name?
Now rolleth the ship the way whence it came.

The mariner looked, and he saw with dread,
   A face he knew too well;
And the cold eyes glared, the eyes of the dead,
And its long hair out on the wave was spread.
   Was there a tale to tell?
The stout ship rocked with reeling speed,
And the mariner groaned, as well he need,
For ever down, as she plunged on her side,
The dead face gleamed from the briny tide.

Bethink thee, mariner, well of the past,
   A voice calls loud for thee—
There's a stifled prayer, the first, the last,
The plunging ship on her beam is cast,
   Oh, where shall thy burial be?
Bethink thee of oaths that were lightly spoken,
Bethink thee of vows that were lightly broken,
Bethink thee of all that is dear to thee—
For thou art alone on the raging sea:

Alone in the dark, alone on the wave,
   To buffet the storm alone—
To struggle aghast at the watery grave,
To struggle, and feel there is none to save—
   God shield thee, helpless one!
The stout limbs yield, for their strength is past,
The trembling hands on the deep are cast,
The white brow gleams a moment more,
Then slowly sinks—the struggle is o'er.

Down, down where the storm is hushed to sleep,
   Where the sea its dirge shall swell,
Where the amber drops for thee shall weep,
And the rose-lipped shell her music keep,
   There thou shalt slumber well.
The gem and the pearl be heaped at thy side,
They fell from the neck of the beautiful bride,
From the strong man's hand, from the maiden's brow,
As they slowly sunk to the wave below.

A peopled home is the ocean bed,
   The mother and child are there—
The fervent youth and the hoary head,

The maid, with her floating locks outspread,
  The babe with its silken hair,
As the water movest they lightly sway,
And the tranquil lights on their features play;
And there is each cherished and beautiful form,
Away from decay, and away from the storm.

Unlike so many poems concerning the sea at this time (sea poems were a popular type among both male and female magazine writers), the storm and water images of "The Drowned Mariner" have a ring of authenticity, perhaps because the Smith family experienced a violent storm during an 1839 midwinter voyage from Portland, Maine, to Charleston, South Carolina:

> We encountered one fearful storm that broke in the cabin windows and deluged it with water. For a time I sat by the taffrail, flat on the ship's deck where I could watch the storm. We were "laying to" under close reefed canvas, the wind howling and shrieking, and we, now engulfed in the bottom of the abysm of sea, and anon riding on the crest.
>
> . . . Looking to the topmast there was a pale blue flame, spectrelike, shining through the darkness. . . . The rain came down in torrents and I was wet to the backbone, but joyous.[21]

The imaginative presentation of the "watergazer" on the masthead is undoubtedly what attracted Melville to this poem. Melville's watergazer, however, contemplates pantheism and its implication of the loss of personal identity. He ultimately saves himself from death. Smith's watergazer sees the face and hair of the young woman he has deceived in the waves of the storm, and does finally fall to his death—a melodramatic touch, in keeping with much imaginative literature of the early nineteenth century. Although the intellectual implications of Melville's passage are certainly more interesting than Smith's, the wave/hair images of the poem are imaginatively integrated, and the hypnotic effect of the sea for the sailor on the masthead is successfully suggested.

"The Sinless Child" is historically a notable contribution to American literature. Although Smith admitted and contemporary critics agreed that the poem suggests Wordsworth, it actually owes more to the early Emerson and to the early nineteenth-century feminist movement. In its own way, the poem is successful, certainly Smith's best poetry. As its title suggests, "The Sinless Child" is based upon a theme common in both English and American poetry at this time. However, among the many treatments of this theme, there are a number of significant variations. In the poems of Wordsworth, for example, the innocent and sinless child dies without maturing.[22] In Whitman's "Out of the Cradle Endlessly Rocking" and "There Was a Child Went Forth," the innocent child matures by experience and discovery, by a certain necessary loss of innocence. In Smith's poem, and indeed in the early Emerson as Smith seems to have read and interpreted *Nature*, the child matures, maintains her innocence, and gives her message to the world.

That Smith's poem is an extension of early Emersonian transcendentalism is clear. The arguments before each of the seven sections contain passages which might well have been footnoted to *Nature*:

[Part I.] She sees the world, not merely with mortal eyes, but looks within to the pure internal life, of which the outward is but a type.

[Part II.] Even from infancy she seems to have penetrated the spiritual through the material; to have beheld the heavenly, not through a glass darkly, but face to face, by means of that singleness and truth, that look within the veil.

[Part III.] Alas! that to assimilate to the good and beautiful should debar us from human sympathy!

And so on. Smith's "Sinless Child" (Eva) is the Emersonian child of *Nature* whose eye and heart "the sun illuminates." She is the child who finds "perpetual youth" in the woods, who demonstrates Emerson's "invariable mark of wisdom . . . to see the miraculous in the common" (*Nature*).

But Smith differs theologically from Emerson in the Christian imagery so profusely scattered throughout the poem. For example, a passage from Part III begins with Emerson but ends with Calvinism and a verbal echo from Sigourney:

The little child at dawn of life
  A holy impress bears,
The signet-mark by heaven affixed
  Upon his forehead wears;
And naught that impress can efface,
  Save his own wilful sin,
Which first begins to draw the veil
  That shuts the spirit in.

Moreover, the mythology of prelapsarian Eve and Marian worship permeates Eva's character. Even though Smith was a Unitarian, one of her notes to "The Sinless Child" urges American women to practice the worship of Mary in the home:

> The worship of the Madonna is in the true spirit of poetry. She has become to the christian world what the Penates had been to the classical. In confining ourselves to the abstractions of religion, we run the hazard of making it one of thought rather than of emotion. A woman must always worship through her affections, and one may readily conceive the comfort which the household faith in the presence of the Madonna is likely to inspire.[23]

On one hand, the Edenic/Marian mythology corresponds to the Adamic theme developed by the men, as well as to the standard nineteenth-century concept of wives as mothers/virgins. On the other hand, Smith extends the mythology beyond the traditional limits and creates a sinless child who embodies Smith's own feminist tendencies. In 1839 Smith dragged an unwilling husband to hear a lecture by Frances Wright, the English reformer. By 1848, she had been active enough in feminist circles to be seriously considered as president of the National Women's Rights Convention. In 1851, Horace Greeley commissioned Smith to write a series of articles concerning the feminist movement for his *Tribune*. The articles were later issued in a twenty-five-cent pamphlet, *Woman and Her Needs*, and widely distributed. Smith then took the feminist cause before the lyceum audience, one of the first women (if not the first) to speak in that public forum.

Not really considered a radical militant,[24] Smith told her lyceum audience just what she had written for the *Tribune*: "What I claim for woman is the removal of the interdict. Accept her as a citizen. Now she is denied the rights of citizen and all the lumbering legislation of centuries will not adjust her relations harmoniously in the world till she is thus recognized. She cannot reach the true dignity of her being till she is invested with the sanctities and privileges of a good citizen." Moreover, "I do not see that the sexes greatly differ, the strong of each and the harmonious of each being the exception and not the rule . . ."[25]

"The Sinless Child," however, expresses not the equality of women but the superiority of women. Eva is the daughter of a poor widow who lives in a cottage in the woods. She grows up without any relationship whatsoever with a male—no father, no brother, no minister, no male friend. Her only companions are the living beings

of the natural world, through whom she finds God. She does somehow learn stories concerning the relationship of men and women: in
Part IV, she corrects her mother's version of a local scandal, the
story of evil Old Richard (the melodramatic plot is based upon the
popular prose melodramas of the time). And Eva is sensitive to the
relationship of other mothers and children (Part V). In Part VI, Eva
becomes a woman, as the argument tells us: "Then cometh the mystery of womanhood; its gentle going forth of the affections seeking
for that holiest of companionship, a kindred spirit, responding to all
its finer essences, and yet lifting it above itself." Eva's first proselyte
is Albert Linne, a young man "whose errors are those of an ardent
and inexperienced nature, rather than of an assenting will." Eva
turns Albert from his former life of "What once he called delight,/
The goblet, oath, and stolen joy." Their physical relationship never
passes beyond a kiss on the brow. Others learn of the message of
"The Sinless Child," but Albert (Adam) is Smith's allegorical rep-
resentation that "The mission of woman, is to the erring of man."
Eva does not really die, but rather "cease[s] to be present," with
Smith herself interjecting, "Eva, mine own, my beautiful."[26]

Eva is really neither prelapsarian Eve nor Mary:[27] she is a female
Christ. She is not searching for equality; she is already superior. She
is the early Emerson's dream of the eternal child in the woods, but
she is a woman and it is the men whom she will convert. To a large
extent, she is the female counterpart of Natty Bumppo and Billy
Budd. She is, of course, a dead end—an unreal fantasy who is not
very attractive in her self-righteous moralizing. She is a "dream," in
which the other American women poets have refused to indulge
themselves. It should be remembered, however, that Eva is also
Emerson's self-reliant person, a woman who maintains her own integrity and sense of purpose. Yet she essentially remains a child-
woman, a person for whom sin is a priori an impossibility.

Although this study is concerned with poetry, it is necessary to
examine Smith's later treatment in a novel of the sinless child to
see just what happens to such a creature when she ventures into the
world outside the woods and when marriage becomes a possibility.
The major female characters of Smith's feminist novel *Bertha and
Lily* (1858) are nearly all manifestations of the sinless child or of
Smith herself. The heroine, Bertha, is the sinless child as a woman
who has had a brief love affair with an older man, Underhill. Underhill (who physically resembles Seba Smith) has "deceived" Bertha
but still loves her and returns to attempt to win her again. (He fails
and dies on the spot.) Bertha is a poet (who writes poems whenever
she is unhappy), with wealth enough to live comfortably. She ulti-

mately marries the local minister, Ernest Helfenstein (one of Smith's pseudonyms in the 1830's and 1840's), who must however be "converted" before marriage. Lily is the sinless child herself again, this time apparently an orphan, with a difficult little brother. Lily is immediately in "soul-communication" with Bertha. Julia, Ernest's cousin, is a beautiful woman to whom Ernest first proposes. But Ernest is not worldly enough for Julia, who eventually marries a wealthy and fashionable man in New York and, with conscious hypocrisy, writes "love poems" for the New York journals (Smith's commentary, one suspects, on her colleagues' poetry). Defiance True represents the Puritan housewife, happy to be keeping a clean house and praying regularly. Statements from the feminist movement are scattered throughout the text.

The various personality splits should not be related to such post-Freudian poems as Elinor Wylie's "Little Eclogue" or Denise Levertov's "An Embroidery (I)."[28] What Smith's novel implies is that the sinless child can only marry herself. She is, however, not really so different from the unmarried Natty Bumppo or Billy Budd. Although the women poets following Smith rejected the myth, the myth itself had to be tried, I suspect. It is the outgrowth of an aspect of early Emersonian Transcendentalism, of certain aspects of a still powerful Calvinism, of the Adamic myth which was by this time permeating the literature of the American men, and, finally, of nineteenth-century feminism.

As poetry, Smith's "The Sinless Child" contains her best work. Her image development at times indicates a progress toward the image concentration in Dickinson:

> She early marked the butterfly,
>   That gay, mysterious thing,
> That, bursting from its prison-house
>   Appeared on golden wing;
> It had no voice to speak delight,
>   Yet on the floweret's breast,
> She saw it mute and motionless,
>   In long, long rapture rest.
>
> .   .   .   .
>
> It crawled no more a sluggish thing
>   Upon the lowly earth;
> A brief, brief sleep, and then she saw
>   A new and radiant birth,
> And thus she learned without a doubt,

> That man from death would rise,
> As did the butterfly on wings,
>   To claim its native skies.

The image itself is not original with Smith: Caroline Gilman had used it (in a great many more words) a few years earlier in "Mother What Is Death?" On the other hand, Smith was able to compact the image in a manner not often achieved by women poets at this time. This kind of single-image development, with the controlled reference and lesson from nature, is scattered throughout the opening sections of the poem.

Smith is important as a poet who offered a feminine parallel to the male poetry and mythology of her day. Her poem was extremely popular, and Smith was a successful lecturer. Her ideas and her poem were well known to both men and women. The feminist ideas she shared with others in the early nineteenth century have survived, but her mythology was rejected by the women poets. They were going in a different direction.

Frances Sargent Locke Osgood (1811–1850)

Not only by talent but also by poetic interest, Osgood is separated from her male and female contemporaries nearly as much as Dickinson is separated from hers. Dickinson, however, explored her inner landscape, while Osgood wrote of her outer landscape, her relationships with other people. Both were incredibly honest and personal in their poetry. However, while Dickinson's poetry is consistently of high quality, Osgood often allowed her poetry to slip into the clichés of the magazine trade, through which she (like Smith and Sigourney) was feeding her family. Highly personal poetry which deals honestly with interpersonal relationships (even to the point of "embarrassment") was not judged "valuable" by the arbiters of American literature until Robert Lowell made "confessional" poetry respectable. Previous to Lowell, poets of this inclination have nearly all been women (with the influence of Sappho) and, like Osgood, have been forgotten or, like Millay, have been scorned.

Frances Osgood, the wife of the painter Samuel Stillman Osgood, is remembered today only as a woman with whom Poe may have had some kind of affair (1845–1846) and whose poems Poe praised. If her poetry is read at all, it is by those scholars who are studying Poe and, from what I can tell, only those poems by Osgood related to her affair are studied. Nevertheless, she is generally considered to be one of the best of the women poets with whom Poe surrounded himself in the 1840's.[29] On the other hand, Hervey Allen draws the rather surprising conclusion that "her verse was compounded by a bombastic rhetoric, sentimentality, and a certain 'grace' for which Poe chiefly praised her."[30]

Like Lydia Sigourney, Osgood had published poetry before her marriage (in 1825, in *Juvenile Miscellany*), but her major work came after her marriage in 1835 to Samuel Osgood. With her husband, she lived several years in England, making friends of painters and of such women as Harriet Martineau. She published two books and gave birth to a daughter in England. After she returned to America in 1840, she had another daughter and began to publish widely in the American journals. In the 1840's, she wrote or edited six books; the seventh, her (not complete) *Poems* appeared the year of her death.[31] Her third child, born in 1846, apparently caused the cessation of whatever kind of affair she was having with Poe.

It is clear that many of Osgood's poems reflect the magazine trade: "The Triumph of the Spiritual over the Sensual," the temptress/ sinless-child dichotomy; "The Life-Voyage," a Christian morality piece; "The Child and Its Angel-Playmate," the dead child floating to heaven; "The Spirit's Voyage," an Indian legend; and "New England's Mountain-Child," a sister to Bryant's "O Fairest of the Rural Maids." Yet even in these poems there is a unique voice. The padded lines, the inverted grammar, the stilted diction, the heavy hand are only occasionally noticeable, despite her use of overworked themes.

The great bulk of Osgood's verse is amatory, but she also wrote poems to her mother, her sister, her children, her husband, her friends, both male and female, and other associates. I say "poems to," because her best poems read like intimate letters, so personal and apparently spontaneous are they. Like Sappho, she is forthright and obvious. She said things in verse that would not be said again in America by a woman until the 1890's. She was not a member of the feminist movement, yet she was aggressively herself.

Until the mid-1840's, when her marriage began to disintegrate, her love poems are light and joyous:

> Your heart is a music-box, dearest!
>   With exquisite tunes at command,
> Of melody sweetest and clearest,
>   If tried by a delicate hand;
> But its workmanship, love, is so fine,
>   At a single rude touch it would break,

Then oh! be the magic key mine,
  Its fairy like whispers to wake!
And there's one little tune it can play,
  That I fancy all others above—
You learned it of Cupid one day—
  It begins with and ends with "I love!"
          "I love!"
  My heart echoes to it "I love."

The brief, trimetric lines, filled with anapests, and the device of the
concluding three lines indicate a command of prosody beyond that
of most American writers in the early nineteenth century.

Moreover, Osgood can tease her lover (and her reader). In "A
Song," Osgood juxtaposes the overworked images of early-nineteenth-
century love verse with the rather unsophisticated and undignified
refrain, "Call me pet names." All this she fits into lines of irregular
(although basically anapestic) tetrameter, which move easily and
perhaps, because of the metric irregularities and refrain, were once
set to music:

Call me pet names, dearest! Call me a bird,
That flies to thy breast at one cherishing word,
That folds its wild wings there, ne'er dreaming of flight,
That tenderly sings there in loving delight!
Oh! my sad heart keeps pining for one fond word,—
Call me pet names, dearest! Call me thy bird!

Call me sweet names, darling! Call me a flower,
That lives in the light of thy smile each hour,
That droops when its heaven—thy heart—grows cold,
That shrinks from the wicked, the false and bold,
That blooms for thee only, through sunlight and shower;
Call me pet names, darling! Call me thy flower!

Call me fond names, dearest! Call me a star,
Whose smile's beaming welcome thou feel'st from afar,
Whose light is the clearest, the truest to thee,
When the "night-time of sorrow" steals o'er life's sea:
Oh! trust thy rich bark, where its warm rays are,
Call me pet names, darling! Call me thy star!

Call me dear names, darling! Call me thine own!
Speak to me always in Love's low tone!
Let not thy look nor thy voice grow cold:

Let my fond worship thy being enfold;
Love me forever, and love me alone!
Call me pet names, darling! Call me thine own!

Although there are other poems which express the joy of "Your
Heart Is a Music-Box, Dearest" and the silliness of "A Song," Osgood also wrote cynical and sophisticated verses, which are intima-
tions of Millay's *A Few Figs from Thistles*, as in the following
poems:[32]

UNTITLED

Have I caught you at last, gentle rover?
  Do I see you at length at my feet?
Will you own yourself, sighing, my lover?
  This triumph is sudden as sweet!

Long vainly I strove to allure him;
  That tender endeavour is past;
My task must be *now, to endure him!*
  Heighho! but I've caught him at last!

UNTITLED

Nay! ours is not the morning
  Of love, when all is fresh and sweet,
I often catch you yawning,
  You know, whene'er we meet.

For me, I must confess, love,
  I'm growing rather bored—and so
Take back this golden tress, love,
  And let me—let me—go!

FORGIVE AND FORGET

"Forgive—forget! I own the wrong!"
  You fondly sigh'd when last I met you;
The task is neither hard nor long—
  I *do* forgive—I *will* forget you!

HE BADE ME BE HAPPY

He bade me, "Be happy," he whisper'd "Forget me;"
  He vow'd my affection was cherish'd in vain,
"Be happy!" "Forget me!" I would, if he let me—
  Why will he keep coming to say so again?

He came—it was not the first time, by a dozen—
  To take, as he said, "an eternal adieu;"
He went, and, for comfort, I turn'd to—my cousin,
  When back stalked the torment his vows to renew.

"You must love me no longer!" he said but this morning.
  "I love you no longer!" I meekly replied.
"Is this my reward?" he cried; "falsehood and scorning
  From her who was ever my idol, my pride!"

He bade me, "Be happy," he murmur'd "Forget me!"—
  "Go into the gayest society, Jane!"
And I would obey him, right well, if he let me;
  But, the moment I do, he comes loving again!

Like Millay, Osgood obviously had a strong and realistic sense of herself, not as an extension of a man, her home, or her children. The difficulties in erotic or marital male and female relationships occur, according to Osgood, when the woman becomes a "worshipper" or loses her identity in the man, although, as we have seen in her poetry, there is nothing wrong with love per se.

A number of her poems emphasize that a woman must not lose her sense of herself as an individual in any love relationship. Her most successful poems on this theme are built with irony, as in "The Fetter 'neath the Flower" and the following, "The Lily's Delusion":

A cold, calm star look'd out of heaven,
  And smiled upon a tranquil lake,
Where, pure as angel's dream at even,
  A lily lay but half awake.

The flower felt that fatal smile
  And lowlier bow'd her conscious head;
"Why does he gaze on me the while?"
  The light, deluded Lily said.

Poor dreaming flower!—too soon beguiled,
  She cast nor thought nor looked elsewhere,
Else she had known the star but smiled
  To see himself reflected there.

Along with such development by analogy, Osgood treated the same subject in a more conversational poem. In a long (for her) monologue of an obviously experienced woman, who is speaking "To Sybil," the woman begins:

> Yes! go to him—thy young heart full
>   Of passionate romance,
> And be the fiat of thy fate
>   His lordly word or glance!
>
> Be thy soul's day, his careless smile;
>   His frown, its clouded night;
> His voice, the music of thy life,
>   His love, thy one delight!

And she continues:

> Go—try them all—those girlish wiles!
>   He cannot choose but love,
> He cannot choose but guard from ill
>   His little, nestling dove!

However, she warns, "But if thou think'st, dear dreaming child!/ That he will watch as now," of course, she concludes, he won't:

> If *this* thy dream, enthusiast, be,
>   I can but idly pray
> Heaven shield thee in thy *waking* hour,
>   And keep it long away!

In this poem, the speaker does not urge Sybil to refrain from love; rather she warns her that a love relationship in which the woman is a coquettish, flirting child is doomed to be unsuccessful and that a woman whose "one delight" is the man must someday wake up from her dream.

Osgood also considered the problems of a woman poet whose love affair has collapsed. Like Millay and H. D., she finds that poetic creation is difficult after love has failed, as in "Song," a poem based on her affair with Poe, from which I quote only a part:

> I cannot forget him!
>   I've locked up my soul;
> But not till his image
>   Deep, deep in it stole.
>
> .   .   .   .   .   .
>
> I turn to my books;
>   But his voice rich and rare,
> Is blent with the genius
>   That speaks to me there.

I tune my wild lyre,
  But I think of the praise,
Too precious, too dear,
  Which he lent to my lays!

Certainly, there is a vast difference between Osgood and contemporary poets of amatory verse, such as Elizabeth Barrett Browning. In fact, in one of her early poems, "Ermengarde's Awakening," Osgood made certain that no reader would ever confuse her sentiments and those of the early Mrs. Browning. The epigraph (by "E. B. Barrett") is from "The Lay of the Brown Rosary" (first published in 1840 as "Legend of the Brown Rosary"). In Browning's poem a young woman, Onora, sells her soul to evil spirits in order to remain alive for her wedding day, on which her lover dies, confessing that he has "sinned." Then Onora throws aside the rosary, the symbol of her pact with the devil, and also dies. It is clear that Onora's actions are not wholly motivated by her love of her fiancé. She is also motivated by selfishness and a desire to defeat death. In Osgood's poem (certainly not one of her best), Ermengarde has made a golden idol of her lover ("an altar worthy of a god!/All of pure gold"). She is also a poet who sings "a love-hymn of worship" and, because of her love, "turn'd from all—from friendship and the world." Eventually, of course, the man proves unfaithful, and the singing ceases; the altar is hidden in the night of Ermengarde's soul. She realizes that she has "sinn'd against God."

In Browning's poem, Onora is in a rather unusual situation: she must die before her appointed marriage day but, by supernatural means, is able to circumvent death. In Osgood's poem, Ermengarde has made an idol of her lover and prays to him, rather than to the evil spirits symbolized by Onora's brown rosary. Osgood alters Browning's "legend" to a more real situation and quite obviously insists that woman must never make an idol of her lover. The dream/waking images tie "Ermengarde's Awakening" to Osgood's later poems dealing with this same theme, but the sense of sinfulness against God in the worship of a man was replaced in the later poems by Osgood's insistence that a woman simply retain her own individuality.

God, in fact, is not mentioned at all in "Oh! Hasten to My Side," a poem in which the sensual temptation of adultery is contrasted to the "respectability" of an unsuccessful marriage. The poem needs no explanation, but it is interesting to note that Osgood's husband was often gone (financially unsuccessful as a painter, he spent 1849 in the California gold fields, for example) and that their marriage had collapsed at least by 1843. Although the poet first insists that her attraction for her lover is a "soul" relationship, later stanzas make it as clear as possible (given the censorship of the time) that the attraction was sensual, with the images nearly as sensual as those in Hewitt's "Imitation of Sappho":

Oh! hasten to my side, I pray!
   I dare not be alone!
The smile that tempts, when thou'rt away,
   Is fonder than thine own.

The voice that oftenest charms mine ear
   Hath such beguiling tone,
'Twill steal my very *soul*, I fear;
   Ah! leave me not alone!

It speaks in accents low and deep,
   It murmurs praise too dear,
It makes me passionately weep,
   Then gently soothes my fear;

It calls me sweet, endearing names,
   With Love's own childlike art;
My tears, my doubts, it softly blames—
   'Tis music to my heart!

And dark, deep, eloquent, soul-fill'd eyes
   Speak tenderly to mine;
Beneath that gaze what feelings rise!
   It is more kind than thine!

A hand, even pride can scarce repel,
   Too fondly seeks mine own;
It is not safe!—it is not well!
   Ah! leave me not alone!

I try to calm, in cold repose,
   Beneath his earnest eye,
The heart that thrills, the cheek that glows—
   Alas! in *vain* I try!

Oh trust me not—a woman frail—
   To brave the snares of life!

Lest—lonely, sad, unloved—I *fail*
   And shame the name of wife!

Come back! though cold and harsh to me,
   There's *honour* by thy side!
Better unblest, yet safe to be,
   Than lost to truth, to pride.

Alas! my peril hourly grows,
   In every thought and dream;
Not—not to *thee* my spirit goes,
   But still—yes! still to *him*!

Return with those cold eyes to me,
   And chill my soul once more
Back to the loveless apathy
   It learn'd so well before!

With the nineteenth-century sense of propriety, its concept of women, and the definition of "female poetry," it is natural to wonder just how Osgood could have been able to publish some of these poems. Osgood herself and her contemporaries were aware that she was "bold" for her day, and, in fact, in the preface (dated 1849) to the 1850 edition of her poems, she protected herself by observing that some poems "were written to appear in prose sketches and stories, and are expressions of feeling suitable to the persons and incidents with which they were originally involved." Rufus Griswold says much the same thing in his biographical statement in *The Memorial: Written by Friends of the Late Mrs. Osgood* and then ignores such potentially objectionable poems. But, of course, Osgood's justification for these poems is largely a deception, and, in the sense of the poetry itself, it ultimately makes no difference.

Although love is uncertain, Osgood's relationship with her small daughters is one of pure joy. (There was no problem in publishing such poems, of course.) When Osgood died in 1850, her daughters were fourteen and eleven (the third daughter died sometime soon after her birth); but Osgood had become an invalid, confined to her room, when the girls were eleven and eight. Thus her poems are concerned with the girls as infants or children, and there is none of the mother/adolescent daughter agony evident in the poems of twentieth-century women, such as Shirley Kaufman ("Mothers, Daughters"). More as in Plath's astonished and sometimes happy observations of her children ("Balloons"), Osgood can simply take joy in the children themselves, while she marks important and universal moments in their infant lives:

ELLEN LEARNING TO WALK

My beautiful trembler! how wildly she shrinks!
    And how wistful she looks while she lingers!
Papa is extremely uncivil, she thinks,—
    She but pleaded for one of his fingers!

What eloquent pleading! The hand reaching out,
    As if doubting so strange a refusal;
While her blue eyes say plainly, "What is he about
    That he does not assist me as usual?"

Come on, my pet Ellen! we won't let you slip,—
    Unclasp those soft arms from his knee, love;
I see a faint smile around that exquisite lip,
    A smile half reproach and half glee, love.

So! that's my brave baby! one foot falters forward,
    Half doubtful the other steals by it!
What, shrinking again! Why, you shy little coward,
    'Twon't kill you to walk a bit!—try it!

There! steady, my darling! huzza! I have caught her!
    I clasp her, caress'd and caressing!
And she hides her bright face, as if what we taught her
    Were something to blush for—the blessing!

Now back again! Bravo! that shout of delight,
    How it thrills to the hearts that adore her!
Joy, joy for her mother! and blest be the night,
    When her little light feet first upbore her!

At the same time, however, Osgood muses on the future of this same Ellen more seriously:

THE CHILD PLAYING WITH A WATCH

Art thou playing with Time in thy sweet baby glee?
Will he pause on his pinions to frolic with thee?
Oh! shew him those shadowless, innocent eyes,
    That smile of bewilder'd and beaming surprise;
Let him look on that cheek where thy rich hair reposes,
    Where dimples are playing "bopeep" with the roses;
His wrinkled brow press with light kisses and warm,
And clasp his rough neck with thy soft wreathing arm.

Perhaps thy bewitching and infantine sweetness
May win him, for once, to delay in his fleetness;
To pause, ere he rifle, relentless in flight,
A blossom so growing of bloom and of light.
Then, then would I keep thee, my beautiful child,
With thy blue eyes unshadow'd, thy blush undefiled;
With thy innocence only to guard thee from ill,
In life's sunny dawning, a lily-bud still!
Laugh on, mine own Ellen! that voice, which to me
Gives a warning so solemn, makes music for thee;
And while I at those sounds feel the idler's annoy,
Thou hear'st but the tick of the pretty gold toy;
Thou seest but a smile on the brow of the churl,
May his frown never awe thee, my own baby-girl.
And oh! may his step, as he wanders with thee,
Light and swift as thine own little fairy-tread be!
While still in all seasons, in storms and fair weather,
May Time and my Ellen be playmates together.

There are several such poems: for example, "The Baby and the Breeze" and "Fanny's Error." How far Osgood has advanced beyond Sigourney's poems of dead babes and her few tentative poems concerning live children! Except in isolated passages, Osgood's poems concerning her children are not sentimental but are honest attempts to express thoughts and emotions never so fully expressed before by women in poetry. It is almost certain that Plath, Sexton, and other modern women who have similar interests in their children have never read Osgood's poems, nor had Elinor Wylie. Nevertheless, this kind of poem has been a constant factor among American women since the early nineteenth century.

Osgood also wrote poems for her mother and her sister Lizzie. "What Can Be the Matter with Lizzie?" teases the younger sister who has just fallen in love. "The Exile's Lament" is not the standard tribute to "Mother" (alive or dead), but is rather Osgood's lament that she and her mother cannot share baby Ellen's first years together—Osgood being in England at the time, her mother in America. Osgood also wrote several poems for her female friends, such as "To a Friend." These poems are personal, direct statements, written for a particular friend with a particular problem.

Osgood wrote few nature poems as such. In that sense she resembles Christina Rossetti, who would soon be writing poems in which nature is seen only from behind a window or is inhabited by animals she had seen in a zoo. Two of Osgood's "nature" poems, however, are notable. "May-Day in New England" describes the poet's walk with a child, May, on May Day. But surprisingly (especially for an American poet at this time), they find no flowers at all. With graceful word-play, the poet finds May-Day flowers on the face of her daughter May. The other poem, "To a Dear Little Truant, Who Wouldn't Come Home," associates spring with the longed-for arrival of a truant lover[33] (much as Dickinson would later make a similar association in "If you were coming in the Fall"). I quote the first and last stanzas:

> When are you coming? the flowers have come!
> Bees in the balmy air happily hum;
> In the dim woods where the cool mosses are,
> Gleams the Anemone's little, light star!
> Tenderly, timidly down in the dell,
> Sighs the sweet violet, droops the harebell;—
> Soft in the wavy grass lightens the dew;
> *Spring* keeps her promises,—why do not *you*?
>
> .   .   .   .
>
> Do not delay, darling, 'mid the dark trees,
> "Like a lute" murmurs the musical breeze;
> Sometimes the brook, as it trips by the flowers,
> Hushes its warble to listen for yours.
> Pure as the rivulet,—lovely and true!
> Spring shoud have waited till she could bring *you*!

Osgood did not write poems of patriotism or of national interest; she did not even urge other women to work in charitable groups. Nor was she interested in writing of sinless female children, who would save the world of men from themselves. She was not particularly erudite, and she seems to have been totally untouched by Transcendentalism. She was not only unintellectual, but positively anti-intellectual. Her bias against Reason and Logic appears in short pieces, such as "Love and Logic," but is best expressed in one of her longer poems, "A Flight of Fancy":

> At the bar of Judge Conscience, stood Reason arraign'd,
> The Jury impannell'd—the prisoner chain'd.
> The Judge was facetious, at times, though severe,
> Now waking a smile, and now drawing a tear;
> An old-fashion'd, fidgety, queer-looking wight
> With a clerical air, and an eye quick as light.

"Here, Reason, you vagabond! look in my face!
I'm told you're becoming an idle scapegrace.
They say that young Fancy, that airy coquette,
Has dared to fling round you her luminous net;
That she ran away with you, in spite of yourself,
For pure love of frolic—the mischievous elf.

"The scandal is whisper'd by friends and by foes,
And darkly they hint too, that when they propose
Any questions to *your* ear, so lightly you're led
At once to gay Fancy, you turn your wild head;
And *she* leads you off in some dangerous dance,
As wild as the Polka that gallop'd from France.

"Now up to the stairs with you, laughing, she springs,
With a whirl and a whisk of her changeable wings;
Now dips in some fountain her sun-painted plume,
That gleams thro' the spray, like a rainbow in bloom;
Now floats in a cloud, while her tresses of light
Shine through the frail boat and illumine her flight;
Now glides through the woodland to gather its flowers;
Now darts like a flash to the sea's coral bowers;
In short—cuts such capers, that with her I ween
It's a wonder you are not ashamed to be seen!

"Then she talks such a language!—melodious enough,
To be sure—but a strange sort of outlandish stuff!
I'm told that it licences many a whapper [*sic*],
And when once she commences no frowning can stop her;
Since it's new—I've no doubt it is very improper!
They say that she cares not for order or law;
That of you—you great dunce! she but makes a cat's paw.
I've no sort of objection to fun in it's season,
But it's plain that this Fancy is *fooling* you, Reason!"

Just then into the court flew a strange little sprite,
With wings of all colours and ringlets of light!
She frolick'd round Reason—till Reason grew wild,
Defying the court and caressing the child.
The judge and the jury, the clerk and recorder,
In vain call'd this exquisite creature to order.—
"Unheard of intrusion!"—They bustled about,
To seize her, but, wild with delight, at the rout,
She flew from their touch like a bird from a spray,
And went waltzing and whirling and singing away!

Now up to the ceiling, now down to the floor!
Were never such antics in courtroom before!
But a lawyer, well versed in the tricks of his trade,
A trap for the gay little innocent laid: .
He held up a *mirror*, and Fancy was caught
By her image within it, so lovely, she thought.
What could the fair creature be!—bending its eyes
She flew to embrace it. The lawyer was ready:
He closed round the spirit a grasp cool and steady,
And she sigh'd, while he tied her two luminous wings,
"Ah, Fancy and Falsehood are two different things!"

The witnesses—maidens of uncertain age,
With a critic, a publisher, lawyer and sage—
All scandalized greatly at what they had heard,
Of this poor little Fancy, (who flew like a bird!),
Were call'd to the stand and their evidence gave:
The judge charged the jury, with countenance grave.
Their verdict was "guilty," and Reason look'd down,
As his honor exhorted her thus, with a frown: —

"This Fancy, this vagrant, for life shall be chain'd,
In your own little cell, where *you* should have remain'd;
And you—for *your* punishment—jailer shall be:
Don't let your accomplice come coaxing to me!
I'll none of her nonsense—the little wild witch!
Nor her bribes—although rumor does say she is rich.

"I've heard that all treasures and luxuries rare,
Gather round at her bidding, from earth, sea, and air:
And some go so far as to hint, that the powers
Of darkness attend her more sorrowful hours.
But go!" and Judge Conscience, who never was bought,
Just bow'd the pale prisoner out of the court.

'Tis said,—that poor Reason next morning was found,
At the door of the cell, fast asleep on the ground,
And nothing within, but one plume rich and rare,
Just to show that young Fancy's wing once had been there.
She had dropp'd it, no doubt, while she strove to get through
The hole in the lock which she could not undo.

Underneath the humorous irony is a firm conviction that Fancy is
superior to Reason and Conscience and to the sober members of the
jury. We should not, however, read this poem as a typical nine-

teenth-century pronouncement concerning reason and the imagination or fancy[34] (for example, Poe's "Sonnet To Science" or, later, Whitman's "When I Heard the Learn'd Astronomer"). Osgood's poem is far more complex and subtle than these poems, although their implications are certainly contained within "A Flight of Fancy."

On the most obvious level, Fancy can be understood as Love, an interpretation supported in part by others of Osgood's poems, such as "Love and Logic," but contradicted in such poems as "To Sybil." The physical image of Fancy, however, is based upon Cupid, albeit a female Cupid. In this sense, then, Love (female Love) is seen as an irrepressible and ultimately victorious force.

Fancy, however, can also be understood as poetry—female poetry. In stanza 5, Fancy "talks such a language," a "melodious," but "outlandish" language which is "new." Moreover, among the witnesses are a publisher and a critic. Her "wealth," cited in stanza 10, is traditional imagery for the "wealth" of poetry. Finally, because Osgood calls this "poetry" Fancy, she is obviously rejecting the values of the reigning critical theories of her day: that Imagination was superior to Fancy. Fancy is, to a large extent, an image of Osgood's own poetry.

Finally, Fancy can be seen as a "female principle." Although the poet tells us in stanza 7 that Fancy is "innocent," the Judge knows better: he calls her a witch, who is attended at times by the "powers of darkness." She represents the antirational, intuitive, perhaps even primitive power which American women poets have celebrated in themselves from this time on. Osgood's Fancy is gayer and lighter than later witches, but she magically ensnarls and tricks Reason and Judge Conscience, leaving only her feather. She is, perhaps, Eve in *her* fortunate fall; on the other hand, she is also the female, subversive element in the masculine-feminine dichotomy.[35] She has a long future before her in the poetry of American women, as we will see.

In 1854 or 1855, in a letter to his publisher, William Ticknor, Hawthorne praised the prose writer Fannie Fern because "The woman writes as if the Devil was in her; and that is the only condition under which a woman ever writes anything worth reading." He added, "Generally women write like emasculated men, and are only to be distinguished from male authors by greater feebleness and folly; but when they throw off the restraints of decency, and come before the public stark naked, as it were,—then their books are sure to possess character and value."[36] One must wonder if Hawthorne would not have considered Osgood one of those women writers who had appeared "stark naked" in public. He had, in 1850, contributed one of his short stories ("The Snow-Image: A Childish Miracle") to her *Memorial*. Osgood herself in "Ah! Woman Still" had asserted that women could not yet appear "stark naked," so to speak. They "still/Must veil the shrine," but she looked forward to the day when the "woodbird" could reveal this "tone." For her day, however, Osgood stood before the public "stark naked," and she was fortunately poet enough to express herself in some of the most successful lyric verse written in mid-nineteenth-century America.

Chapter Five

1850–1900
Refinement and Achievement

In 1850, Frances Osgood died, and Emily Dickinson probably wrote her first poem, "Awake ye muses nine, sing me a strain divine"—a poem directly derivative from the pages of the popular journals of her day. Within the next thirty-six years, Dickinson would refine many aspects of previous women's verse and mold them into what is perhaps the finest poetry written by an American, male or female. Dickinson's poetry, in fact, represents the culmination of American women's verse to her day; after her, women poets sought other directions and modes of expression which were still, nevertheless, consonant with the traditions of women's poetry in America.

At the time Dickinson began writing—that decade which Pattee has termed the Feminine Fifties, and up to the Civil War, several developments important to women's verse occurred. First, the women on the frontier found their own poetic voices again. The Cary sisters, Alice (1820–1871) and Phoebe (1824–1871),[1] published their first volume of verse in 1849; Alice moved from the family farm in Ohio to New York in 1850, with Phoebe following the next year. The two women were commercial successes (Alice at her best in prose sketches, Phoebe in poetry), and, until their deaths, were at the center of the New York circle of literati, with regular "salons" in their home. Alice's poetry rarely rose above the popular verse of her day, but Phoebe occasionally overcame the influence of the magazine poetry and of Elizabeth Barrett Browning to produce independent verse in which, for example, she defended her unmarried status in "A Woman's Conclusions"; she defined a woman as

"woman," specifically not as "saint," in "Women"; and she occasionally continued the tradition of honesty and colloquial diction
in children's poetry, as in "The Prairie on Fire."

More significant, however, is the independent and aggressive spirit
exhibited by women who stayed in the West.[2] Although women living west of the Alleghenies did not produce important poetry until
the very late nineteenth and early twentieth centuries, women such
as Frances G. Gage pondered their lot as mothers and housewives. In
"The Housekeeper's Soliloquy," Gage concluded in the final stanzas:

> When I was young I used to earn
>   My living without trouble,
> Had clothes and pocket-money, too,
>   And hours of leisure double.
>
> I never dreamt of such a fate,
>   When I, a-lass! was courted—
> Wife, mother, nurse, seamstress, cook, housekeeper, chamber-maid,
>   laundress, dairy-woman, and scrub generally, doing the work
>   of six,
> For the sake of being supported!

Scattered throughout the verse of other women, such as Laura M.
Thurston, Sarah T. Bolton, and Mary W. Betts, are poems entitled
"I Fear Not Thy Frown," "Paddle Your Own Canoe," and "A Ken-
tuckian Kneels to None but God." Although the last is based upon
an incident in Cuba, the attitude expressed by women in these
poems is the same as that which, Dee Brown speculated, led to the
passage of a bill for woman suffrage first in a Western state.[3]

Another important development is that poetry by black and Jewish women, as well as by women from other ethnic groups, appeared. In the first half of the century, the expansion of woman's
poetry had been vertical: women from every social level were able to
publish. Early in the second half of the century, the expansion became horizontal. The noted black abolitionist, Frances Ellen Watkins Harper (1825–1911), published *Poems on Miscellaneous Subjects*[4] in 1854—a work which was reissued twenty times within the
next twenty years—and in 1869 published *Moses: A Story of the
Nile*. Her poems generally support the abolitionist and temperance
movements. Although, in his preface to her *Poems*, William Lloyd
Garrison felt it necessary to apologize for her verse, there was no
reason to. Her poetry is vigorous and certainly as poetically satisfying as that of the Cary sisters. She was particularly outspoken in

her denunciation of Christians who supported slavery by citation of biblical passages. In other poems she advised young women to marry only men who are "good and kind" and who have "common sense." Harper was the first black woman poet to publish since Wheatley and the first of many black women who have contributed significantly to American verse in the last century.

In 1856, Penina Moise (1797–1880) published her most widely known book, *Hymns Written for the Use of Hebrew Congregations.*[5] She was soon followed by Adah Isaacs Menken (1835–1868)[6] and Emma Lazarus (1849–1887),[7] who carried their Jewish womanhood to a more general audience. Actually, Menken's life is more interesting than her one book of poems, *Infelicia* (1868). She is, however, the only woman of her day whose prosody was influenced by Walt Whitman; but her poems are usually little more than imitations of contemporary amatory, religious, and otherwise melodramatic verse. On the other hand, Lazarus, in her later poems, indicated the kind of vigor and originality which Jewish women have brought to American verse from her day to the present. Lazarus is best known for "The New Colossus" (1883), the final lines of which have been inscribed on the Statue of Liberty:

Not like the brazen giant of Greek fame,
With conquering limbs astride from land to land;
Here at our sea-washed, sunset gates shall stand
A mighty woman with a torch, whose flame
Is the imprisoned lightning, and her name
Mother of Exiles. From her beacon-hand
Glows world-wide welcome; her mild eyes command
The air-bridged harbor that twin cities frame.
"Keep, ancient lands, your storied pomp!" cries she
With silent lips. "Give me your tired, your poor,
Your huddled masses yearning to breathe free,
The wretched refuse of your teeming shore.
Send these, the homeless, tempest-tost to me,
I lift my lamp beside the golden door."

Lazarus's early poetry is highly derivative from the verse of Longfellow and Emerson, but the pogroms in the 1880's in Russia and east-central Europe moved her to speak in her own voice, although she had written some poems concerning Judaism before that time. Her pamphlet of later poems and translations, published in 1882, was entitled *Songs of a Semite*. Most of Lazarus's later poems celebrate Jewish holidays ("The Feast of Lights"—Hanukkah) or Jewish history ("Bar Kochba"). Others, like "The New Colossus" and "1492," recognize that the United States is a sanctuary for exiles, especially Jewish exiles. In "The Banner of the Jew," she urges "Israel" to awake and fight. Lazarus's verse is aggressive and bold, parallel, as we have seen, to the kind of outspokenness women had already exhibited in abolitionist, in feminist, and in "personal" poems.

Prosodically, Lazarus experimented with prose poems, a form which would not really be used widely in America until the 1920's, but which French poets had been using since the 1840's. Although Aloysius Bertrand is generally considered the creator of the modern prose poem, it is certain that Lazarus modeled her prose poems on those of Baudelaire, whose *Petite Poéms en prose*, or *Le Spleen de Paris*, was published in its final form in Paris in 1869. Lazarus's last work published in her lifetime, "By the Waters of Babylon,"[8] was subtitled "Little Poems in Prose." The numbered passages of the seven sections resemble the verse of both Baudelaire and the Bible. (At times, they intimate the vignettes of Ernest Hemingway.)

> I. 1. The Spanish noon is a blaze of azure fire, and the dusty pilgrims crawl like an endless serpent along treeless plains and bleached high-roads, through rock-split ravines and castellated, cathedral-shadowed towns.

> VII. 3. And the world has named him [the Orient-Jew] an ugly worm, shunning the blessed daylight.[9]

In fact, Lazarus's rather innovative and daring experiment with "little poems in prose," as well as her obvious pre-Imagistic tendencies in this late work, indicates that "Imagism" must lie more deeply in late nineteenth-century American verse than even recent critics suppose.

A final circumstance which affected women's poetry at this time was the increasing antagonism of men to any kind of public or political life for women. In the 1850's, for example, the otherwise urbane and popular *United States Magazine* printed articles decrying the active role of women in election campaigns ("Female Politicians," April 1852, and "Female Influence in the Affairs of State—Politics Not Women's Sphere," April 1859), as well as the feminist movement and feminist meetings. In fact, the funny, but nasty, "Woman's Rights" ("Chunk No. 1" of "Human Nature in Chunks," November 1854) bases its satire on several of the same kinds of female types Henry James was later to explore in *The Bostonians*

(1886). It is thus not surprising that, in the September 1855 edition, "Walt Whitman and His Poems" were excitedly welcomed: "An American bard at last! One of the roughs, large, proud, affectionate, eating, drinking, and breeding, his costume manly and free . . ." Such articles in a popular journal reflect increasing activity in the larger social area. In the second half of the nineteenth century, women were rapidly entering many nondomestic fields, with the sympathy and support of a number of men. Other men, however, became increasingly and belligerently vociferous in their opposition to a larger role for women, who often responded in kind. Much as in women's poetry today, both sentiments and vocabulary of this debate sometimes appeared in the verse of women who wrote from 1850 to 1900, as we will see.

Emily Dickinson (1830–1886)

The poetry of Emily Dickinson has received more respectful, scholarly attention than has the verse of any other American woman poet. Several major studies treat her work intelligently and fairly, and we have excellent modern editions of her poems and letters.[10] Numerous articles center on specific aspects of her work. Indeed, it seems that Dickinson's poetry has been mistreated only because it has often been distorted to fit the patterns of male verse and has been viewed in isolation from the verse of her time. Critics have traced her backgrounds to Emerson primarily, but also to, among others, the English metaphysical poets and Elizabeth Barrett Browning. The only American women poets who have been even slightly considered in association with Dickinson are Helen Hunt Jackson (by a number of critics) and Margaret Fuller (by Albert J. Gelpi), and only Henry W. Wells and Thomas H. Johnson have been able or willing to draw any poetic relationships between Dickinson and Jackson or Fuller or any other American woman poet.[11] Moreover, their observations are extremely general and superficial. In a variety of ways, however, Dickinson's poetry stands firmly within the developing tendencies of American female verse.

I have already mentioned several thematic, metaphoric, and prosodic qualities which Dickinson's verse shares with the poetry of other American women. Certainly, the nursery-rhyme quality of her verse, her "feminine realism," and even particular images, such as the chrysalis-butterfly, all suggest such a relationship. Furthermore, other aspects of her verse which have been noted by other critics need to be examined with respect to the development of women's verse in America. For example, in a very obvious parallel, the domestic imagery mentioned by nearly every critic[12] had long been standard poetic imagery for American women poets. Sigourney's "To a Shred of Linen" and many of Osgood's poems cited in Chapter 4 employ such integration of the domestic and poetic. The male poets, of course, practically never used such imagery.

Or, again, when Yvor Winters finds it "curious" that Dickinson "is constantly defining the absolute cleavage between the living and the dead,"[13] we realize that he has not read much women's elegiac verse of the early nineteenth century. The kind of poem which Lydia Sigourney and her many imitators reiterated separates the dead baby or mother from the rest of the family with absolute distinction from the very moment of death. Moreover, when Austin Warren feels compelled to point out that "there is no Biblical warrant for 'fleshless lovers' meeting in heaven,"[14] he is right. However, he apparently does not realize that the warrant for such meetings in the afterlife lies in the elegies of Sigourney and her followers, whose dead mothers and babes eventually meet in heaven and whose dead husbands and wives are to be reunited in the afterlife. In addition, the symbols of royalty which Dickinson associates with the dead are her own method of granting dignity to those many dead who are not otherwise special, much as Sigourney attempted to dignify women and babes.

Another quality of Dickinson's poetry often mentioned is her desire to "communicate" through her poetry, which is her "letter to the World." We have already noted such a familiar and epistolary means of writing poetry in the verse of American women, beginning especially in the eighteenth century; in fact, there is a line of continuity from Bleecker through Osgood to Dickinson. And even though we still may have some difficulty interpreting certain of Dickinson's poems, the great bulk of her poetry is easily understood, communicative as the poetry of American women has been intended to be. It is no wonder that a woman, a fellow female poet, Helen Hunt Jackson, was the person who "had insights about the poetry of Emily Dickinson more penetrating than those of any other qualified judge who, during Dickinson's lifetime, evaluated her poetry."[15]

In short, it is not difficult to select observations and interpretations by which critics (unknowingly, of course) have already related Dickinson's poetry to the verse of her female predecessors in America:

"No pessimist knew the power of blackness more deeply than Emily Dickinson."[16] Gelpi is attempting to relate Dickinson's verse to the "blackness" of the male prose writers, Melville and Hawthorne. However, cosmic pessimism and "blackness" in American women's verse antedate this theme in American male prose or poetry.

"Among the poets of the nineteenth century the romantic idea predominates that nature and God are one. Emily Dickinson is remarkable in the degree to which her clear vision kept the Creator apart from the things created."[17] Her "clear vision" is remarkable only to those who have not read the poetry of such women as Osgood (who could not even find flowers—let alone God—on May Day), or Bleecker, or Bradstreet.

"The God who emerges from these poems is a God who does not answer, an unrevealed God whom one cannot confidently approach through Nature or through doctrine."[18] Such "remarkable" or "curious" qualities of Dickinson's verse are not so remarkable or curious against the background of American women's poetry.

There is, however, much more to be said. Let us examine her river/sea, stream/river, and other such water-related images. Nearly all of these images are involved in poems which concern God and man as lovers. Critics have often noted that God is treated by Dickinson as a lover.[19] Poems which concern God as lover are related by images to a series of poems which express love for human males— poems which have caused critics to speculate as to the identity of her "lover(s)" and also to make such silly observations as this: "Most probably the poems would not have amounted to much if the author had not finally had her own romance, enabling her to fulfill herself like any other woman."[20] That is, if Dickinson had not (presumably) loved a man, she could not have written such wonderful poetry.

The image which unites these two kinds of "amatory" verse (to God and to man) involves a stream (the poet) flowing into a river (God or the human lover) or a river (the poet) flowing into the sea (God or the human lover). In early poems, the poet is a "docile" bark or a "docile" river entering the sea:

NO. 52

Whether my bark went down at sea—
Whether she met with gales—
Whether to isles enchanted
She bent her docile sails—

By what mystic mooring
She is held today—
This is the errand of the eye
Out upon the Bay.

NO. 212

Least Rivers—docile to some sea.
My Caspian—thee.

Such poems should be grouped with those in which the woman is a docile wife who is transformed by the sea:

NO. 732

She rose to His Requirement—dropt
The Playthings of Her Life
To take the honorable Work
Of Woman, and of Wife—

If ought She missed in Her new Day,
Of Amplitude, or Awe—
Or first Prospective—Or the Gold
In using, wear away,

It lay unmentioned—as the Sea
Develope Pearl, and Weed,
But only to Himself—be known
The Fathoms they abide.

Poems such as these form the basis for a "passive" characterization. The woman is "docile" and dominated by the sea or larger body of water. Dickinson's image is of the submergence of the female into the male God or male human.

Mergence images are part of the general Judaic-Christian tradition, of the New England Puritan tradition (e.g., Jonathan Edwards's fountain/river and sun/beam images in *The End for Which God Created the World*), and of Emersonian Transcendentalism ("I become a transparent eyeball.") Dickinson's images represent a submergence rather than a mergence—a loss of personal identity in the woman's passive relationship to the male God or lover. It is this loss of identity which, in other poems, frightens her:

NO. 520

I started Early—Took my Dog—
And visited the Sea—
The Mermaids in the Basement
Came out to look at me—

And Frigates—in the Upper Floor
Extended Hempen Hands—

Presuming Me to be a Mouse—
Aground—upon the Sands—

But no Man moved Me—till the Tide
Went past my simple Shoe—
And past my Apron—and my Belt
And past my Boddice—too—

And made as He would eat me up—
As wholly as a Dew
Upon a Dandelion's Sleeve—
And then—I started—too—

And He—He followed—close behind—
I felt His Silver Heel
Upon my Ancle—Then my Shoes
Would overflow with Pearl—

Until We met the Solid Town—
No One He seemed to know—
And bowing—with a Mighty look—
At me—The Sea Withdrew—[21]

NO. 284

The Drop, that wrestles in the Sea—
Forgets her own locality—
As I—toward Thee—

She knows herself an incense small—
Yet *small*—she sighs—if *All*—is *All*—
How *larger*—be?

The Ocean—smiles—at her Conceit—
But *she*, forgetting Amphitrite—
Pleads—"Me"?

Dickinson thus refuses to be submerged, to be one of "the Mermaids in the Basement," or to be like Amphitrite, the wife of Poseidon.

Of course, the mythological reference associates poem 284 with women's verse, but such water images were also used by a number of women and men at this time. For example, Alice Cary began a section of "Life's Mysteries" with "We are the mariners, and God the Sea." Or out in Ohio, Coates Kinney was depicting "marriage" in brook/river/lake images. In "On Marriage," the brook (woman) flows into the river (man) and together they flow into the "Lake of Love." As far as I can tell, most poets who used such images seemed to accept (or perhaps did not understand) the implications of their images. Dickinson, however, refused to assume such a passive role and, in fact, extended these common images to their logical conclusions in order to declare her own individuality, her refusal to be drowned. Her water images are comparable to the waking and sleeping images in Osgood's verse (discussed in Chapter 4), with the parallel of sleeping and drowning. The assertion of self, the refusal to be submerged, lies at the basis of many poems of both Dickinson and Osgood.

With Dickinson, the assertion of self resulted, in one direction, in the poems which depict God as "Burglar! Banker—Father!" (no. 49), or as a stately gentleman (no. 357) or as a "King, who does not speak" (no. 103), or as a Swindler (no. 476). These and other poems constitute her characterization of a Minerva or Amazon aspect of Woman. Such poems should be grouped with the cluster of poems concerning "Liberty" (nos. 77, 384, 512, 652, 720, 728, 801, and 1082). From the first, however, Dickinson saw the paradox of "Liberty"— that "Captivity is Consciousness—/So's Liberty" (no. 384), and that even what she might have been, "that easy Thing/An independant Man—" (no. 801), was less satisfactory than her own kind of independent artistic "Liberty." In short, neither a passive role nor a Minerva role offers satisfaction.

Thus, in another direction, her assertive sense of self ultimately resulted in self-examination (what do I think and feel and know)— those poems which George Frisbie Whicher has called her "psychic reconnaissance."[22] Many critics have already discussed the poetic expression of her inner landscape, those poems which define moments of psychological time in terms applicable to both men and women. It is in these poems that she is able to reach beyond the feminine to the universal human. I do not mean to slight this kind of poem in my discussion, but the excellence of such poems has, as I have said, already been recognized in other studies. I need only demonstrate that such introspection, coupled with both intellectual and metaphoric objectivity, was not unique in her time to Dickinson, as scholars would have us believe.

The women poets had been attempting to define such states of emotion or consciousness since 1800. For example, Elizabeth Oakes Smith, in a sonnet entitled "Faith," stated: "Faith is the subtle chain/Which binds us to the Infinite." She described "doubt" in another sonnet, "Annihilation":

> Thus, midnight travellers, on some mountain steep,
> Hear far above the avalanche boom down,
> Starting the glacier echoes from their sleep.[23]

This kind of poem certainly prepared the way for such Dickinson images as "Faith—is the Pierless Bridge" (no. 915) and

No man can compass a Despair—
As round a Goalless Road
No faster than a Mile at once
The Traveller proceed—
(no. 477)[24]

Other poems which describe a moment of consciousness also have their predecessors in the verse of earlier women. "After great pain, a formal feeling comes" (no. 341) and "I like a look of Agony" (no. 241) are poems which develop the intimate and personal states expressed in the pre-"confessional" poetry of a woman like Osgood. Such sentiments, so often poorly and incompletely realized in previous women's verse, are just those which Dickinson is attempting to isolate and define.

Indeed, if one were to separate and categorize Dickinson's poems of psychological consciousness and emotional definition, the result would be similar in general structure to the many early nineteenth-century anthologies of "flower sentiment" with their attempts to define such mental states as "Rage," "Sorrow," "Religious Fervor," "Misanthropy," or "Bashful Shame."[25] The editors of such anthologies were almost exclusively women, and most poems contained in such anthologies were written by women, although poems by men also appear. The brief verse which illustrates the emotion is often dramatic or narrative, but just as often an emotion or state of mind is described by a metaphor, as in "Misanthropy," by Anna P. Dinnies, in which misanthropic cares

. . . [gather] up the rills
Of lesser grief, spread real ills;
And with their gloomy shades conceal
The land-marks Hope would else reveal.[26]

Dickinson was able to make precise definitions, to avoid the cliché, and to find the exact image. Her "psychic reconnaissance" has a detached objectivity not often achieved by other women poets, who tended to luxuriate in the emotion or psychic state they were describing. Nevertheless, it seems clear to me that such poems are refinements of similar verse written by her sister poets of America. She combined the naked honesty of a poet like Osgood with the poems of "sentiment" attempted by so many American women before her. Like the other women, she expressed her mental states directly, not clouding her meaning with the complex and confused symbols which the men needed to describe their inner worlds.[27] Her accuracy and her metaphors of inner landscape are thus an intelligent and artistic refinement of methods and themes which many women had already been exploring in the early nineteenth century.

Although we have apparently preferred not to notice, Emily Dickinson was well aware of American women's verse. She even imitated some of its worst elements quite directly, as, for instance, in nos. 196 and 923, and yet, as I have shown, she refined themes, metaphors, and poetic types to create her best poetry. It should be no surprise that she also explored other specific themes and types of female poetry already established in the earlier nineteenth century. This large number of poems has generally been ignored. Such poems fall into several categories:

    1. The poem of admiration for another woman: for example, no. 14 ("One Sister have I in our house"). A type common in the verse of both English and American women, such a poem reflects Sappho's influence. In England, this type of poem is notable early in the work of Katherine Philips, "the matchless Orinda," and it first appeared in America in the verse of Jane Turell. Such poems, with increasing emotional intensity, appear in the verse of nearly every woman in the early nineteenth century (see the discussion of Osgood in Chapter 4). Such poems by women have been ignored by male critics because they often appear to be Lesbian (as, of course, some may very well be) and, in fact, are sometimes the cause of interpretive confusion, as in John Cody's *After Great Pain: The Inner Life of Emily Dickinson*.

    2. Poems expressing a woman's "special attributes" or "unique" vision: for example, no. 24 ("There is a morn by men unseen") and no. 271, which concludes:

> And then—the size of this "small" life—
> The Sages—call it small —
> Swelled, like Horizons—in my breast—
> And I sneered—softly—"small"!

Increasingly, in the nineteenth century, such poems tended to represent a subversive attack on the critical restrictions of "female poetry." That is, when the women were told they could write only certain types of poems, they eventually responded with "Yes, you are right, but you really do not understand just how special our verse can be." In "Ah! Woman still," Osgood, for example, believed that women had important things to say, but realized that they had not the freedom to speak. Developing more after 1850, such poems as Dickinson's represent the kind of exclusiveness occasionally implied in women's verse.

3. Poems expressing the narrow roles of women, which fall into two kinds: a role over which women have little choice: for example, no. 146, "On such a night, or such a night," and the poems which employ brook/river and river/sea images; and a role which women have chosen for themselves: for example, no. 401, "What Soft—Cherubic Creatures—/These Gentlewomen are—," and no. 354, "From Cocoon forth a Butterfly/As Lady from her Door." As early as Mercy Warren, however, women poets had expressed the reality of both externally imposed and self-imposed role limitations. I should note that there are also poems celebrating traditional marriage and love: for example, no. 208, "The Rose did caper on her cheek," and no. 387, "The Sweetest Heresy recieved." Such poems were common in popular male and female verse at this time.

4. Poems expressing the attraction of suicide: for example, no. 277, "What if I say I shall not wait!" and no. 1062, "He scanned it—staggered." There is a surprising number of such poems (also nos. 279, 296, 670, and 786). In American women's poetry, the theme extends from Brooks's *Zóphiël; or, The Bride of Seven* to the verse of Sylvia Plath. I have not found such self-destructive tendencies expressed by male American poets in their verse until the twentieth century. Until recently, we have tended to ignore women's poems of suicide or to regard them as "attitudinizing," but Plath's and Sexton's deaths should have shocked us into viewing such poems more seriously.[28]

Along with these poems of suicide is a cluster of verses which express psychic dislocation, poems which suggest at one level mental breakdown[29] or, on another level, psychic insecurity bordering on despair. Critics have noted and examined certain of these poems, and a few, especially no. 556, "The Brain, within it's Groove," are regularly anthologized. Generally such poems are understood to be another example of poems describing states of emotion or consciousness (or "psychic reconnaissance"), and they have been tied to that aspect of the romantic sensibility in which madness or perversion is explored. Such interpretations seem generally accurate, but I suggest that a more thorough analysis is necessary.

Dickinson's poems of dislocation are not simply mental (that is, expression of psychic dislocation for the poet herself), but involve a view of the universe. Construction images (planks and grooves, which in the later poems become cleavages or schism) dominate in these poems (nos. 556, 937, 997, and 1343, for example), and tie them to other poems in which the poet asserts that the world is dislocated also (nos. 891 and 1569). In these poems, the poet's dislocation is parallel to God's dislocation, with the result that the world is full of unreasonable cruelties and has in fact been carelessly constructed:

NO. 848

Just as He spoke it from his Hands
This Edifice remain—
A Turret more, a Turret less
Dishonor his Design—

According as his skill prefer
It perish, or endure—
Content, soe'er, it ornament
His absent character.

God the Swindler (no. 476) and His world stand in stark contrast to the Edenic world projected in the poems of American men at this time (especially Whitman and Emerson) and are more closely related to the poems of earlier American women, even to those poems for children in which Piatt, Dickinson's contemporary, confessed that had there been a choice, she would not have "made the world at all."

5. Poems concerning witchcraft. Dickinson never settled on any meaning for witchcraft. In two early poems, God is associated with witchcraft (nos. 155 and 593); in no. 1046, "Witchcraft" is Death. Yet in no. 1158 ("Best Witchcraft is Geometry/To the magician's mind"), witchery becomes a natural mode of life, at least for a magician. This concept is extended in no. 1583:

Witchcraft was hung, in History,
But History and I
Find all the Witchcraft that we need
Around us, every Day—

And, finally, in no. 1708, witchcraft is a person's most human quality, which, in fact, must escape at the moment of death. Witchcraft is, therefore, a minor theme in Dickinson's verse which developed through the years. In the end, Dickinson comes closer to the concept of "witch" more generally celebrated by women poets.

Thus a substantial number of poems relate specifically and directly to the verse women had been and were writing in America. Dickinson was simply the best poet of them all. (One senses that she is speaking directly to her many sisters who poetically described sunrises when she writes no. 318, "I'll tell you how the Sun rose.") Furthermore, to this point in my discussion, I have generally examined only those poems which relate directly to "adult" verse by American women. The influence of poems written by women for their children (children's and adult verse was still published together in the same volume or collection at this time) is evident in the nursery-rhyme quality of her verse, as well as in poems which are descriptions of nature's creatures, such as nos. 328, 986, and 1463.[30] Certain poems deal sentimentally with children (nos. 196, 1020, and 1185); and, even though critics contend that Emily Dickinson poetically ignored her own mother (a quiet woman, submissive to Emily's dominant father), a number of happy and kind "Mamas" (certainly not "Papas") are scattered throughout her verse (as in so much of American children's literature at this time), as in nos. 164, 790, 1085, and 1143. These "Mamas" are often Mother Nature, but the maternal image is kind, understanding, and generous. Indeed, the "Typic Mother" (no. 1115) who brings the fall is gentle and prophetic (as opposed to the irrationally cruel male image of Frost in no. 1624).

The light and simple tone of no. 59 ("A little East of Jordan") is surely descended from the poems for children which are based on scripture, such as Sigourney's "The Ark and Dove." Another early poem (no. 9) is reminiscent of several children's fairy tales. That curious poem, no. 274 ("The only Ghost I ever saw"), can easily be understood when juxtaposed to those poems which women in the nineteenth century wrote for their children in order to alleviate childish fears of ghosts, elves, or other such folk (see Piatt's poems). In short, the cross-fertilization of women's "adult" and "children's" verse is evident in the work of Dickinson, as it has continued to be in the verse of Gertrude Stein, Edna St. Vincent Millay, and Sylvia Plath.

This kind of poem is certainly more joyous and exuberant than others of Dickinson's poems we have been discussing. Critics have, in fact, so consistently emphasized her psychological, philosophical, and amatory verse (so much of it "black" or sardonic) that we have overlooked the happiness and joy in this group of other poems. Indeed, even "the little Tippler/Leaning against the—Sun—" (no. 214; variant reading) is too often seen in terms of "ecstasy" rather than joy. For, despite the cosmic pessimism in so much women's verse,

there does exist the other side—the joyous side. Thus Dickinson
herself could be a "Tippler," an "Inebriate of Air," at the same time
she viewed God as a Swindler. Osgood could poetically and happily
mark her daughter's first steps, while living with "a doubt in less
than perfect faith" in "Reflections." The exuberance of life, the
joy of others and of nature, the "intoxicating" quality which James
Gray[31] noted in the verse of Edna St. Vincent Millay, for example—
does not constitute a schizophrenia when juxtaposed to the more
pessimistic poems. Rather, the women poets we have been discussing
seem to have accepted an unhappy cosmos, but at the same time to
have found and celebrated the available joys. The joys are more
valuable, in fact, as they exist within the cosmic frame (in contrast,
for example, to the simple-minded exuberance in Whitman's "Song
of Myself," which lacks such underlying complexity). Such joy is,
of course, another aspect of "feminine realism," and allows the
women poets to assert a complex and often paradoxical angle of
vision.

Thus, rather than being "masculine," as Adrienne Rich would
have her in "I Am in Danger—Sir—,"[32] Dickinson is eminently
feminine in her approach to herself, her cosmos, her immediate environment, and her poetry. For her, poetry was a "dwelling in
Possibility." She was not the arrogant Namer or Sayer whom Emerson sought (although she, like Elizabeth Oakes Smith, certainly
studied Emerson). Like Osgood, she realized that women could not
yet speak as openly as they wished:

NO. 1129

Tell all the Truth but tell it slant—
Success in Circuit lies
Too bright for our infirm Delight
The Truth's superb surprise
As Lightning to the Children eased
With explanation kind
The Truth must dazzle gradually
Or every man be blind—

Above all, she wanted to communicate, and she was willing to let
the world wait (no. 883); she knew that eventually her "fuller tune"
would be heard (no. 250). She was an artist who was fully aware of
the importance of the "word" (nos. 1126 and 1212). Like American
women poets before her, she wanted to be a poet who "Distills
amazing sense/From ordinary Meanings" (no. 448). Like other

women poets, she sang "To Keep the Dark away" (no. 850). She was a more intelligent and talented poet than her female predecessors, but, without such earlier verse, without the previous development of American female poetry, we would not have had such a poet as Emily Dickinson.

Bogart-Baldwin-Guiney

While Emily Dickinson was refining certain themes and types of feminine verse, several other women were developing other aspects. The verse of these women is only occasionally successful poetically, but it points to the work of several important poets in the twentieth century, such as Amy Lowell, Sara Teasdale, and some verses of H. D. In the poetry of these women of the late nineteenth century, several nuances of old themes gradually emerge as major themes, emphases shift, and another variety of female verse develops. Emerging as a by-product of the feminist movement (in part, the "sour-grapes" division) and as a reaction to the increasingly noisy antagonism to any nondomestic role for women (evident, for example, in *United States Magazine*), the first hint of this trend is a rejection of the world of men, especially the commercial world. Up to 1850, the women poets had not rejected the nondomestic world as such but had happily competed with the men whenever they could, as educators, as editors, and increasingly in other enterprises (as more jobs were opened to them in the later nineteenth century). However, opposition to what these women poets considered negative and destructive traits of men in the commercial-legal-political world, such as ambition and moral "violence," came to be more and more commonly expressed. The poetry of Elizabeth Bogart (1806–18??)[33] defines the commercial world as "the spirit-stirring warfare," "the wild commingling strife," "thick-clashing interests," all of which she terms *"man's* pursuits" in "Estrangement." In such a world, men may be successful, but they lose their health, in "The Price of Success." Or, in "The Broken Promise," the man believes "that the whole world was made for *him!*"

It is, of course, just this sort of antagonism to the commercial world which Roy Harvey Pearce and others have suggested is to a large degree at the basis of the American Adamic myth. Indeed, it is possible to find more poems by men (both major and minor poets) than women who condemn harshly the attitudes and activities of the American businessman.[34] While the male poet thus affected envisaged himself as a hero-martyr to the system, the women poets who followed this line of social criticism asserted the superiority of their "femininity." We have already seen in Chapter 4 the attempt by Elizabeth Oakes Smith to define an American Eve, who would reform the men. Bogart, however, pointed to another alternative for a woman confronted with the "hostile" world of businessmen. She continually contrasted the ambitious male with woman's "vast ocean of uncertainty," as in "The Broken Promise," and her "pale exotics of the mind," in "Moonlight." Thus we find developing the strange combination of harsh, outspoken, vindictive, antimale verse published along with dainty and fragile poems of feminine "withdrawal."

Another developing characteristic in this type of poet can be seen in the verse of Emily Foote Baldwin, whose one volume of verse (476 pages), is entitled *Flora and Other Poems, Grave and Humorous, for the Domestic Circle* (1879). The wife of a prominent Protestant minister of the time, Baldwin is incredibly outspoken in her condemnation of the male world, as well as of the traditional role of wife, especially for a book of poems intended for the "domestic circle." Again we find the harshly negative poems, such as "Woman" and "The Model Wife, As Some Would Call Her," along with fragile and more "exotic" pieces, such as "To Hesperus."

One new quality is added, however: Baldwin rejects her own sister poets of America. In a long poem, "My Husband's Library," the Queen is Felicia Hemans (there are many Kings); and it is only *The British Female Poets*, an anthology collected by George Washington Bethune in 1848, which supports her view that *"Woman has talent,"* although, of course, woman's talent is not in "metaphysics" but rather in *"the warm affections."* No American woman poet is even mentioned. It is certain that Baldwin read the poems of American women regularly: the bulk of her poetry reflects both "adult" and "children's" verse (still thoroughly permeating the journals and rolling from the presses). Nor is this poem a condemnation of her husband's library.

Baldwin stands at the beginning of a group of American women poets who outwardly rejected their own tradition of female verse, while continuing to write their poems within it. Such denigration of their own tradition by American women has continually been reinforced by the American male critics, who had, as we have seen, for a long time publicly condescended to the "ladies" and privately, like Hawthorne, considered their verse "trash." Shortly after Baldwin's book appeared, Edmund Clarence Stedman and Ellen Mackay Hutchinson began gathering materials for their eleven-volume *Library of American Literature from the Earliest Settlement to the*

Present Time (to appear in 1888-1891, only ten years after Baldwin's book of verse); Stedman's "gallant" hypocrisy toward the "ladies" was recognized even by Alfred Kreymborg.[35] Much like Stedman, Amy Lowell in "The Sisters" would later praise the verses only of Emily Dickinson from among the many volumes of poetry written by American women.[36] American poets such as Baldwin and Lowell were thus only aligning themselves with the male school of American criticism.

Later in the century, Louise Imogen Guiney (1861–1920) pursued one poetic path leading from Bogart and Baldwin—the "exotic" route.[37] The verse of Guiney is generally associated with the *fin de siècle* movement in England, with a further basis in the Pre-Raphaelite verse of the Rossettis. (Along with friends, she is even reported to have had a mass said for the soul of Aubrey Beardsley.) She urged Americans to find other cultural values in other lands,[38] and her early verse, especially, represents a conscious (even self-conscious) attempt to reflect "international" or more general humanistic qualities. Although it is easy enough to associate her verse with that of the male humanists in England and America at this time, we must also remember that American women's verse has always expressed a more general humanism than that of the male poets.
The humanistic tendencies of earlier American women, evident, for example, in their interest in and personal association with female mythological characters, is manifest in Guiney's "Heathenesse." Furthermore, Guiney extended this interest in poems like those of "Alexandriana"—a series of epitaphs for both men and women (called "Fifteen Epitaphs" in later editions). In such poems, H. D.'s early verse is so clearly suggested that one must wonder whether or not H. D.'s poetry would have been any different had she never met Ezra Pound. Here, for example, is Guiney's "Alexandriana XII":

Cows in the narrowing August marshes,
Cows in a stretch of water
Motionless,
Neck on neck overlapped and drooping;

These in their troubled and dumb communion,
Thou on the steep bank yonder,
Pastora!
No more ever to lead and love them,

No more ever. Thine innocent mourners
Pass thy tree in the evening

Heavily,
Hearing another herd-girl calling.

Moreover, Guiney writes a number of delicate pieces of exquisite emotion, as in "Spring Nightfall," which begins "April is sad, as if the end she knew," or "The Still of the Year," which begins:

Up from the willow-root
Subduing agonies leap;
The squirrel and the purple moth
Turn over amid their sleep;
The icicled rocks aloft
Burn amber and blue alway,
And trickling and tinkling
The snows of the drift decay.

Like Teasdale, she emphasizes gentle, resigned melancholy—not Poe's melancholy, but a melancholy which, like Teasdale, she associates with moon and snow.[39]

As we understand when we read through Teasdale's verse,[40] this kind of poem is ultimately restrictive. It is not a "dwelling in Possibility" or poetry of extension; rather, it is a retreat, a closing in. And, although Guiney and Teasdale (and, to some extent, other women, such as Edith M. Thomas and Louise Chandler Moulton) wrote several remarkable and successful poems, the restrictive and continually repeated tone and theme eventually become dull. The emotional and intellectual vigor which characterizes so much verse by American women is lacking. We should thus not be surprised that certain male critics, such as Allen Tate, believe Teasdale to be "one of the best lyric poets of her generation."[41] And when other critics[42] favorably note, for example, that Teasdale remained independently aloof from the styles of the new poetry in the twentieth century and then trace her verse to Christina Rossetti, we must remember that her fragile poetry should also be understood against the background of verse written by earlier American women, such as Bogart, Baldwin, and Guiney.

Jackson-Wilcox-Reese

The less delicate and less fragile feminine line, the more vigorous verse, was continued by a large number of women in the late nineteenth century, the best of whom, besides Dickinson, were her friend

Helen Hunt Jackson (1830–1885), Ella Wheeler Wilcox (1850–1919), and Lizette Woodworth Reese (1856–1935). These women wrote a large number of poems specifically for the popular journals, and they profited financially from their verse.

Jackson wrote most of her poetry during the early part of her career and later concentrated on prose.[43] She is best known, in fact, for *Ramona* (1884), a novel which explored the plight of the American Indian. Because she was a correspondent and friend of Emily Dickinson, she has also been discussed by Dickinson scholars, as noted earlier in this chapter. In Jackson's own verse, several tendencies can be traced. In poems like "Best" and "When the Baby Died," she carries Sigourney's elegies into the late nineteenth century, but Jackson had not the intelligence or ability to reshape such a form in her own poetic voice, as Dickinson did. In poems such as "Ariadne's Farewell," "Oenone," and "Demeter," she interprets the ancient legends in her own way, as had the American women before her. Historical women, such as "Esther," are extolled, and Jackson worries about "A Woman's Battle." In fact, I find Jackson's verse so directly imitative of American women's verse in the earlier nineteenth century and, in poems such as "A Woman's Death-Wound," so derivative from the verse of Elizabeth Barrett Browning, that I cannot understand how Thomas H. Johnson could claim for her "independence of thought."[44] But it is not difficult to discover why she was popular in her own day and her verse so valued by Emerson. She carefully moved within the confines of traditional "feminine verse" while toying with Emersonian Transcendentalism ("Tribute to R. W. E.").

She did, however, write with "elegance and feeling," as Johnson claims. Her elegance lies in her language, in her general avoidance of verbal clichés, and in the traditional "international" tendencies we have already noted in American women's verse. Her "feeling" is not simply that of Elizabeth Browning, but a broader expression on a variety of topics. Her use of the sonnet is to be traced not just to Browning's primarily amatory sonnets, but even more to the discursive sonnet used by earlier American women (such as Elizabeth Oakes Smith).

Her primary contribution to women's verse is in none of these areas, but rather in her desire to give a specific prosodic "form," an artistic discipline, to her themes and "feelings." While the Romantic and Transcendental poets sought an "organic" poetic structure, Jackson (and Dickinson) reaffirmed the value of traditional verse forms. It is possible to understand such a tendency in terms of a "reactionary" movement at this time in the verse of both men and women in the ebb and flow of "the meter-making argument," which Edwin Fussell has identified as "the soul of American poetry."[45] I have no doubt that Dickinson and Jackson and others (both men and women) were reacting against the poetic excesses of Whitman; it is true, moveover, that, except for Menken, no American woman poet imitated Whitman's prosody until the beginning of the twentieth century.

Actually, Jackson and Dickinson and Guiney and Lazarus seem to represent the growing awareness among American women of the relationship of prosodic structure and meaning. Only Osgood in the early nineteenth century had seemed aware (or poetically capable) enough to combine form and meaning. As women's poetry developed throughout the nineteenth century, the poets had emphasized meaning, thoughts, and themes and ignored prosody. Again and again, we find that the bold and often original content is buried in poorly contrived metrics (inappropriate anapests and jerky trochees) and common rhyme patterns. On the other hand, from 1880 to 1900, there existed in the verse of American women four distinct kinds of prosodic methods, none of which is related to the prosody of Emerson or Whitman or other American male poets at this time. Women's verse was certainly more rich in this sense at this time than that of the American men, and it is clear just how the twentieth century could produce Marianne Moore and Gertrude Stein. The four kinds of prosodic methods evident in the verse of American women at the end of the century are these:

1. The prose poem of Lazarus, based on French models, not to be generally popular in America until just before World War I.

2. The use of brief iambic lines, with which Guiney discovered she could express fragile emotions. Like the irregular lines in her "Alexandriana," the iambic line as used by Guiney seems to be based in the prosody of the ancient Alexandrian (Greek) poets.

3. Emily Dickinson's accentual emphasis upon the word, with, at most, a sense of line structure. Despite all the attempts to figure out her prosodic backgrounds, we still are unable to isolate just how she moved from the Protestant hymnals or from the nineteenth-century declamation techniques to her specific kind of verse. Dickinson's influence on the prosody of twentieth-century men and women is well known.

4. Jackson's emphasis on a tight stanzaic structure, through which vigorous emotions or thoughts are allowed to play. Such a resolution of prosodic problems is exactly what certain kinds of women poets needed at this time. Jackson herself believed that underlying

the universe was a "Form" (the poem is vaguely, but not necessarily, Emersonian) and applied such a standard to her own poetry. Her discursive sonnets, of course, exhibit her attempts to structure thoughts through form, but other poems clearly indicate her emphasis upon the stanza as a means of controlling feeling and thought. Following her in one direction is the poetry of Marianne Moore and in another direction the lyrics of Edna St. Vincent Millay, who announced, "I will put Chaos in fourteen lines" (*Mine the Harvest*).

It is possible to see Ella Wheeler Wilcox's conversational line in *Three Women* (1897) as another kind of prosodic development, but it seems to me to extend back through Osgood to Bleecker (and has few characteristics of the pentametric conversational line developed by Robert Browning). *Three Women*, a narrative poem of approximately 3,500 lines, is predominantly written in rhyming anapestic tetrameter, with its conversational tone created by shifting caesurae, common diction, intermingled iambs and trochees, and generous use of enjambment. Wilcox can vary her lines, as, for example, the speaker shifts from a reflective to an assertive mood, as in this passage, in which Ruth, one of the three women, leaves her home to begin medical training:

> Once I thought
> Men cared for the women who found home the spot
> Next to heaven for happiness; women who knew
> No ambition beyond being loyal and true,
> And who loved all the tasks of the housewife. I learn
> Instead, that from women of that kind men turn,
> With a yawn, unto those that are useless; who live
> For the poor hollow world and for what it can give,
> And who make home the spot where, when other joys cease,
> One sleeps late when one wishes.
> .   .   .   .
> Well, I'm done with the role of housewife. I see
> There is nothing in being domestic. The part
> Is unpicturesque, and at war with all art.
> The senile old Century leers with dim eyes
> At our sex and demands that we shock or surprise
> His thin blood into motion. . . .

However, if Wilcox is remembered at all, it is for her short poems. Generally popular in her own day, by the 1930's she had been critically relegated by Alfred Kreymborg to "the leader of fireside sentiment and household editions."[46] More recently, Louise Bogan has praised Wilcox's *Poems of Passion* (1883) for having "brought into popular love poetry the element of 'sin.' . . . By 1900 a whole feminine school of rather daring verse on the subject of feminine and masculine emotions had followed Mrs. Wilcox's lead."[47] Wilcox gained a reputation as a "sinful poet" when a Chicago firm refused to publish *Poems of Passion* in 1883. After a great deal of publicity, another Chicago publisher quickly issued the book. It was amazingly popular, selling sixty thousand copies in its first two years.

Concerning Wilcox, both Kreymborg and Bogan are accurate in a sense: Wilcox was read in the "household," and she did project a sense of "sin," but such, as we have seen, was nothing new for the women poets of the nineteenth century. Her shorter poems are simply more blunt than those of preceding women writers of amatory verse ("blunt," in the sense that Piatt's poems to her children were "blunt"); in theme and attitude, she represents a bridge between Osgood and Millay. Wilcox was less capable artistically and more willing to rely on verbal clichés than Jackson and Guiney, for example, but her poetry continues the same vigorous traditions as that of Jackson and other earlier poets. She certainly never wrote a "fragile" or "delicate" poem, but rather in her best poems represents a development from the rough and highly independent verse of frontier women in the middle of the century. She was from a poor family in Wisconsin and published her books with Chicago firms. More sardonic and sensual than the hopeful Jackson, Wilcox wrote some aggressive and interesting poems.

Wilcox wrote two distinct kinds of "adult" poems: those which might appeal today to the television soap-opera set and those which are poetically and intellectually interesting in themselves. She mixed the two together in her volumes of poetry, along with poems apparently meant for children. Thus she tuned her verse directly to the housewife and mixed poems asserting a tough and aggressive individualism (and feminism) with poems of sentimentalism and traditional values. Nevertheless, her firm belief in woman and in her talents springs from the tendencies of earlier American women poets and marks a step to women's poetry today. In her own way, she foreshadows the verse of Edna St. Vincent Millay and, later, Sylvia Plath.

For example, in *Poems of Passion*, several poems, such as "Individuality," demand that a woman must retain a sense of self, of "individuality," a "subtle part" of her being, even in a happy love situation. In "An Answer," the poet rejects marriage:

If all the year was summer time,
And all the aim of life
Was just to lilt on like a rhyme,
Then I would be your wife.

Sexual passion (of both women and men) is symbolized throughout her poems as a tiger, not as in the naturalistic novels as a "beast within," but as a "splendid creature," which "Once having tasted human flesh, ah! then,/Woe, woe unto the whole rash world of men" ("The Tiger"). Nine years later, in "Three and One," published in *Poems of Pleasure* (1892), Wilcox admits that, for her, sex is "all the tiger in my blood." On the other hand, in "At Eleusis" (*Poems of Passion*), motherhood is praised and welcomed, but Persephone is passive, a "rescued maid," led "by the hand." In "A Gray Mood" (*Poems of Pleasure*), the world is a tragic place: "This world is a vaporous jest at best,/Tossed off by the gods in laughter." In this poem, such cosmic cruelty is moderated only by the hope of a better world in the hereafter. At times, in these short poems, Wilcox toys with the traditional concept of feminine duality ("Angel or Demon," *Poems of Pleasure*), and in her first long (3,200 lines) poem, *Maurine* (*Maurine, and Other Poems*, 1888), Wilcox introduced two types of women: Helen, a passive, weak woman, who bears a daughter and soon dies; and Maurine, an aggressive, intelligent artist, who eventually marries an American poet-intellectual after a trip to Europe, where her paintings receive respectable notices and a European nobleman proposes marriage to her. Helen and Maurine reappear, in far more complex form, as Mable and Ruth, two of the women in *Three Women*.

Lizette Woodworth Reese[48] is a better poet than Jackson. She more fully understood how to put "Chaos in fourteen lines," so to speak. Although her poetry occasionally suggests the fragile and delicate verse of Guiney (who was her contemporary), she has none of Guiney's "exotic" tendencies, nor Guiney's conscious striving for humanism (Reese did not need to strive for this quality), nor Guiney's cultured urbanity. Reese's verse is permeated with the sun and summer rather than with the moon and snow of Guiney and, later, of Teasdale. Her verse is generally treated at least with respect by critics, and it is interesting that Hyatt H. Waggoner makes a special point to mention her "unique virtues,"[49] but admits that he really cannot fit her into his *American Poets from the Puritans to the Present*. Of course, she is not "unique," but is one of the best women poets writing this kind of verse at this time. A native of Maryland, she spent her life writing poetry and prose and teaching in the Baltimore public schools.

I could list elements of her verse which reflect the poetry of earlier American women, much as I did for Jackson, but at this point such a listing seems redundant. Her poems also seem to have been influenced by Robert Herrick and Sappho, as other critics have noted.[50] She introduced an epigrammatic quality into women's verse at this time and was willing to take certain prosodic risks. For example, in *A Branch of May* (1887), we find these two poems (here given in their entirety):

DOUBT

Creeds grow so thick along the way,
  Their boughs hide God; I cannot pray.

TRUTH

The old faiths light their candles all about.
  But busy Truth comes by and blows them out.

She also wrote several excellent sonnets, such as "August," which is a descriptive sonnet in *A Branch of May*, and "Ellen Hanging Clothes," which is a "domestic" sonnet (for want of a better term) in *Spicewood* (1921). Like Sylvia Plath (several poems in *Ariel*), but unlike Emily Dickinson, she associates bees with death ("Telling the Bees" in *A Quiet Road*, 1896) and presents the custom used before in such a sentimental fashion by Whittier ("Telling the Bees") in a more sparse and striking image. In *Wild Cherry* (1923), she condemned "A Puritan Lady," who "stared to tears/Tall, golden Helen." And even though she is termed a "late-Romantic," she could not find God in the woods in "The Daffodils" (*A Wayside Lute*, 1916).

The presence of a number of fine women poets in the latter half of the nineteenth century—that is, the presence of an obviously major poet like Dickinson as well as a number of talented minor poets like Reese and Guiney—indicates that American women's poetry had assumed a maturity and dignity of its own. The broad basis of women's verse (rich and poor; black and white; Catholic, Protestant, and Jew) which had been established throughout the nineteenth century gave women's verse a richness and complexity which is not observed in the verse of the men at this time. When we speak disparagingly of *fin de siècle* or decadent verse at the end of the century, we are speaking primarily of male verse. The verse of American women was obviously vigorous both intellectually and prosodically. Unlike the men, the poetic momentum of the women was carrying them naturally into the twentieth century.

Chapter Six

1900-1945

A Rose Is a Rose with Thorns

As Wilcox's lecherously leering "senile old Century" came to an end, American women such as Guiney and Reese continued to write their own kind of poetry, and Emily Dickinson's verse began to appear. New women poets were also publishing, however, and American male poets were soon to recognize what we are still in the process of understanding: that the poetry of American women had, in fact, something to tell the twentieth century and had already found several ways to say it. As T. S. Eliot realized, Sweeney had finally to confront Mrs. Porter.

Except for the verse of Edwin Arlington Robinson, poems by American men from the last work of Whitman and Melville to Ezra Pound's proclamation of "Imagism" in 1912 are generally ignored. However, as we have seen, the final years of the nineteenth century were important for the verse of American women—and so were the first ten years of the twentieth century. Jessie Belle Rittenhouse's *The Younger American Poets* (1904)[1] not only demonstrates the richness of women's verse (as opposed to the male verse) at this time, but also anticipates both tendencies and problems of poetry to come. For example, among the eleven men she discusses are the late Romantics Richard Hovey, Bliss Carman, George E. Santayana, Madison Cawein, and Ridgeley Torrence; among the seven women are Reese, Guiney, Josephine Preston Peabody, and Edith M. Thomas.

Concerning Reese, Rittenhouse observes that her best poems are those of the "poet-singer" (p. 33), who can communicate with a

large audience. Rittenhouse then deplores what she sees as the growing exclusiveness of poets. "Poetry grows more and more an intellectual pleasure for the cultivated classes, less and less a possession
of the people. . . . the spirit of poetic art has suffered a sea-change"
(p. 34). Her remarks were made only ten years before Ezra Pound
so arrogantly announced in "The Audience" (*Poetry*, October 1914)
that "It is true that the great artist has in the end, always, his audience, for the Lord of the universe sends into the world in each
generation a few intelligent spirits, and these ultimately manage the
rest."[2] Such an attitude eventually alienated much of the American
reading public in the first half of the twentieth century. After all, it
is generally assumed that the chief "sin" of Amy Lowell's "Amygism"
was that she wanted to "popularize" Imagism, to free what she considered a valuable poetic technique from the tight and esoteric
clutches of Ezra Pound.

Concerning Guiney, Rittenhouse notes her "internationalism":
she "has little to do with the times and conditions in which she finds
herself" (p. 76). Moreover, Guiney's best poems are "pictures," based
firmly on visual images (p. 82). Rittenhouse especially praises Guiney
for her "fibre," "nerve," and "individuality" (p. 93). Both the adult
and children's poems of Josephine Peabody (1874–1922)[3] are discussed, but Rittenhouse saves much of her highest praise for Edith
M. Thomas (1854–1925), who, she declares, often writes verse which
"has a vivid energy of style, masculine in its force." Nevertheless,
Rittenhouse concludes, ultimately "Miss Thomas' work in the main
proves the woman" (p. 162).

Many of the poems of Thomas (twenty-one separate volumes of
adult and children's verse published between 1895 and 1915) are
pre-Imagist and pre-Modern. One poem Rittenhouse specifically
cites from Thomas's *The Dancers and Other Legends and Lyrics*
(1903)[4] is "The Deep-Sea Pearl":

> The love of my life came not
>   As love unto others is cast;
> For mine was a secret wound—
>   But the wound grew a pearl, at last.
>
> The divers may come and go,
>   The tides they arise and fall;
> The pearl in its shell lies sealed,
>   And the Deep Sea covers all.

In the same volume is the haunting "Shield Me, Dark Nurse."
Thomas eventually proved to be an uneven poet, vacillating be-

tween imitations of Longfellow and Poe and her own original kind of poetry which Rittenhouse noted and praised. Her later verse, written shortly before World War I, is notable for its pacifism (*The White Messenger, and Other War Poems*).

Rittenhouse's volume was apparently prepared too early to note the publication of *April Twilights* (1903), the first book by Willa Cather (1876–1947).[5] The 1903 edition exemplifies aspects of both the quality and the tendencies of women's poetry at this time. Although her modern editor, Bernice Slote, is careful to note Cather's poetic forefathers as A. E. Housman, Virgil (especially the Arcadian world of the "Eclogues"), Shakespeare, and others, we can readily identify her foremothers in the verse of her American sisters, as in "Dedicatory" and "Grandmither, Think Not I Forget." We find the now familiar image of a female mythological figure, "Eurydice"; and in "Winter at Delphi," the poet-oracle herself complains that Apollo has left her, that "Service of gods is hard."

Without the advice of Ezra Pound, Cather wrote "Prairie Dawn":

A crimson fire that vanquishes the stars;
A pungent odor from the dusty sage;
A sudden stirring of the huddled herds;
A breaking of the distant table-lands
Through purple mists ascending, and the flare
Of water ditches silver in the light;
A swift, bright lance hurled low across the world;
A sudden sickness for the hills of home.

Without the help of Jessie L. Weston's *From Ritual to Romance* (1920) and T. S. Eliot, she wrote of knights seeking the Grail, Eastern kings seeking the Rose, and a merchant seeking the Pearl in "Thou Art the Pearl." In "White Birch in Wyoming," as Slote points out (p. xxvi), Cather begins with a painting by Sir Edward Coley Burne-Jones and ends with a female/birch/Brunhilda in a land "Where heat has drunk the living water dry," where she is "girdled by the burning sand."

Within the same decade, another woman also now known primarily for her prose, Edith Wharton (1862–1937), published *Artemis to Actaeon and Other Verse* (1909). Wharton's prose is generally discussed in terms of the novels of her friend Henry James, although one critic, Alfred Kazin, credits her with being "among the few of her generation to attain the sense of tragedy, even the sense of the world of pure evil."[6] (Kazin obviously does not know a great deal about the other woman poets of her generation.) Her poetry reflects this same sense of tragedy and evil, although she depends on nineteenth-century poetic diction far more than did Cather or the poets discussed by Rittenhouse.

The poetic concerns we recognize as common in the verse of American women are there, with the title poem declaring that Artemis is superior to and more powerful than Actaeon and that, in fact, Actaeon must lose himself in her. Perhaps most interesting, however, is her poetic thrust toward free verse, as in this passage (from section I of "An Autumn Sunset"):

> Leaguered in fire
> The wild black promontories of the coast extend
> Their savage silhouettes;
> The sun in universal carnage sets,
> And, halting higher,
> The motionless storm-clouds mass their sullen threats,
> Like an advancing mob in sword-points penned,
> That, balked, yet stands at bay.

She was not quite able to break away from rhyme and meter. Nevertheless, "An Autumn Sunset" anticipates Imagism in several ways: consecutive lines are generally in different meters; the rhyme follows no set pattern; and the parallel structure and alliteration which unify H. D's "free verse" are well established. The attempt to create sharp images, the "impersonal" approach to description, and the short lines of the Imagist poem (as opposed to Whitman's longer, expanding line) are already present.[7]

H. D. (Hilda Doolittle Aldington, 1886–1961)

Among Imagist poems, the verse of H. D. stands apart.[8] Although she has been called "the perfect Imagist," she was never really an Imagist, as Pound defined that term anyway. Although she is credited with being one of the formulators of the three Imagist principles, she was hardly any more a "follower" of them than Guiney, Cather, or Reese. Some critics have recognized that her verse is not really Imagistic,[9] while other critics have claimed that "Actually . . . it was not Hulme but H. D., who had provided Pound with the direct inspiration for the new school of 'Imagistes,' "[10] and that Imagism was only a term "invented to launch H. D."[11]

If we examine the three original principles of Imagism as stated by F. S. Flint in the March 1913 issue of *Poetry*, we find that H. D.'s verse is related to, undoubtedly should stand as the original inspiration of, Imagism, but is in fact something else besides. The first principle is "1. Direct treatment of the 'thing,' whether subjective or objective." In a general sense, this principle in fact reflects much of women's verse in the nineteenth century. If taken literally, for example, it describes much of Dickinson's verse. Flint means, however, "direct" in the sense of being without the poet's presence or personal interjection, an impersonal poetry, such as Pound achieved in "In a Station of the Metro" or William Carlos Williams in "Poem" or "The Locust Tree in Flower." However, even in one of the first "Imagist" poems ever published, H. D.'s "Orchard" (originally titled "Priapus") in the January 1913 issue of *Poetry*, H. D. did not even try to achieve such an "impersonal" or "scientific" distance: "Orchard" begins "I saw the first pear/as it fell."

"2. To use absolutely no word that [does] not contribute to the presentation." This is a rule of good poetry in general and can be applied to anyone from Shakespeare to Alexander Pope. Flint meant, however, no "ornaments" or "decorations," only the "necessary" words. Pound could write this kind of poetry, as could Williams. H. D., however, could not: her parallel syntactical constructions and her careful alliterations in *Sea Garden* and *Hymen* are a different kind of word economy from that which Pound intended and which he himself practiced at this time.

"3. As regarding rhythm: to compose in sequence of the musical phrase, not in sequence of a metronome." Regardless of what Flint (and Pound) meant—and the meaning is debatable[12]—H. D.'s prosody is more "traditional" than this principle might suggest. H. D.'s meters are based roughly on Greek meters (much as Guiney's "Alexandriana" were), but, more specifically in the very early poems, her "free verse" is simply consecutive lines of different meters, such as Wharton had already been writing. Harvey Gross (*Sound and Form in Modern Poetry*, p. 108) has noted that H. D. used basically iambic meters, with occasional rhymes. In an early poem like "Hermes of the Ways," a close analysis reveals only a slight development from the kind of prosody Wharton was attempting (and which, we should remember, was the kind of prosodic experiment first tried in America in 1804 by Susanna Rowson).

However, if we assume that such critics as William Pratt and Hugh Kenner are even partially correct, then an American woman poet, H. D., was the inspiration for and an active collaborator in the formation of a major movement in American poetry which affected male poets. On the other hand, it is also apparent that H. D.'s verse is a culmination of certain aspects of previous American women's verse. Thus, for example, her early verse especially is permeated with female figures from classical mythology. What was a new and exciting source of poetic images for Pound, Eliot, Yeats, and other men in the early twentieth century was, in fact, for H. D., a natural and traditional source of images.[13] Moreover, like earlier American women poets, H. D. reinterpreted the classical figures in her own way. Unlike the male poets, she did not use myth as an expression of traditional (or even archetypal) values or as a vehicle for cosmic transcendence.

In *Hymen* (1921), "Leda" is an active and happy participant in what has traditionally been seen by male poets as a forcible rape which ultimately produced glorious children—a process in which Leda was no more than a vessel. "Demeter" is the "Great Mother," but men to her are now "useless" and she sings a mournful song:

> Do I sit in the market place—
> do I smile, does a noble brow
> bend like the brow of Zeus—
> am I a spouse, his or any,
> am I a woman, or goddess or queen,
> to be met by a god with a smile—and left?

In other poems in *Hymen*, H. D. establishes a pair in contrast, Phaedra and Hippolyta (in a series of three grouped poems, "Phaedra," "She Contrasts with Herself Hippolyta," and "She Rebukes Hippolyta"): Phaedra has committed suicide for love, but Hippolyta the Amazon has never known love and, at least from Phaedra's point of view, Hippolyta suffers.

The witch Circe is in depair after her failure to enchant Ulysses:

> It was easy enough
> to bend them to my wish,
>
> .   .   .   .   .   .
>
> but you
> adrift on the great sea,
> how shall I call you back?
>   (from "Circe")

The only reasonably happy woman besides Leda is Evadne, who has, like Leda, enjoyed her sexual union with a god. In fact, the drowsy, relaxed, and sensuous interior monologues of Leda and Evadne as they recall the sexual act probably represent the first realistic rendering of a woman's consciousness immediately after a satisfying orgasm. For H. D., the use of female mythological characters was a means of probing reality, especially for the various images of women. As she herself pointed out, "Isis takes many forms, as does Osiris."[14]

One major difference, however, between H. D.'s treatment of mythological characters and their use by earlier American women poets is the complex, layered texture of H. D.'s poetry. Indeed, the major problem for the modern reader of H. D.'s verse is that we are not familiar with classical mythology and its vocabulary. In her early verse, I think that H. D. expected her reader to respond much as the ancient Athenians responded to the tragedies of Aeschylus. For the Greek tragedians and their audience, the "story" was not important (everyone knew the story of Orestes and Electra), but the method of presentation was the significant creative factor. Thus, when one reads H. D.'s *Hymen,* the presentation and nuances are striking, but only to one who has a firm understanding of the myths. It is possible that H. D. misjudged her audience; after all, women poets in America had been using mythological figures as personal images since 1800. On the other hand, H.D., like Pound and Eliot, may have intended to write arrogantly esoteric verse.

Unlike her fellow American women poets from 1800 to her own day, H. D. did not deal exclusively with the major female mythological characters (some are minor), nor was she careful to provide the backgrounds of their stories, as preceding women poets had. On the basis of her late poetry, it appears that H. D. originally made the mistake of assuming that many of her readers understood the classical myths as fully as she did. In her War Trilogy (1944–1946), she shifted to the better-known Christian myth of the Virgin Mary; in her final major work, *Helen in Egypt* (1961), she meticulously explained the entire myth, with all its various implications.

With her return to the classical myths in *Helen in Egypt,* H. D. continued a symbolic exploration evident throughout much of her career. Even in her earliest poetry, she had symbolically juxtaposed the values of Greece (male, rational principles) and Egypt (female, passionate principles). The early Phaedra poems, section 3 of her novel *Palimpsest* (1926), and even the title of her 1931 collection of poems, *Red Roses for Bronze,* indicate her continuing attempt to discover the "intermediate state" between Greece and Rome. In *Helen in Egypt* she finally succeeded.

One of the few long poems written by an American woman in the twentieth century, *Helen in Egypt* is a mixture of poetry and prose, divided into three large sections (twenty "books"). H. D.'s story is based in obscure classical mythology: even before the Trojan

War, Helen had been wafted to Egypt, where a ship-wrecked Achilles had been washed to shore. Achilles is no longer a war hero, but simply a mortal man. (His mortality is his true Achilles' heel.) They marry and have two children. Achilles represents the Grecian/ rational view which Helen (originally from Sparta) must balance with values found in Egypt. At one point, Achilles accuses Helen of being a witch, a Hecate, which she is and is not, since she has become Isis, all-women, the "intermediate ground," which H. D.'s young scholar was attempting to find at the end of *Palimpsest*. Helen wishes to "bring Egypt and Greece together," as apparently only a woman (not a man) can. Nevertheless, against Achilles' male, Grecian eyes, Helen must struggle for her identity ("I must fight for Helena"). Significantly, Achilles admits that "The whole heroic sequence is over."

H. D. describes three modes of being clearly and explicitly: "Helen says, 'I am awake, I see things clearly; it is dawn.' If the Helen of our first sequence was translated to a transcendental plane, . . . and the Helen of our second sequence contacted a guide or guardian, near to her in time, Theseus, the hero-King and 'Master of Argo,' our third Helen having realized 'all myth, the one reality,' is concerned with the human content of the drama" (p. 265). The human, female content is the "intermediate ground":

the seasons revolve around
a pause in the infinite rhythm
of the heart and of heaven.
                    (p. 315)

In short, men seem to fall into two categories ("heaven" and "heart"), which women can and do imitate. The third category of being is the woman who is concerned with the "human content." She is assertive and intelligent; she contains qualities of the other types of men and women. She is a mother (although H. D.'s Helen is amazingly unresponsive to her children; she simply has them) . And, although H. D. seems to have reached, in Helen anyway, some kind of satisfactory definition of Woman, Helen's relationship with men is never very happy. In the course of the poem, she remembers all her various lovers; it is, however, Achilles whom she loves and whose children she bears in Egypt, but she does not like him very much and her new sense of self-value is threatened by him.

The poem is an attempt by H. D. to explore abstract and complex concepts; her intent is didactic. H. D., as narrator, explains what is happening or what the characters are thinking in prose, in declarative sentences, and then poetically describes the same event or thought, with a heavy reliance upon image patterns. An example of the modern poetic sequence,[15] *Helen in Egypt* is the climax of H. D.'s career, both intellectually and poetically.

Not only did H. D. anticipate Modern (male and female) poetry in the various ways we have already discussed, her early attempts to incorporate techniques from the plastic arts into her verse seem also to have been innovative and seminal. In certain early poems, H. D. was working as close as she could to a mingling of the art forms. She seems to have tried to "see," to represent the visual poetic image with reference to or by means of techniques of paintings she had viewed in Europe. Such a means of expanding the visual presentation of either poetry or prose was to become more and more common in the twentieth century, both for expatriate Americans and for those who stayed in the United States.[16]

H. D.'s early verse seems to be the first modern American verse to display such an interdisciplinary tendency. For example, her "Pear Tree" seems based on certain principles of French Impressionist painters:

Silver dust
lifted from the earth,
higher than my arms reach,
you have mounted,
O silver,
higher than my arms reach
you front us with great mass;

no flower ever opened
so staunch a white leaf,
no flower ever parted silver
from such rare silver;

O white pear,
your flower-tufts
thick on the branch
bring summer and ripe fruits
in their purple hearts.

In "Vorticism" (1914), Pound certainly encouraged such a tendency in all Modern poets, but I do want to point out that, from 1800, the women poets were constantly aware of the visual arts. Although we are accustomed to think of the nineteenth-century American poet-painter relationship in terms of Bryant's nature poetry and the landscapes of the Hudson River School, the literary historians seem to have completely overlooked the relationship of American women's poetry and the American and English genre and portrait painters, whose works were often used as illustrations for the popular journals like *Godey's Lady's Book*, as well as for gift-books, annuals, and the deluxe editions of the women poets (such as Osgood, Welby, even Griswold's anthology, *The Female Poets of America*).[17] Sometimes a poem was inspired by a print; sometimes a print was commissioned for a poem. With our present ignorance of this aspect of American literature and art, such relationships remain like that of the proverbial chicken and egg.

Osgood, whose husband was a painter and illustrator, wrote a number of such poems, as did Elizabeth Oakes Smith and the Cary sisters. Generally, the poems were descriptive or narrative, but Osgood occasionally seemed to be attempting to achieve visual effects. Later in the century, Guiney, whose poems Rittenhouse rightly described as "visual," occasionally anticipated the twentieth-century trend in a poem such as "A Madonna of Domenico Ghirlandajo." Cather's interest in the painting of Burne-Jones has already been mentioned. In short, even before H. D., American women's verse had for a century already reflected a more than superficial interest in the visual arts. However, H. D.'s attempt to incorporate the techniques of a visual art into her own verse seems a truly pioneering achievement in Modern American poetry.[18]

Thus, in several ways, H. D.'s verse represents the very earliest expression of those tendencies by which we identify poetry as Modern. Nevertheless, with her interest in mythological women, her "international" and broad humanistic tendencies, her type of prosodic experimentation, her sense of the visual image, and her refusal to be "cosmic"—her verse represents a development from many poems written by American women throughout the nineteenth century, with, as I have shown, a basis especially in the late nineteenth and early twentieth centuries. That H. D.'s verse does not completely correspond to Pound's three dicta is evidence of her independence and originality—a poetic individualism which continued until her death. The verse of H. D. had unquestionably affected the Modern poetry of many (both men and women) whom we now consider major American poets. Sweeney had met Mrs. Porter.

Lowell-Crapsey-Moore

As could be expected, a number of women poets were affected by the Imagist movement and, as is usual for American women, quickly

veered off in a variety of individual directions, while still advocating
and reflecting the modes and interests of their sisters.

Amy Lowell (1874–1925) is the most complex of this group.[19] In
one sense, she is the Sarah Wentworth Morton of her day, careful
to comply in much of her poetry and criticism to the reigning male
standards; yet, as in "Amygism," she is independent enough to assert her own values and critical beliefs. Her *Tendencies in Modern
American Poetry* (1917) states much that is valuable and much that
is foolish. In her poetry, we find a continual and disturbing shift of
directions: to Whitman, to Keats, to feminine protest in "Patterns,"
to the New England regionalism of Robert Frost, to Imagism, to
Symbolism. Her consciousness in her amatory verse shifts from male
to female (with more male than female, as Clement Wood, *Amy
Lowell*, pp. 139–179, has noted). What we miss in Lowell is her own
poetic voice. Her shifting position is not the result of a paradoxical
or at least convincing multiple angle of vision (as was Dickinson's),
but rather of a poet in search of her own speech and themes.

Nevertheless, she wrote a number of fine poems: "Patterns," in
which she was able to voice her protest in words and images within
a suitable structure; "Behind a Wall"; "Market Day"; "Lilacs"; and
"Nuit Blanche." She was willing to attempt difficult poems involv-
ing integration of the visual arts, as in "Lacquer Prints" and "Impressionist Picture of a Garden," and music, as in "Violin Sonata by
Vincent D'Indy" and "Stravinsky's Three Pieces 'Grotesques,' For
String Movement." Her better poems certainly reflect interests consonant with those of preceding American women poets: poems concerning female mythological characters, "The Captured Goddess"
and "Venus Transiens" (with a male poetic consciousness and voice);
poems of religious uncertainty and doubt, "Folie de Minuit" and
"Ely Cathedral"; poems of admiration of other women, "Eleanora
Duse" and "On Looking At a Copy of Alice Meynell's Poems"; poems
of independence, both poetic, such as "Astigmatism. To Ezra
Pound," and feminine, as in "Evelyn Ray"; many children's poems,
such as "A Roxbury Garden" and "The Painted Ceiling," some even
published in a book of "adult" poems, according to the nineteenth-
century practice (*A Dome of Many-Coloured Glass*) .

If her poetic voice was uncertain, we should still value her work
for those poems which do succeed; for her willingness to experiment
with various poetic techniques; and for her outspoken defense of
new poetic methods as well as of women poets. In fact, even though
she was somewhat narrow-minded concerning women poets in "The
Sisters" (1925), in *A Critical Fable* (1922) she defended women poets
as they are (not as they *should* be) and also indicted American male

critics for their treatment of women poets. In these two ways, *A Critical Fable* is a pioneering effort. The dialogue in the poem is between the poet ("A Poker of Fun") and her ancestor, James Russell Lowell (whose *Fable for Critics* appeared in 1848). The "Poker of Fun" has just defended Whitman, Poe, and Dickinson as the best poets in the nineteenth century, and James Russell Lowell responds:

> ["] For the men, I'll admit there is room for dispute;
> But the choice of Miss Dickinson I must refute."
> Then seeing me shrug, he observed, "I am human,
> And hardly can bear to allow that a woman
> Is ever quite equal to man in the arts;
> The two sexes cannot be ranked counterparts."
> "My dear Sir," I exclaimed, "if you'd not been afraid
> Of Margaret Fuller's success, you'd have stayed
> Your hand in her case and more justly have rated her."
> Here he murmured morosely, "My God, how I hated her!
> But have you no women whom you must hate too?
> I shall think all the better of you if you do,
> And of them, I may add." I assured him, "A few.
> But I scarcely think man feels the same contradictory
> Desire to love them and shear them of victory?"
> "You think wrong, my young friend," he declared with a frown,
> "Man will always love woman and always pull down
> What she does." "Well, of course, if you will hug the cynical,
> It is quite your affair, but there is the pinnacle.
> She's welcome to climb with man if she wishes."
> "And fall with a crash like a trayful of dishes,"
> He answered at once . . .

The "Poker of Fun" then goes on to praise several women (herself, H. D., and Sara Teasdale) as poets who have something valuable to say and who have said it well. For the first time since the early nineteenth century, women poets were not told that they had to write of the "affections," and they were not treated with condescension. Their special interests and types of poems were praised. Laura Riding, Muriel Rukeyser (*The Life of Poetry*, 1949), Louise Bogan, and Mary Ellman (*Thinking About Women*, 1968) were to follow in this critical line.

Adelaide Crapsey (1878–1914)[20] is best known for her imitations (in 1911–1913) of the Japanese haiku and tanka, which she called "cinquains." Her "Triad" is a favorite of anthologists, but other "cinquains" are equally interesting:

TRAPPED

Well and
If day on day
Follows, and weary year
On year . . . and ever days and years . . .
Well?

NOVEMBER NIGHT

Listen . . .
With faint dry sound,
Like steps of passing ghosts,
The leaves, frost crisp'd, break from the trees
And fall.

FOR LUCAS CRANACH'S *Eve*

Oh me,
Was there a time
When Paradise knew Eve
In this sweet guise, so placid and
so young?

Nor should we forget that she also wrote this kind of poem:

THE WITCH

When I was a girl by Nilus stream
    I watched the desert stars arise;
My lover, he who dreamed the Sphinx,
    Learned all his dreaming from my eyes.

I bore in Greece a burning name,
    And I have been in Italy
Madonna to a painter-lad,
    And mistress to a Medici.

And have you heard (and I have heard)
    Of puzzled men with decorous mien,
Who judged—The wench knows far too much—
    And hanged her on the Salem green?[21]

She died, just as her career was beginning.

The poetry of Marianne Moore (1887–1972) does not need to be introduced. We have a collected edition of her verse and several full-length studies.[22] She is a poet who is a favorite of critics and other poets, male and female. By the end of her life, she had won nearly every major poetry award and was applauded by baseball fans in Brooklyn's old Ebbets Field, but it is doubtful that many in the stadium had read her poetry. Although her poems are widely anthologized, she never had a broad readership in her lifetime. Even now, her reputation seems to be slipping. Yet, when we think of potential major poets in the twentieth century, we keep coming around to Marianne Moore.

The consensus of critical opinion is highly favorable. The essays gathered by Charles Tomlinson in *Marianne Moore: A Collection of Critical Essays* provide a summary of male opinion. (This entire volume, except for a 1919 letter by Moore herself to Pound, is a display of all-male judgment and contains articles by the Great Names of the twentieth-century canon of literary criticism: Eliot, Blackmur, Kenner, Ransom, among others.) Generally, we find the same words recurring throughout the articles: "clarity," "craftsman," "precision," "restraint," "fastidious," "feminine," "compact," "chaste," "reality," and "particular." The conclusion of one of the two articles by Eliot is this: "And there is one final, and 'magnificent' compliment: Miss Moore's poetry is as 'feminine' as Christina Rossetti's, one never forgets that it is written by a woman; but with both one never thinks of this particularly as anything but a positive virtue" (p. 51). There is a general tone of condescension.[23] A number of women critics have discussed Moore's poetry, with less condescension, but also with somewhat less praise and celebration.[24] She was, nevertheless, as Jean Garrigue has observed, "with the *Zeitgeist*."[25] In the major studies of American poetry written in the 1960's, her verse is still praised, but we can see her reputation beginning to evaporate. Pearce finds her aware of the "Adamic predicament," but uncommitted; Waggoner labels Moore (rather than H. D.) as the true Imagist.[26]

Everyone seems to admire her craftsmanship—her sense of poetic form and of the proper word—and her sense of herself as a poet. Although some of her poems are in free verse, most are written in her own original prosody—the syllabic line in a firm stanza pattern: according to the stanzaic pattern established by the poet, each line is allowed only a certain number of syllables. As we have seen, an emphasis upon the stanza (rather than the word or line) was an interest of several women poets, such as Jackson, at the end of the nineteenth century. In Moore's poems, however, the prosody sometimes becomes a mechanical device, and I believe that Waggoner rightly questions its poetic effectiveness.

Her search for the right word is admirable and certainly ties her to the Imagist movement. But her search often leads to strange words, vague word associations, and obscure word derivations— sometimes to confusion and sometimes to an esoteric exclusiveness akin to that of many twentieth-century male poets. She is, however, not particularly esoteric in her use of quotations, which come from newspapers and journals. Her use of quotations seems to represent a kind of middle ground between Eliot's use of quotations, which not even recourse to the source can always clarify, and that of E. E. Cummings, who poetically employed advertising slogans and bits from popular American songs.

The same critics have also recognized in Moore's poetry "Americanism," "Protestantism," "feminine realism," and "moralizing." Perhaps because we have wanted too much to make Moore a Modern, we have overlooked that long tradition in America of poetry which found morality in things (especially nature). This tendency begins with Puritan natural typology, as evident in Edward Taylor's "Upon a Spider Catching a Fly"; continues in the early Romantic period with poems such as Freneau's "The Wild Honeysuckle"; and develops into Emerson's "The Rhodora." The structure of these poems and that of many of Moore's "analytic" poems (as opposed to her "descriptive" and more "Imagistic" verse) is the same: the observation of the event or thing, and then, after some reflection or analysis, the statement of the specific moral conclusion. One significant difference between Moore and these earlier poets, however, is that her source is not nature so often as books, pictures, a horse race, a ball game, animals in a zoo, or whatever. Such poems are many and her most interesting: "His Shield," "Charity Overcoming Evil," "No Swan So Fine," and "Elephants." Thus, in a sense, she has "modernized" an old form: she has developed her morality from elements of civilization (from people) rather than from nature. (This is not the same as William Carlos Williams's "no ideas but in things," because the "ideas" in Moore's poems are about "things/people" and come ultimately from herself.)

On the other hand, it is a fact that few of the best American women poets have written the kind of poem which begins with nature and ends with a moral. Anne Bradstreet's "Contemplations" is one exception; several of the poems of Elizabeth Oakes Smith and of the women who imitated Bryant and Emerson (such as Peirson and Welby) also employ this device. Most women, including Dickinson, if they are working toward a moral, move as Moore does—

from people or civilized objects or situations to a moral. We remember Bleecker's poem concerning her husband's drunken friends on New Year's Day; or Warren's poems based on philosophical principles; or Osgood's poems of personal relationships (in which morals can be drawn from a child playing with a watch); or Dickinson's poems, most of which use nature as an image or symbol rather than as a starting point for moralizing; or H. D. The reason for this different trend, this different way of moralizing, is that separation between God and nature which the critics have noted in Dickinson—and which, as we have seen, has been insisted upon by most American women poets. It is further evident in the interest of the nineteenth-century American women poets in genre and portrait painting rather than in the landscapes of the Hudson River School. It is interesting that, later in her career, Moore found her starting points more and more often in everyday life (the Brooklyn Dodgers, Yul Brynner, an old amusement park) rather than in the statistics and strange bits of fact evident in her early verse.

The concluding moral which Moore reaches is never very profound and is certainly not "cosmic" (hence her "feminine realism"): "Whatever it is, let it be without affectation" ("Love in America?"); "Ecstasy affords/the occasion and expediency determines the form" ("The Past Is the Present"); New York is " 'accessibility to experience' " ("New York"); although occasionally we find, "This is mortality,/this is eternity"—"this" being the "captive" bird who knows "how pure a thing is joy" ("What Are Years?"). In short, she is very "real" and thus, in the context of American poetry, very "feminine." Naturally, this quality, despite her craftsmanship, is in part the cause of her evaporating reputation in such recent major and cosmically oriented studies of American verse as Pearce's and Waggoner's.

As the critics have recognized, her "feminine realism" is accompanied by "restraint." In this sense, she is unlike those women poets, such as Millay, who frightened Ransom ("The Woman as Poet," quoted in Chapter 3) and who never achieved a high reputation among the male critics to begin with. She appears to be rational and logical. Moreover, she says nothing very new, nothing particularly challenging, nothing even profound. Her verse, in fact, is not a challenge to male or female either intellectually or emotionally, although her intricacy of irony is interesting. She works very hard to come to her conclusions and, in the end, one must often ask whether or not it was all worth it.

In short, it seems clear that, although certain aspects of Moore are related to previous women's verse, much of her poetry also conforms to the strictures of twentieth-century literary criticism, a field dominated by men like Ransom and Eliot. And yet she maintains her independence from them by refusing to sacrifice her "realism" for their "cosmic" qualities; it is, however, a very narrow "realism," which I feel will ultimately be unacceptable. Thus, although R. P. Blackmur thought "Marriage" an excellent poem, it is, as Randall Jarrell pointed out,[27] limited in its intellectual complexity. Moore took few emotional, intellectual, or prosodic risks. In fact, her emphasis has been on structure, on the mode of expression, and on a defense of herself as a poet ("Poetry"). Her devotion to her craft has clearly influenced a number of later poets, both men and women (such as Elizabeth Bishop and Jean Garrigue). Her poetry resembles the snail she describes in "To a Snail":

> If "compression is the first grace of style,"
> you have it. Contractibility is a virtue
> as modesty is a virtue.
> It is not the acquisition of any one thing
> that is able to adorn,
> or the incidental quality that occurs
> as a concomitant of something well said,
> that we value in style,
> but the principle that is hid:
> in the absence of feet, "a method of conclusions";
> "a knowledge of principles,"
> in the curious phenomenon of your occipital horn.

Gertrude Stein (1875–1946) and *Laura Riding* (1901–)

Gertrude Stein[28] and her most direct literary descendant, Laura Riding, represent a new direction in American women's verse in the twentieth century. Both, but especially Stein, are the first philosophical poets among American women after Mercy Otis Warren. Even in her philosophic, poetic meditations, Stein is not a "cosmic" poet; her world is either godless or, according to one reading of that lyrical passage from *Four Saints in Three Acts*, "Pigeons on the grass alas," dominated by a distant and unattractive deity.[29] Stein is, in fact, as much a "feminine realist" as any of her female poetic predecessors in America. Her emphasis is upon the mind and its experience—the "continuous present." Moreover, her emphasis is also upon the particular experience of a woman, a highly intelligent and sensitive woman, who is a reflection of many women: herself, in her poetic meditations, or, for example, "Many, Many Women" (written 1910–1912) or the women in *Three Lives* (1909). Her love of children and their interests is evident in the number of poems and books she wrote for them.

On the other hand, Stein's poetry is certainly not "communicative" in the sense that most women's poetry has been in America. If we were to apply the generally accepted definition of public and private poets to her work, Stein would be the ultimate private poet —one who attempts to resolve the conflicts of her age in a language which people must "learn." It should be noted, however, that at the beginning and end of her career (in the first decade of the twentieth century and in the 1930's and 1940's) she wrote works which are obviously more "communicative" in the sense that women's poetry in America has tended to be. In between, she generally wrote in her own "hermetic" technique and wondered why her works did not sell better.

Stein's poetry often sounds and looks very much like her prose. As Michael J. Hoffman has shown in *The Development of Abstractionism in the Writings of Gertrude Stein*, the line between her prose and her poetry is not always clear—a general tendency not uncommon in twentieth-century poetry or prose.[30] *The Autobiography of Alice B. Toklas* is prose, and *Stanzas in Meditation* is poetry. On the other hand, we may read *Tender Buttons* or *The Mother of Us All* as poetry or prose. Although, in "Poetry and Grammar,"[31] Stein insisted that poetry is essentially lyrical and that the poetic line should be short and repetitive, it is clear that she herself did not always follow such a course.

Another quality which distinguishes Stein's poetry, especially that written after 1910, is her obvious and often discussed integration of the visual arts into her verbal techniques. Her well-known advice to Ernest Hemingway to study Cézanne is indicative of many of her own methods. Her "continuous present" of simultaneity, her use of words as pigment, her abstraction, her "Cubist" style—all of these qualities force her readers to a sensual expansion, to a synesthetic mosaic of experience comparable to that expressed in much twentieth-century painting (Cubism) and literature (Hemingway and Faulkner). In fact, her experiments in such a multimedia approach extend beyond the use of techniques from painting (as was then being attempted independently by H. D. and would soon be attempted by Wallace Stevens) to a more thoroughgoing effort to unite all the art forms. In this way, she anticipated the expression and examination of a unitary sense of art evident later among the French Dadaists and Surrealists (of whom, by the way, Stein did not approve).

Gertrude Stein's significance in twentieth-century literature is generally restricted by critics to her influence on the work of a number of her contemporaries, not the least of whom was Hemingway. Thus her theories of writing are seen as a significant aspect in the development of twentieth-century literature[32] (much as H. D.'s verse has been credited with being essential to another aspect of twentieth-century poetry). However, it seems to me that Stein is important in the development of women's verse in three other important ways:

First, Stein's experiments with language and punctuation, as well as her concern with poetic attitude, influenced a number of younger women poets, the most important of whom is Laura Riding. Riding published defenses and interpretations of Stein in the 1920's (see below). For these younger women, Stein represented an approach to poetry and language different from (even in direct conflict with) the Pound-Eliot poets, the Fugitive poets, and the regionalists—the dominant poetic voices in America in the 1920's.

Second, as I have said, she is the first philosophical woman poet since Warren. Unlike Warren, however, Stein rejected traditional philosophical positions, as her Jamesian pragmatism directed, and began all over again (just, of course, the kind of process to which Warren objected). Nevertheless, the meditative and philosophical tendency in both Stein and Warren resulted in a conclusion of the importance of "liberty" (in all its various modes) and in an affirmation of the abilities and attitudes of women. Each approached her age with erudition and intelligence.

Third, in Stein's best work, there is a continual movement, even if, as in the "continuous present," things (events, thoughts) keep beginning again. As Stein stated in "The Gradual Making of *The Making of Americans*" (1935), "Think of anything, of cowboys, of movies, of detective stories, of anybody who goes anywhere or stays at home and is an American and you will realize that it is something strictly American to conceive a space that is filled with moving, a space of time that is filled always filled with moving . . . an American thing."[33] Stein saw women as "moving" too—not as sedentary passive creatures. They are not Warren's "Roman matrons," but there seems to be little they cannot do, or at least attempt.

Stein's poetry is not often anthologized, because it is difficult to understand and because it is difficult to select a cutting from her often long and involved poems. Perhaps the best presentation of her poetry concerning Picasso is *Gertrude Stein on Picasso*, edited by Edward Burns. Here is both prose and poetry, carefully selected and enriched with a number of drawings and paintings by Picasso. The generally available *Last Operas and Plays*, edited by Carl Van Vechten, contains some of her more easily understood poetry, including *Four Saints in Three Acts* and *The Mother of Us All*. Her best poetry, however, seems to me to be her *Stanzas in Meditation, and Other Poems* [*1929–1933*], vol. 6 of *The Yale Edition of the Unpublished Writings of Gertrude Stein*. Here are poems discussing color relationships in modern art ("Stanzas in Meditation," Part V, Stanza XIII); literary theory ("A stanza should be thought," "Stanzas in Meditation," Part V, Stanza XXIX); historical meditation ("History misses pansies" in "A French Rooster. *A History*"); and her usual observations on women ("In many women wedding is an offering" from "A Ballad").

Laura Riding (Gottschalk Jackson)[34] was one of the few writers and critics in the 1920's publicly and vehemently to defend Stein and then to adopt certain of her poetic techniques and attitudes. In *Contemporaries and Snobs,* Riding praises Stein for her "barbarism" and juxtaposes Stein's poetry to the critical standards of T. E. Hulme. In *A Survey of Modernist Poetry* (written in 1927 with Robert Graves) she explained that Stein's only fault was that "she took primitiveness too literally."

Laura Riding seems to be an almost totally forgotten poet. For a time (roughly 1923–1925) she was associated with the Fugitive group, but she deserted them because she felt that they were too concerned with "composition."[35] During the late 1920's and the 1930's, having left her husband, she lived in Europe in close personal and professional association with Robert Graves. In 1939, she "renounced" poetry, remarried, and returned to the United States.

Riding's introduction to her *Collected Poems* is her own defense against the charge of "obscurity," which was in the 1920's and 1930's directed against her work by a number of critics. Ransom and the other Fugitives felt that her poetry was too formless; even Alfred Kreymborg, who was generally an intelligent reader, confessed that he could not understand her then famous "The Quids," which had originally appeared in the February 1924 issue of *The Fugitive*.[36] She defends her poetry as "our own proper immediacies" (like Stein's "continuous present") but also suggests that readers often come to poetry for the wrong reasons and that poets often write poetry for the wrong reasons. She is, nevertheless, disturbed that people— many people—do not understand her verse. In *A Survey of Modernist Poetry*, she defends her verse from charges of obscurity and, in turn, accuses other poets of an intentional and snobbish obscurity. For readers today, it is difficult to understand just how her poems could have been so universally considered "obscure."

There are a few difficult poems, chiefly those in which she imitates what she calls the "nursery-rhyme" quality of Stein's verse—poems such as "Forgotten Girlhood" and "Poem Only." These are indeed obscure poems, with both the technical and intellectual complexity of Stein, although Riding generally writes in a workable free verse form. However, we can also find a large number of more easily understood poems which seem to echo Dickinson, especially in those poems concerning death, such as "Chloe Or . . . " and "Second-Death," or in other poems, such as "The Rugged Black of Anger," which begins "The rugged black of anger/Has an uncertain smile-border."

There is a wealth of material concerning women in these poems:

Mothering innocents to monsters is
Not of fertility but fascination
In women.
                    (from "Echoes")

Woman, reviling term
Of Man unto the female germ,
And Man, reproach of Woman
In this colloquy,
Have grown so contrary
That to have love
We must combine chastely next
Among the languages
Where calling is obscene
And words no more than mean.
                    (from "Rhythms of Love")

CARE IN CALLING

Who, then, is child,
And who is man?
Child is the first man still,
Man is the last man not yet.
And the first man is seed,
And the last man is seed silenced.
The last man is womanish:
Woman which before man
Was silent word alone—
That breeding silence she.
Let it be a care

How man or child
Be called man or child,
Or woman, woman.

She wrote a number of excellent amatory poems, especially "Midsummer Duet," in which the First Voice is Riding and the Second Voice Robert Graves.

Her philosophical poems are usually attempts to define questions of personal identity and relationship of self to the world, as in "The World and I" and "I Am." Or she considers history, in a way different from T. S. Eliot, in "The Forgiven Past." She seems to accept the value of traditional religious doctrine ("Christmas, 1937"), but, like preceding American women poets, she can make no personal contact with the Deity, nor does she ever "transcend."

Obviously, she is a poet who is not so secretive or difficult as many critics have led us to believe. Allen Tate has commented that Riding is "an international poet who happens to write in English."[37] As we have seen, however, this observation could be applied to a large number of American women poets. Tate continues: Riding "is one of the best living poets." I agree with him.

Edna St. Vincent Millay (1892–1950) and Elinor Wylie (1885–1928)

Millay and Wylie were good friends, and their poetry is often considered together as "female Lyrist," apparently a new twentieth-century category of poetry which has been conceived especially for women poets such as Millay, Wylie, Teasdale, Reese, and others. Here is a typical definition of this term by Thomas A. Gray from his study of Elinor Wylie: ". . . these 'Lyrists' wrote in a common style, the chief hallmark of which, aside from its traditionalism, is its femininity. The preference for the smallest, neatest verse forms; the meticulous technical finish; the habitual use of imagery for pure decoration; and the prevalence of certain kinds of images—dainty, pretty, rare, refined, precious, and exquisite ones—inevitably suggest the feminine taste."[38] This is, Gray assures us, the "common feminine lyric style," a development from the nineteenth century.

Well, yes, a development from the nineteenth century, but only as we have seen the poetry of twentieth-century American women as developing from the women poets of the nineteenth century. Actually, the term *Lyrist* itself is a catchall and condescending critical term which is a development from the concept of "female poetry" of the nineteenth century. Moreover, the generalization which this term demands is wrong. Sara Teasdale is not Lizette Woodworth Reese is not Elinor Wylie is certainly not Edna St. Vincent Millay.

Actually, of all these women, Wylie[39] does most closely resemble the "Lyrist" poet as that term is defined: she did wish to produce small, neat, meticulous poems; she did use traditional meters; and her images are often not essential to the poem. With influence from Shelley, her style is poetically between those of Teasdale and Millay. Poems such as "Pity Me" and "Let No Charitable Hope" are reminiscent of Teasdale's poetry of withdrawal; "Where, O, Where?" and "Enchanter's Handmaiden" suggest the independent and vigorous poetry of expansion of Millay and Dickinson. One of her most interesting poems is "Letter to V——," addressed to Millay—a listing of their theological and hence for them essentially personal differences. In certain of her ballads and her self-conscious thrust toward a more general humanism, Wylie also resembles Guiney, who was writing her best poetry when Wylie was a teenager. Waggoner[40] has rightly noted her poetic debt to Emerson, but Wylie never "transcended," nor could she be considered a "cosmic" poet.

Wylie did not understand the dynamic power of words (in the way, for example, Dickinson did), but she is sensitive to their sound and connotative qualities, as is evident in "Pretty Words." She mixes an emotional softness, as in "Bread Alone," with types of poems which critics like to term "masculine," such as "Peregrine." At times, as in "Heroics," she believes that the world is a wasteland, but she is also able to accept the truth of simple, optimistic morality ("The Lion and the Lamb") and, in other poems, is willing to assert that the reality of the world is certain and "lovely," even though it is "a thin gold mask" ("Sunset on the Spire"). In poems such as "Nancy" and "Francie's Fingers," there are traces of nursery rhymes in her verse. She asserts her individuality, her sense of self-value in "Unfinished Portrait" and "False Prophet"; offers a gift from a "sorceress" to the familiar female mythological figure in "To Aphrodite, with a Talisman"; and honors other women, as, for example, in "On a Singing Girl" and "To Claudia Homonoea." As she grew older, she came to love London; and, as in "One Person," her poems began to resemble those of Elizabeth Barrett Browning. Most critics have preferred her verse to that of Edna St. Vincent Millay.

Millay[41] was extremely popular in the 1920's, especially with the young women who viewed her "as symbolic figure—the 'free woman' of the age."[42] It was she who galvanized Ransom in the 1930's to write "The Poet as Woman" and about whom Kreymborg snorted such words as these: "The ballad about 'my true love's rover' and 'my true love is false' invites women to play the game as men play it"; and "here is a girl, a woman, who does not kneel to her lover."[43] In the general context of women's poetry in America, she was not saying anything unique, but she said it well and she said it in such a way that a good many people listened. It was not until the 1960's that the critics began to discuss her work again. However, if the sales of her verse mean anything, people continued to read her.[44] Millay must be considered important, if only because her voice demonstrated to many people that women could and should write with freedom and bluntness—and talent. She encouraged other women to expand both their verse and their lives. We should remember that many women writing today are daughters of those women who looked upon Millay as a "symbolic figure."

We also should, moreover, remember to look upon Millay as a poet. "Renascence," the poem which first brought her critical attention, expresses a "cosmic" or "mystical" vision, consonant with male verse, but then Millay found her own poetic voice and never again expressed such a theme. *A Few Figs from Thistles* (1922), which has caused such critical nastiness, is the work of a young woman and is indeed hedonistic. I do not need to praise her poems, nor should I have to mention at this point those poems which relate her verse to that of previous women in America.

Millay did write one very significant poem which has generally been ignored. *Conservation at Midnight* (1937) is a closet drama and contains the voices only of men. The all-male cast is a daring device, because, although male writers have written words for women to speak for centuries, few women poets have attempted to create significant and serious voices for men. Women playwrights and novelists have written dialogue for men, but women poets (with the exception of some brief lyrics by Amy Lowell and one or two others) have generally maintained a female voice. What is more important, however, is that *Conversation at Midnight* is an attempt to understand the "male" world. Millay has chosen to characterize a group of intelligent and urbane men: a capitalist, a poet, a painter, a Roman Catholic priest, and so on. The situation is all quite contrived, the analysis is at times not very profound, and the poetry often reads like prose. At the same time, however, she consciously undercuts and thus plays havoc with those images which many of the radical poets of the 1930's were using in their political verse.[45]

Her poem is thus working on two levels. First, she is attempting to understand the male world, as no other woman poet had. She has not simply viewed man as "Man," nor does she hate him. Obviously, the poetry of American women had reached a point at which it was secure and confident enough not to be defensive or aggressively hostile. Second, she is constantly defending different kinds of values, not the least interesting of which is that of the businessman Merton, who is juxtaposed to the poet-communist Carl. Like Cummings, Stein, Riding, and others in the 1930's, Millay opposed the radical line.[46]

Some of Millay's best discursive poetry is contained in *Conversation at Midnight*, although it is unfair to quote only separate passages from the context of this poem, which is carefully organized and integrated:

> JOHN [a painter]
> Belief, perhaps, is at the opposite pole
> From thought; and their functions cannot be combined;
> Believing being the office of the soul,
> As reasoning is the office of the mind.
> The man who reads a book asks of the eye
> Alone its service; he does not exact
> Help from the ear as well; if he should cry,
> "I do not hear it!—therefore it is no fact!"
> When speaking of a book, we must confess
> This man unbalanced; persisting, he would be
> A source of pity, not unmixed with—yes
> Annoyance, to persons functioning properly.
> Belief has its own logic; I divide
> Apples by pears, when I set that fact aside.

See also the speech of Anselmo the priest which begins, "If you live in the street called *Now*, in a house called *Here*—." Other passages deal with the men's opinions of women.

"With Signs of Belief"

In her own way, Millay prepared for and anticipated the new group of women poets already beginning to emerge in the 1930's, such as Muriel Rukeyser. World War II created a break in women's verse, much as it did in the poetry of the men.

During the war, however, two little-noticed books of poems by American women appeared. They anticipated the poems of women today[47] and signaled new emphases in women's verse. The first is Margaret Walker's *For My People* (1942). The colloquial diction (in Walker's verse, of blacks) and the emphasis upon traditions and stories of the people as in "Stagolee," which are combined with the sense of herself as an individual and a woman ("Lineage" and "Kissie Lee") and with a protest for her people ("We Have Been Believers"), introduced a multifaceted poetry which would eventually appeal to a wide audience and maintain a firm intellectual basis. Her spontaneity, her witch "Molly Means," her direct and honest expression, and (as Stephen Vincent Benét noted in his introduction) her sense of "reality"—all suggest her heritage in the verse of earlier American women. Walker is poet enough that, in writing for her people, she ultimately influenced a wide variety of white and black American poets. In particular, *For My People* marks a resurgence of poetic expression by black women.

The other short volume to appear during the war is Muriel Rukeyser's *Beast in View* (1944).[48] Rukeyser had already published three volumes of poetry before *Beast in View*, but in this volume she seemed to find her own poetic voice. In her early poetry, she aligned herself with the radical poets of the 1930's and wrote in the styles of Eliot, Whitman, Yeats, and John Dos Passos. Interest in social or political causes has, as we have seen, always been at least a peripheral concern of American women poets from the eighteenth-century farces of Mercy Warren through Lydia Sigourney, surfacing in the twentieth century in the pre–World War I pacifist verse of Edith M. Thomas and in the more radical verse of Lola Ridge in the 1920's.[49] Even Millay joined the protest surrounding the execution of Sacco and Vanzetti both personally and poetically in "Justice Denied in Massachusetts." Ridge's *Sun-Up, and Other Poems* (1920), however, contains truly radical political poetry which, it appears, directly influenced the verse of political poets (both men and Rukeyser) in the 1930's.

In her first book of poems, *Theory of Flight* (1935), Rukeyser announced in "Poem Out of Childhood" that her poetry was to be "Not Sappho, Sacco," but one poem in this volume suggests a broader scope as well as a unique poetic voice: "Four in a Family." In her second book of verse, *U.S. 1* (1938), three poems are exceptional and, in fact, strikingly anticipate some of the poems Sylvia Plath would later write: "Girl at the Play," "In Hades, Orpheus," and, perhaps even more indicative of American women's poetry at the present, "More of a Corpse Than a Woman." In her third volume, *A Turning Wind* (1939), a serious concern with the family (all members: father, mother, children) is evident in "The Victims: A Play for the Home"; and, instead of Whitman or Yeats, we hear the nursery rhyme ("M-Day's Child Is Fair of Face"). A woman, "Ann Burlak," is celebrated, and the "ten greatest American women" are listed as various "anonymous" women.

Finally, in *Beast in View,* there is less Sacco and more Sappho: a celebration of love in "Mortal Girl" (a poem similar in theme to H. D.'s "Leda"); "Suicide Blues" (a poem which stands between the poems of suicide written by American women since the early nineteenth century and similar poems by Sylvia Plath and Anne Sexton); "Wreath of Women" (in which she defines Woman as four-fold: "Whores, artists, saints, and wives"); "Holy Family"; and "Letters to the Front," which combines a sense of womanhood and ethnic identity (here, Judaism) and which concludes:

> Surely it is time for the true grace of women
> Emerging, in their lives' colors, from the rooms, from the harvests,
> From the delicate prisons, to speak their promises.
> The spirit's dreaming delight and the fluid senses'
> Involvement in the world. Surely the day's beginning
> In midnight, in time of war, flickers upon the wind.
>
> O on the wasted midnight of our pain
> Remember the wasted ones, lost as surely as soldiers
> Surrendered to the barbarians, gone down under centuries
> Of the starved spirit, in desperate mortal midnight
> With the pure throats and cries of blessing, the clearest
> Fountains of mercy and continual love.
>
> These years know separation. O the future shining
> In far countries or suddenly at home in a look, in a season,
> In music freeing a new myth among the male
> Steep landscapes, the familiar cliffs, trees, towers
> That stand and assert the earth, saying: "Come here, come to me.
> Here are your children." Not as traditional man
> But love's great insight—"your children and your song."
>
> Coming close to the source of belief, these have created
> Resistance, the flowering face of memory,
> Given the bread and the dance and the breathing midnight.
> Nothing has been begun. No peace, no word of marvellous
> Possible hillsides, the warm lips of the living
> Who fought for the spirit's grace among despair,
> Beginning with signs of belief, offered in time of war,
> As I now send you, for a beginning, praise.

Rukeyser thus made her "Beginning with signs of belief." The next year Gwendolyn Brooks's *A Street in Bronzeville* and Elizabeth

Bishop's *North and South* appeared, and the poetry of American women had begun another period of vigorous achievement.

 Although I have emphasized the thematic contributions of women to American poetry throughout my study, I do not mean to imply that their verse has been limited to self-definition, or to women-centered and domestic themes. Clearly, however, the American women have never hesitated to explore that poetically new area—their homes and their children. They have, indeed, discovered a still expanding source of vibrant metaphors and vital themes. "Domestic" verse, now a significant element in contemporary poetry by men as well as by women, strikingly represents the different ways in which poetry by American men and women has developed historically.

 A number of other significant tendencies, however, are now obvious in the verse of American women. For example, as I have pointed out throughout this study, poetry by American women has tended to concern itself primarily with "international" or "universal" themes rather than with "nativist" or American concerns. While the men were concerned with creating an American myth—the American Adam—the women created a poetry in which the persona often has no identifiable nationality and whose subject and images (Osgood's children or Dickinson's soulscape) are common to a broad group of humanity. The "failure" of the American women to write a national epic can certainly be traced to their collective lack of a "national consciousness."

 However, a discussion of women's contributions to American poetry need not be limited to theme. Their significance is evident in a number of different ways: in terms of prosodic innovation, at several historical points, but especially in the late nineteenth century, as a number of diverse prosodic tendencies among women poets anticipated H. D. and the Modern age; in terms of poetic structure and inspiration, the continuing interrelationship of the plastic arts and poetry, evident in women's verse, even before the Knickerbocker Poets responded to the Hudson River School of painters (Chapter 6); and in terms of literary criticism, the implications and consequences of that critical definition of "female poetry," developed by men and women in the early nineteenth century—a definition which, of course, also tells us something about "male poetry."

 On the basis of such evidence, we can only conclude that American women have contributed significantly to American poetry. We must now begin to understand that complex interrelationship between male and female poets of America.

Notes

Introduction

1 See also the many women poets in the anthology *Local and National Poets of America*, ed. Thomas W. Herringshaw. Or read an American hymnal of almost any Protestant faith to find the unfamiliar names of women who also expressed themselves poetically. Many poems written for children by women since the eighteenth century have never been catalogued, because they were published in the same volumes as "adult" verse.

2 Most recently: Roy Harvey Pearce, *The Continuity of American Poetry*; Hyatt H. Waggoner, *American Poets from the Puritans to the Present*; and Edwin Fussell, *Lucifer in Harness: American Meter, Metaphor, and Diction*.

3 American poets have never become wealthy only from the sale of verse. However, in *The Profession of Authorship in America, 1800–1870*, William Charvat shows that poetry by women sold better than that of men in America before the Civil War. No comparable study has been done for the industry since 1870, but we know, for instance, that in the 1890's Ella Wheeler Wilcox's poems were "best sellers," and that, beginning in the 1920's, Edna St. Vincent Millay certainly supported herself with her verse. In fact, her sister, Norma Millay Ellis, recently observed that "Her royalties have helped me live for the last 24 years" (*New York Times*, February 20, 1974, p. 26).

4 Originally developed in R. W. B. Lewis's *The American Adam: Innocence, Tragedy, and Tradition in the Nineteenth Century*, the American Adam is further explored in Pearce's *The Continuity of American Poetry*. Leslie Fiedler has recognized certain limitations of the American Adam as this image has developed in American prose (*Love and Death in the American Novel*).

5 Pearce, *The Continuity of American Poetry*, p. 181.

1. 1632–1758: Anne Dudley Bradstreet and the Other Puritan Poets

1 For a condensed survey of poetry by English women before 1650, see Elizabeth Wade White, *Anne Bradstreet: "The Tenth Muse,"* pp. 273–282.

2 For all practical purposes, the poetry of English women has been ignored almost as carefully as that of American women.

3 The definitive edition of her poetry and prose is *The Works of Anne Bradstreet*, ed. Jeannine Hensley. *Poems of Anne Bradstreet*, ed. Robert Hutchinson, makes available a wide selection of her work in an inexpensive paperback edition. The best critical-biographical studies are Josephine K. Piercy's *Anne Bradstreet* and White's *Anne Bradstreet: "The Tenth Muse."* Piercy has also edited a facsimile reproduction of *The Tenth Muse*. A brief and intelligent analysis of Bradstreet's themes, verse forms, and certain poetic techniques is Rosemary M. Laughlin's "Anne Bradstreet: Poet in Search of Form," *American Literature* 42 (March 1970): 1–17. See also Ann Stanford, "An Annotated Check-List of Works by and about Anne Bradstreet," *Early American Literature* 3 (Winter 1968–1969): 217–228.

4 Roy Harvey Pearce, *The Continuity of American Poetry*, p. 24. Re-

cently, a curious criticism of Bradstreet's poetry has been offered by Kenneth A. Requa, "Anne Bradstreet's Poetic Voices," *Early American Literature* 9 (Spring 1974): 3–18. Requa claims that Bradstreet's "The Four Monarchies" fails because of "the conflict between the historian and housewife, the Raleigh-like master of times past and the self-conscious poet who doubts her abilities as historian poet" (p. 6).

[5] A pirated edition of Katherine Philips's poems and translations, which had been circulating in manuscript among her friends for several years, appeared in 1664, followed by a corrected edition in 1667. Although she is generally termed neo-Platonic, her verse suggests Sappho just as well. A 1904 volume of her poetry, *Katherine Philips, "the Matchless Orinda": Selected Poems*, was edited by the American poet Louise Imogen Guiney.

[6] When White designates Bradstreet as a "middle-class woman" (*Anne Bradstreet: "The Tenth Muse,"* p. 291), she overlooks the fact that in Puritan America the daughter of a governor who was also the wife of a governor was "upper-class." White herself notes that Simon Bradstreet is the only "free House Houlder" listed as "Mr." in the early records of the plantation on the Cochichewick Brook (now North Andover), where the Bradstreets moved sometime in the mid-1640's (pp. 224–227).

[7] Only the nonvirgin Semiramis ("The Four Monarchies," ll. 70–147) ruled alone, but she killed her husband with whom she had shared power for a time. Although Bradstreet worries a bit about "her life licentious, and unchaste," she nevertheless admires the ancient queen.

[8] For stylistic relationships between these poems, see Piercy, *Anne Bradstreet*, p. 62.

[9] Ibid., pp. 32–33.

[10] As Philippe Ariés has shown in *Centuries of Childhood: A Social History of Family Life*, trans. Robert Baldick, a similar development was taking place in French portraiture (see especially pp. 44–46).

[11] John Wilson, *A Song of Deliverance*, reprinted in *Handkerchiefs from Paul*, ed. Kenneth B. Murdock, pp. 23–75. For general information concerning the history of poems for children at this time, see Cornelia Meigs et al., *A Critical History of Children's Literature: A Survey of Children's Books in English from Earliest Times to the Present*, especially pp. 119–128, 152–155.

[12] Piercy (*Anne Bradstreet*, p. 86) accuses Anne of "jealousy" of Simon's second wife—unjustly, I think.

[13] The English author of educational books Sarah Kirby Trimmer (1741–1810) denounced the Cinderella myth as prejudicial to stepmothers, but the American women paid no attention to her (Meigs et al., *A Critical History of Children's Literature*, p. 79).

[14] After all, the male poets, at least until recently, have never shown any interest in fatherhood—especially those poets who like Emerson celebrated "plain old Adam, the simple genuine self against the whole world" (as quoted by Pearce, *The Continuity of American Poetry*, p. 153).

[15] *The Letters of Emily Dickinson*, ed. Thomas H. Johnson, 1:210.

[16] For Edwards's *Personal Narrative*, a convenient and accurate text is *Jonathan Edwards: Representative Selections*, ed. Clarence H. Faust and Thomas H. Johnson, pp. 57–72. For Taylor's poetry, consult *The Poetical Works of Edward Taylor*, ed. Thomas H. Johnson. Emerson's "transparent eyeball" appears in *Nature*; the standard text for Emerson's work is *The Complete Works*, ed. Edward W. Emerson.

17 Throughout this paragraph, I am quoting from Bradstreet's prose letter to her children (*The Works of Anne Bradstreet*, ed. Hensley, pp. 240–245).

18 For a brief review of such critical speculation, see White, *Anne Bradstreet: "The Tenth Muse,"* p. 337. More recently, Anne Hildebrand has recognized the Deistic tendencies of this poem: "Anne Bradstreet's Quaternions and 'Contemplations,'" *Early American Literature* 8 (Fall 1973): 117–125.

19 For an explanation of Puritan typology, see Sacvan Bercovitch, ed., *Typology and Early American Literature*, especially Thomas M. Davis, "The Traditions of Puritan Typology," pp. 11–45. For a discussion of various modes of Deism, see Alfred Owen Aldridge, *Benjamin Franklin and Nature's God*.

20 The standard text for Winthrop's *History* is John Winthrop, *History of New England, 1630–1649*, ed. James Savage. *Winthrop's Journal: "History of New England," 1630–1649*, ed. James Kendall Hosmer, has been reprinted from Hosmer's 1908 edition, in which the quoted passage appears in vol. 2, p. 225. The best bibliography of Puritan verse is Harold S. Jantz, "The First Century of New England Verse," *Proceedings of the American Antiquarian Society*, n.s. 53, pt. 2 (October 1943): 219–523.

21 Samuel Kettell, ed., *Specimens of American Poetry*, 1: xxvii–xxviii.

22 Several modern editions are available. I am using Sarah Kemble Knight, *The Journal of Madam Knight* (1972).

23 Anna Tompson Hayden (or Haiden), "Upon the Death of . . . Elizabeth Tompson" and "Verses on Benjamin Tompson . . . ," in Joseph Tompson's manuscript journal, published in *Handkerchiefs from Paul*, ed. Murdock, pp. 6–7, 20–22.

24 Winthrop's "little speech" on "liberty" was delivered in 1645 and is widely anthologized. It is found in *Winthrop's Journal*, ed. Hosmer, 2:239.

25 Samuel Eliot Morison, *The Intellectual Life of Colonial New England*, p. 82.

26 Ibid., p. 85.

27 Thomas Jefferson Wertenbaker, *The Puritan Oligarchy: The Founding of American Civilization*, p. 150.

28 For a brief description of Puritan homes, see ibid., pp. 117–127.

29 This biographical information is from Murdock's introduction to *Handkerchiefs from Paul*, pp. xxxvi–xxxvii.

30 See note 23 above.

31 Brewster's "On the Four Ages of Man" could just as easily have been influenced by the almanac poems of the Puritan men. See, for example, the almanac poems in Harrison T. Meserole, ed., *Seventeenth-Century American Poetry*.

2. 1735–1804: Another Kind of Independence

1 Roy Harvey Pearce, *The Continuity of American Poetry*, p. 56. See also Hyatt H. Waggoner, *American Poets from the Puritans to the Present*, pp. 24–34; Vernon Louis Parrington, *The Colonial Mind 1620–1800*, vol. 1 of *Main Currents in American Thought: An Interpretation of American Literature from the Beginnings to 1920*, pp. 357–395; Alfred Kreymborg, *A History of American Poetry: Our Singing Strength*, pp. 19–26; the first

third of Benjamin T. Spencer's *The Quest for Nationality: An American Literary Campaign*; and so on.

² Page Smith, *Daughters of the Promised Land: Women in American History*, pp. 41, 57 ff.

³ There is no definitive biography. The best modern edition and biography is *The Poems of Phillis Wheatley*, ed. Julian D. Mason, Jr. *Phillis Wheatley (Phillis Peters): Poems and Letters (1915)*, ed. Charles F. Heartman, is a facsimile reproduction of a 1915 edition. Four new poems and a holograph version of a published poem have been published by Robert C. Kuncio, "Some Unpublished Poems of Phillis Wheatley," *New England Quarterly* 43 (June 1970): 287–297.

⁴ Mason, ed., *The Poems of Phillis Wheatley*, pp. xv–xvi.

⁵ Kuncio, "Some Unpublished Poems," p. 293. The Revolution eventually raised many poetic voices, of both men and women. See Samuel White Patterson, ed., *The Spirit of the American Revolution As Revealed in the Poetry of the Period*.

⁶ See Mason, ed., *The Poems of Phillis Wheatley*, pp. xlv–xlvii.

⁷ Alice Brown's *Women of Colonial and Revolutionary Times: Mercy Warren* is the source for much of Katharine Anthony's *First Lady of the Revolution: The Life of Mercy Otis Warren*, but Anthony's book contains a bibliography of Warren's works, as well as a critical bibliography. Warren's *The Group: A Farce* is available in a facsimile reproduction by the William L. Clements Library, University of Michigan. *The Adulateur* was reprinted in *The Magazine of History with Notes and Queries*, Extra Number 63 (1918): 225–259. The most recent commentary concerning Warren's *History* is William R. Smith, *History as Argument: Three Patriotic Historians of the American Revolution*, especially pp. 73–119. Warren's plays and poems are briefly discussed in chapters 1 and 2 of Ernest Earnest's *The American Eve in Fact and Fiction, 1775–1914*. Concerning her prose drama *The Blockheads* (1776), see John J. Teunissen, "Blockheadism and the Propaganda Plays of the American Revolution," *Early American Literature* 7 (Fall 1972): 148–161.

⁸ Upon publication of her *History* in 1805, there was some bitterness between John Adams and Mercy Warren. In *History as Argument*, Smith defends Warren against Adams's charges. Matters were eventually smoothed over.

⁹ For Warren's friendship with Catharine Macaulay (who Wollstonecraft said had been her inspiration for *Vindication of the Rights of Women*) and her letters discussing feminist views, see Anthony, *First Lady of the Revolution*, pp. 186–191.

¹⁰ The best discussion of the various modes of Deism, especially of those in America at this time, is Alfred Owen Aldridge's *Benjamin Franklin and Nature's God*. Actually, Warren and Franklin often overlap in their ideas. I find no evidence that they knew each other, but Franklin did write of his beliefs to Warren's friend John Adams (ibid., p. 74). Ironically, Newton's work ultimately contributed to the Deistic movement; see Edwin A. Burtt, *The Metaphysical Foundations of Modern Physical Science*, especially pp. 17–19, 282–297.

¹¹ "Simplicity" is the only poem of Warren's anthologized by Samuel Kettell, ed., *Specimens of American Poetry*. Kettell does, however, omit the epilogue concerning woman's "narrow bounds."

12 *The Posthumous Works of Ann Eliza Bleecker, in Prose and Verse: To which is added, A Collection of Essays, Prose and Poetical, by Margaretta V. Faugères* (1793). Faugères, who was Bleecker's daughter, will be discussed in the next section of this chapter. The biographical material concerning Bleecker is based on Faugères's sketch of her mother contained in this same volume. The only modern treatments of any work of Bleecker's are mentions of "The History of Maria Kittle" in Leslie Fiedler's *The Return of the Vanishing American*, pp. 92–93, and in Henri Petter's *The Early American Novel*, pp. 35, 373–376. For some reason, Fiedler considers Bleecker's story pure fiction.

13 Sarah Wentworth Morton (see the next section of this chapter) imitated this poem in her hypocritically entitled "Impromptu, For a Lady to a Riotous and Insensible Company," in *My Mind and Its Thoughts, in Sketches, Fragments, and Essays* (1823). It is one of her best poems.

14 For Franklin, the most complete text at present is *The Writings of Benjamin Franklin*, ed. A. H. Smyth. A modern edition, projected as 40 vols., is now in preparation: *The Papers of Benjamin Franklin*, ed. Leonard W. Larabee et al. A representative selection of Freneau's work is *Poems of Freneau*, ed. Harry Hayden Clark.

15 Judith Sargent Stevens Murray, *The Gleaner: A Miscellaneous Production*, is a collection of her essays (with some poems used as prefaces for the prose). The only modern biography is Vena Bernadette Field's *Constantia: A Study of the Life and Works of Judith Sargent Murray, 1751–1820*. Like Warren, Murray advocated feminine equality before Wollstonecraft's *Vindication* appeared. See *The Gleaner*, vol. 3, nos. lxxxviii–xci (reprinted from the March and April 1790 issues of *Massachusetts Magazine*).

16 See W. J. Free, *The Columbian Magazine and American Literary Nationalism*.

17 Margaretta V. Faugères, "Ode," in *An Oration Delivered on the Fourth of July, etc., 1798 by George Clinton, Junior*. The sketch of Faugères's life is based on Rufus Griswold, ed., *The Female Poets of America*, p. 35.

18 In one of her prose essays, "Fine Feelings" (from the 1793 edition of her works included in *The Posthumous Works of Ann Eliza Bleecker*), Faugères is willing to grant humanity to slaves and at least vaguely urges abolition of slavery.

19 A convenient and accurate source for Poe's poetry is *The Poems of Edgar Allan Poe*, ed. Floyd Stovall.

20 There is no modern edition of her work, but, for her biography and a bibliography, see Emily Pendleton and Milton Ellis, *Philenia: The Life and Works of Sarah Wentworth Morton, 1759–1846*. *My Mind and Its Thoughts* contains much of her otherwise uncollected prose and poetry.

21 This anthology is designated as vol. 1. There was, however, no subsequent volume.

22 Ola Winslow, "Sarah Wentworth (Apthorp) Morton," in *Notable American Women: A Biographical Dictionary*, ed. Edward T. James, Janet Wilson James, and Paul S. Boyer, 2: 587.

23 *Ouâbi* has been most recently considered critically by Roy Harvey Pearce in *The Savages of America: A Study of the Indian and the Idea of Civilization*, pp. 185–188.

[24] Arthur Hobson Quinn, *A History of the American Drama from the Beginning to the Civil War*, pp. 121–123. There is neither a modern biography nor a modern edition of Rowson's poetry and surviving play, although there are several modern editions of *Charlotte Temple*. For a bibliography of her works, see R. W. G. Vail, "Susanna Haswell Rowson, the Author of *Charlotte Temple*: A Bibliographical Study," *Proceedings of the American Antiquarian Society*, n.s. 42 (April–October 1932): 47–160. I have based my biographical information on Vail and on Elias Nason, *A Memoir of Susanna Rowson*. The most recent discussions of *Charlotte Temple* are in Petter's *The Early American Novel*, pp. 22–45, and in Earnest's *The American Eve in Fact and Fiction*, pp. 30–31.

[25] See Harvey Gross, *Sound and Form in Modern Poetry: A Study of Prosody from Thomas Hardy to Robert Lowell*, especially Chapter 4, "Nineteenth-Century Precursors," pp. 79–99. It is possible that Rowson was influenced in her experimentation by Abraham Cowley's odes, but I find nothing else in her verse to suggest that she had even read Cowley. For a discussion of the structure of Cowley's odes, see Carol Maddison, *Apollo and the Nine: A History of the Ode*, pp. 371–372.

3. 1800–1850: The Rise of Female Poetry

[1] Many scholars have examined the American cultural inferiority complex and its nineteenth-century critical spokesmen in a variety of works: Benjamin T. Spencer, *The Quest for Nationality: An American Literary Campaign*; Leon Howard, *Literature and the American Tradition*; Henry Steele Commager, *The American Mind: An Interpretation of American Thought since the 1880's*; F. O. Matthiessen, *American Renaissance*. The best examination of critical writings from this time is John Stafford, *The Literary Criticism of "Young America": A Study in the Relationship of Politics and Literature, 1837–1850*. However, Stafford omits entirely the development of the critical prescriptions for "female poetry." See also Clarence Brown, ed., *The Achievement of American Criticism: Representative Selections from Three Hundred Years of American Criticism*, pts. 1–2.

[2] Quoted in Spencer, *The Quest for Nationality*, p. 32.

[3] Margaret Fuller's poetry is derivative from Emerson's and, in several poems, such as "Lines Written in Illinois," seems to repeat the Edenic myth of America. Her poetry has none of the intellectual vigor evident in her literary criticism or in her *Woman in the Nineteenth Century*.

[4] Lydia Jane Peirson published two books, *Forest Leaves* (1845) and *The Forest Minstrel*, ed. Rev. B. S. Schneck (1846). Both the variety and the limitations of poetry by women on the frontier at this time are evident in *Selections from the Poetical Literature of the West*, ed. William D. Gallagher, originally published in 1841, but available in a modern facsimile edition.

[5] Amelia Welby's verse is collected in *Poems* (1850).

[6] See *The Poetical Works of William Cullen Bryant*, ed. Parke Godwin.

[7] The only woman poet, however, who wrote in all of the categories is a later and highly derivative writer, Ellen Clementine Howarth, *The Wind Harp, and Other Poems* (1864). Her broader interests can be attributed, in large part, to the patriotic fervor leading up to and including the Civil War.

8 The standard text is *The Writings of John Greenleaf Whittier*, ed. Horace C. Scudder. The poetry is collected in vols. 1–4.

9 Caroline Gilman, *Verses of a Life Time*. Gilman was a very popular writer in her own day, in both poetry and prose. In 1832, she published *Rose-bud, or Youth's Gazette*, one of the earliest American magazines for children. *Rose-bud* eventually became a family magazine, *Southern Rose* (1835–1839). Jay B. Hubbell cites Gilman as one of "the best [early] Southern women writers" (*The South in American Literature, 1607–1900*, p. 604).

10 The most concise statement of the epic thrust in American poetry is Roy Harvey Pearce's "The Long View: An American Epic," in *The Continuity of American Poetry*, pp. 59–136. Of course, no woman poet is mentioned in this chapter.

11 Aaron Kramer's *The Prophetic Tradition in American Poetry, 1835–1900* mentions more men than women as authors of poems directed against the Mexican War, the mistreatment of fugitive slaves, mobbism, mistreatment of the Indians, and the Spanish-American War—but not many more. Most of the poems he cites are from 1850–1900, a time of national crisis when, as I have said, the poetry of American men and women tended to overlap. Many of the poems which Kramer cites are a continuation in form and tone of such poems written by women (and, of course, by men) in 1800–1850. One major area of concern for the women which Kramer simply overlooks is feminism, in all its various poetic manifestations. It should be noted, finally, that, although Kramer calls Sigourney a "hack" writer (her usual epitaph from male critics), he mentions her often (mostly poems written after 1832) and that, incredibly, he attempts to squeeze Dickinson's poems into his thesis.

12 Only Margaret Fuller, who, Vernon Louis Parrington feels, might have been happier "if she married early" seems to have sensed the "main currents" (*Main Currents in American Thought: An Interpretation of American Literature from the Beginnings to 1920*, 2: 428). As for women other than Fuller, Parrington mentions more English women than he does American in his uncompleted three-volume study.

13 Spencer, *The Quest for Nationality*, p. 68.

14 The standard text for Longfellow's work is *The Complete Poetical and Prose Works of Henry Wadsworth Longfellow*, Riverside ed.

15 The "American myth" of the superior artist of integrity who is misunderstood and unappreciated by society and thus must starve and suffer in his garret or cold-water flat is a male myth, from Freneau's "Advice to Authors" (1788) to Kurt Vonnegut, Jr.'s Kilgore Trout.

16 See Hawthorne's letter of January 1855 to his publisher, William D. Ticknor, in Caroline Ticknor, ed., *Hawthorne and His Publisher*, p. 141. Hawthorne admits that his own chances of publishing success are slight and says, "[I] should be ashamed of myself if I did succeed" in competition with the women's "trash."

17 See Bradford A. Booth's "Taste in the Annuals," *American Literature* 14 (November 1942): 299–302. Sigourney is by far the most popular, at least in Booth's quantitative analysis of the annuals and gift-books. Eight women are among the top nine contributors.

18 For other sociological and intellectual implications of Emerson's statement, see William Charvat, *The Profession of Authorship in America, 1800–1870*, ed. Matthew J. Bruccoli. Charvat concludes his discussion of

this aspect of Emerson with the observation, "The whole romantic movement in America may be considered as a protest against the new bourgeoisie" (p. 66).

[19] See Perry Miller, Foreword to *Margaret Fuller: American Romantic*, pp. xi, xxiv–xxv.

[20] Howard Mumford Jones, *The Theory of American Literature*, p. 86.

[21] Hannah F. Gould was the most talented of the unmarried women poets at this time. The most complete collection of her verse is the two-volume *Poems by Miss H. F. Gould* (1839–1841). Gould did write occasionally of topics unusual for her day (e.g., a celebration of "The Steam-Boat") and in one poem, "The Great Refiner," developed a conceit in an effective manner (similar to the then unknown Edward Taylor's "Huswifery"). The rest of her poems, however, are highly derivative and redundant.

[22] The bitterness continued throughout the nineteenth century. See, for example, Paul H. Hayne's "Literature at the South: The Fungous School; 'Christian Reid's' Novels," *Southern Magazine* 14, no. 6 (June 1874): 651–655.

[23] For the response of a twentieth-century woman poet to "Casabianca," see Elizabeth Bishop's "Casabianca," in which the boy who "stood on the burning deck" has become "Love" (*The Complete Poems*, 1969).

[24] E. C. Stedman, ed., *An American Anthology, 1787–1900: Selections Illustrating the Editor's Critical Review of American Poetry in the Nineteenth Century*. However, vols. 4–6 of Stedman's eleven-volume *Library of American Literature from the Earliest Settlement to the Present Time*, compiled and edited with Ellen Mackay Hutchinson, more clearly indicate just how dependent Stedman was on the anthologies.

[25] Louise Bogan, *Achievement in American Poetry, 1900–1950*, p. 24.

[26] Fred Lewis Pattee, *The Feminine Fifties*, p. 307.

[27] Rufus Wilmot Griswold, "Frances Sargent Osgood," in *The Memorial: Written by the Friends of the Late Mrs. Osgood*, ed. Mary E. Hewitt, pp. 13–14. Griswold's observation that intellectual women are incapable of affection was a common assumption of the day, as, for example, in Chapter 13 of Hawthorne's *The Scarlet Letter*.

[28] John Crowe Ransom, "The Poet as Woman," in *The World's Body*, pp. 76–78.

[92] Howard, *Literature and the American Tradition*, p. 200.

[30] Albert J. Gelpi, *Emily Dickinson: The Mind of the Poet*; Hyatt H. Waggoner, *American Poets from the Puritans to the Present*, especially pp. 181–222.

[31] Pearce, *The Continuity of American Poetry*, p. 190.

[32] Even Mercy Warren had condemned Anne's family for having produced Thomas. As Rapatio (Thomas) says in *The Adulateur*, "Could I have tho't my stars would be so kind/As thus to bring my deeplaid schemes to bear,/Tho' from my youth ambition's path I trod,/Suck'd the contagion from my mother's breast;/The early taint has rankled my veins;/Despotic rule my first my sov'reign wish" (act 4, scene 2). Especially with the rise of feminism in the early nineteenth century, "mothers" have periodically been blamed for nearly every evil in American society. Notable instances are Walt Whitman's *Democratic Vistas* (1871) and Philip Wylie's *Generation of Vipers* (1942).

33 Maria Gowen Brooks, *Judith, Esther and Other Poems.* Brooks's *Zóphiël; or, The Bride of Seven* (first published in 1833) is the first book-length poem written by an American woman. Although highly praised by the English poet Robert Southey and by Rufus Griswold, the poem never sold well in America, and Brooks withdrew it from the market. Deeply pessimistic, especially concerning the situation of women, the poem contains some remarkable passages, such as "Egla's Song" in Canto VI. Other notable long (500 or more lines) poems were written in the nineteenth century by Elizabeth Oakes Smith, Emma Lazarus, Helen Hunt Jackson, Emily Foote Baldwin, and Ella Wheeler Wilcox. In the 1850's, Sigourney was unable to finish her epic concerning Pocahontas. Long poems by American women have centered upon international or universal concerns, with little or no emphasis upon national and traditionally epic themes.

34 Harriette Fanning Read, *Dramatic Poems.*

35 "La Vie de Sapho" is a section of *Poësies d'Anacréon et de Sapho* by Anne Lefèvre (later Mme Dacier). There were many editions of this work, and I have been unable to ascertain which one Hewitt read. It is interesting to note, however, that Dacier comments, "Mais c'estoit trouvé peu, ou point de tout de femmes qui eussent voulu en venir à cette extremité; c'est pourquoi les Poëtes l'ont appellée *Mascula Sapho*, la courageuse Sapho [But there had been few women, or none at all, who would have wanted to come to this extremity; this is why the Poets have called her *Mascula Sapho*, courageous Sapho]" (from the 1681 Paris edition, pp. 400–401). The most complete edition of Hewitt's poems is *Poems: Sacred, Passionate, and Legendary* (1853).

36 A more literal rendering of Sappho's poem is Robert Lowell's translation, part 1 of "Three Letters of Anaktoria," in *Imitations.*

37 For Melville's poetry, consult *Collected Poems of Herman Melville*, ed. Howard P. Vincent.

4. 1800–1850: Sigourney, Smith, and Osgood

1 Bryant's father had published some of William's earlier poems in a pamphlet in 1809.

2 Roy Harvey Pearce, *The Continuity of American Poetry*, p. 197.

3 Jay B. Hubbell, *The South in American Literature, 1607–1900*, p. 608.

4 Louise Bogan, *Selected Criticism: Prose, Poetry*, p. 338.

5 Sigourney's verse which is "prophetic" (which contains social commentary) has been mentioned by Aaron Kramer in *The Prophetic Tradition in American Poetry, 1835–1900*. Most of the poems he cites were written after 1832. Her verse is also cited often as an example of the "hack" work of her time; in the anthology *American Life in the 1840's*, ed. Carl Bode, in which the editor claims to treat "the daily life of the average American," only a poem by "the hack poet Mrs. Sigourney" (p. xix) and two selections from *The Lowell Offering* (a journal of articles, stories, and poems written by factory girls in Lowell, Massachusetts) are used to represent the daily life of women!

6 Gordon S. Haight, *Mrs. Sigourney: The Sweet Singer of Hartford*, p. 35.

7 Ibid., pp. 77–89.

8 In progress is *The Collected Writings of Walt Whitman*, ed. Gay Wilson Allen and E. Sculley Bradley. For a convenient and accurate text, see *Complete Poetry and Selected Prose*, ed. James E. Miller, Jr.

9 One notable exception is Thomas Holley Chivers's "To Florence Allegra in Heaven," a poem closely related in sentiment and diction to Sigourney's elegies, although rhythmically associated with Poe's verse. "To Florence Allegra in Heaven" has been republished in Richard Croom Beatty et al., eds., *The Literature of the South*, pp. 175–177.

10 Philippe Ariés found that the modern family did not really emerge until the eighteenth century, when, among other characteristics, children began to be valued for themselves (not ignored as potential ephemera or enjoyed as playthings) and to be treated as equals with one another (*Centuries of Childhood: A Social History of Family Life*, trans. Robert Baldick, pp. 398–403). We have already seen affirmation of this kind of evaluation of children in the poetry of Bradstreet, Wheatley, and Bleecker.

11 In the elegies written by men from 1800 to 1850, fathers are more often present, especially when the mother has died and the poet is the son. The most famous father's elegy of the period is Emerson's "Threnody." The first part of Emerson's poem is a listing of his dead son's toys—a bit of sentimentality beyond even Sigourney's sensibility. The second part of the poem is a meditation upon death and its place in Transcendentalism. Emerson's resolution is similar to that of the traditionally Christian Sigourney: his son will be assumed in the godhead, while Sigourney's babes will join Christ in heaven.

12 It is interesting that Sigourney received requests from both men and women for poems concerning the death of a child, wife, or husband (Haight, *Mrs. Sigourney*, pp. 103–104).

13 Robert J. Lifton, "Woman as Knower: Some Psychohistorical Perspectives," in *The Woman in America*, ed. idem, p. 45.

14 It is ironic that Hemans wrote more poems praising America than did Sigourney or other American women at this time. Hemans's "The Landing of the Pilgrim Fathers in New England" was a poem widely reprinted and praised in America. Indeed, one must wonder whether the great rush of similar poems by American male poets in the 1820's and 1830's was not inspired by such poems of Hemans.

15 See Leo Marx, *The Machine in the Garden: Technology and the Pastoral Ideal in America*. As usual, the views of women have been almost wholly excluded from this study.

16 This poem was often attributed to Hemans and, in fact, appeared by mistake in an 1827 edition of her poems. It is, however, unlike much of Hemans's work. Moreover, the poem is evidence of Sigourney's tendency to "experiment" with verse form—something Hemans never did.

17 This poem was written sometime between 1833 and 1837 and appears in Lydia Huntley Sigourney, *Select Poems* (1845).

18 Sarah Morgan Bryan Piatt, "If I Had Made the World," from *Poems in Company with Children* (1877). In *A Voyage to the Fortunate Isles* (1874), Piatt introduces her children to communism and, in effect, supports a revolutionary spirit ("The Palace-Burner: A Picture in a Newspaper"). Her husband, John James Piatt, was also a poet but had none of his wife's spirit and vigor. His poems concern the rural Midwest and are

highly traditional and derivative. Nevertheless, it was Mr. Piatt's poems which were chosen for praise and anthologizing by contemporary critics. See, for example, Douglas Sladen's anthology, *Younger American Poets, 1830–1890.* The Piatts were friends of William Dean Howells and are mentioned several times in Howells's *Literary Friends and Acquaintance: A Personal Retrospect of American Authorship.*

19 *Selections from the Autobiography of Elizabeth Oakes Smith,* ed. Mary Alice Wyman, p. 46. Wyman has also written a biography of both Seba and Elizabeth Smith, *Two American Pioneers: Seba Smith and Elizabeth Oakes Smith,* in which there is a partial bibliography of Mrs. Smith's work (pp. 237–242). There is no complete edition of her poems. The earliest collected edition is *The Sinless Child and Other Poems,* ed. John Keese (1843). A larger selection is contained in *The Poetical Writings,* ed. Rufus Griswold (1845). The rest of her poems are scattered throughout the journals.

20 For example, in the December 1845 number of *Godey's Lady's Book,* Poe praised "The Sinless Child." Hervey Allen contends, however, that Poe's praise of "The Sinless Child" was the result of Smith's kindness to Poe and his mother-in-law, Mrs. Clemm. As a result, argues Allen, the verses of Smith's poem "were vaguely eulogized through a veil of gauzy irony" (*Israfel: The Life and Times of Edgar Allan Poe,* p. 560). On the other hand, in her *Autobiography,* Smith stated: "Mr. Poe in conversation warmly commended 'The Sinless Child,' and when his 'Eureka' appeared, he called upon me and said, 'In "Eureka" I am in the spirit what you are in "The Sinless Child." ' He talked long in his most weird, lovely strain, saying, I remember, ' "The Sinless Child" is what all women should be, and then we men would be more what we are designed to be, what we are at our best, all of us' " (p. 124). For a comparison of Poe's "Eureka" and "The Sinless Child," see Wyman, *Two American Pioneers,* pp. 169–170.

21 Smith, *Autobiography,* p. 76.

22 In fiction, such is also generally the case. Moreover, so close are Smith's sinless child Eva and Harriet Beecher Stowe's Little Eva (*Uncle Tom's Cabin*) that I suspect Smith's quite popular poem was the source for Stowe's character. The relationships between Smith's poem and Longfellow's "Evangeline" (written and published during the time of Smith's greatest literary popularity) have never been investigated.

23 The only American woman poet who has been as interested in Mary is H. D., especially in *The Flowering of the Rod,* the third volume of her War Trilogy (1946). H. D.'s Mary, however, is hardly a cousin to Smith's Eva. H. D.'s Mary weeps "bitterly" (section XVI), appears "disordered, dishevelled" (XVIII), and is gossiped about (XX).

24 Except by her husband and by a few of the older women, such as Hale and Sigourney. Had she really been an aggressive feminist, Smith would never have been so successful on the lyceum circuit. She was also able to get along with Emerson and spent an extended visit in his home in 1851.

25 Smith, *Autobiography,* pp. 153, 119. For a fuller discussion of Smith's role in the feminist movement and her career on the lyceum circuit, see Wyman, *Two American Pioneers,* pp. 189–210.

26 Smith later confessed that the sinless child represented "some things in my own life and experience . . . my love of nature, my early harmony

with her, by which birds gathered around me, and even the snakes did not run from me" (*Autobiography*, p. 100).

[27] In a brief essay called "Characterless Women," *Graham's Magazine* 21, no. 4 (October 1842): 199–200, Smith supports Coleridge's statement, "The perfection of a woman's character is to be characterless." In defining the characterless woman, Smith states that "A characterless woman is, assuredly, anything but an imbecile one. She must be one equal to all contingencies, whose faculties or powers are developed by circumstances, rather than by spontaneous action; and this implies the possession of all that is peculiar to her sex, but all in harmonious adjustment." The characterless woman must suffer, does not marry, is lonely, and reforms men. The most "characterless" women in history are Mary the "meek" sister of Lazarus, Mary the mother of Jesus, and Eve before the fall, a "type" for all women.

[28] See Florence Howe's introduction to *No More Masks! An Anthology of Poems by Women*, ed. idem and Ellen Bass, pp. 27–30.

[29] Arthur Hobson Quinn, *Edgar Allan Poe: A Critical Biography*, especially pp. 477–479. Other critics see Osgood's work only as derivative of Poe's; see, for example, Alfred Kreymborg, *A History of American Poetry: Our Singing Strength*, p. 47. Critics generally agree that the best poet of Poe's "ladies" was his fiancée, Sarah Helen Whitman, but, for the most part, Whitman's poems are highly derivative from Poe and Bryant. Although she wrote with a certain ease and tried to vary meters with some success, her dependence for content, theme, and diction upon Poe and Bryant makes her an undistinguished writer. Only very late in life, in the 1860's and 1870's, when she finally found her own voice, was she capable of verse which was original and interesting. A poem for children, "Christmas Eve," is notable, but "Science" is worth quoting:

> While the dull fates sit nodding at their loom,
> Benumbed and drowsy with its ceaseless boom,
> I hear, as in a dream, the monody
> Of life's tumultuous, ever-ebbing sea;
> The iron tramp of armies hurrying by
> Forever and forever but to die;
> The tragedies of time, the dreary years,
> The frantic carnival of hopes and fears,
> The wild waltz-music wailing through the gloom,
> The slow death-agonies, the yawning tomb,
> The loved ones lost forever to our sight,
> In the wild waste of chaos and old night;
> Earth's long, long dream of martyrdom and pain;
> No God in heaven to rend the welded chain
> Of endless evolution!
>
>   Is this *all*?
> And mole-eyed "Science," gloating over bones,
> The skulls of monkeys and the Age of Stones,

> Blinks at the golden lamps that light the hall
> Of dusty death, and answers: "It is all."

The most complete edition of Whitman's verse is *Poems* (1879).

30 Allen, *Israfel*, p. 515.

31 Unless otherwise noted, my text for Osgood's work is the posthumous *Poems* (1850). The most complete contemporary biography of Osgood was written by Rufus Griswold and appeared in a memorial for Osgood which contained the work of her friends. I should not need to point out that Griswold and I have different favorites among Osgood's poems. See Rufus Wilmot Griswold, "Frances Sargent Osgood," in *The Memorial: Written by Friends of the Late Mrs. Osgood*, ed. Mary E. Hewitt, pp. 13–30.

32 The first two untitled poems are from Frances Sargent Locke Osgood, ed., *The Poetry of Flowers and Flowers of Poetry*. They were not included in the 1850 *Poems*.

33 Undoubtedly, Poe, that "Israfel," whose heart strings were "like a lute."

34 In *Biographia Literaria*, Coleridge had distinctly separated Imagination and Fancy (Chapters 4 and 13), and Americans were familiar with his definitions. Fancy, for Coleridge, is inferior to Imagination; unchecked by Reason, Fancy becomes "delirium."

35 Other than the general acceptance of Medea, witches were at this time turned into rather attractive and innocent creatures (à la Shelley's "The Witch of Atlas"). For example, in Smith's prose sketch, "The Witch of Endor" (*Graham's Magazine*, April 1843), the Witch is not evil, although she has "learned the knowledge of the East." In fact, she helps Soul and is an example of "woman's great tenderness."

36 Caroline Ticknor, ed., *Hawthorne and His Publisher*, p. 142.

5. 1850–1900: Refinement and Achievement

1 Biographical information and their poems are contained in *The Poetical Works of Alice and Phoebe Cary with a Memoir of Their Lives* by Mary Clemmer.

2 William T. Coggeshall's anthology, *The Poets and Poetry of the West: With Biographical and Critical Notices*, contains the work of 58 women poets (and 101 male poets).

3 Dee Brown, *The Gentle Tamers: Women of the Old Wild West*.

4 Frances Ellen Watkins Harper, *Poems on Miscellaneous Subjects* (1854), available in a modern facsimile edition, ed. Maxwell Whiteman. Whiteman includes a brief biographical and bibliographical discussion in this edition. Some of Harper's poetry is contained in William Henry Robinson, Jr., ed., *Early Black American Poets*. A more recent discussion of her work is contained in Joan R. Sherman's *Invisible Poets: Afro-Americans of the Nineteenth Century*, pp. 62–74. Sherman also discusses other black women poets of the nineteenth century, such as Ann Plato and Charlotte L. Forten Grimké.

5 For a discussion of early Jewish women poets, see Joseph Mersand, *Traditions in American Literature: A Study of Jewish Characters and*

Authors, especially pp. 118–127. Theodore L. Gross, ed., *The Literature of the Jews*, contains a brief selection of the poems of Moise, Menken, and Lazarus.

⁶ Menken has two modern biographers: Bernard Falk, *The Naked Lady*, and Allen Lesser, *Enchanting Rebel*.

⁷ Her poems are collected in a two-volume edition, *The Poems of Emma Lazarus* (1889). A modern paperback selection of poems and prose has been published by the Emma Lazarus Federation of Jewish Women's Clubs: *Emma Lazarus: Selections from Her Poetry and Prose*, 3d rev. ed., ed. Morris U. Schappes. *Songs of a Semite* (1882) has been reissued by Literature House.

⁸ It first appeared in the March 1887 edition of *The Century*.

⁹ It is worth noting that Lazarus's Orient-Jew chrysalis bursts forth as a butterfly into immortality, an image, as we have already seen, used earlier in the century by Caroline Gilman and Elizabeth Oakes Smith. Three of Dickinson's poems (nos. 66, 129, and 1099—all written probably between 1859 and 1866, but not published until later) are based upon this same image, which seems to have held a fascination for the women.

¹⁰ The definitive edition for her poems is *The Poems of Emily Dickinson*, ed. Thomas H. Johnson, 3 vols. (1955), but Johnson has also edited *The Complete Poems of Emily Dickinson* in a reliable and more convenient one-volume edition (1960). The standard edition for her letters is *The Letters of Emily Dickinson*, ed. Thomas H. Johnson, 3 vols. (1958). Of several fine biographical and critical studies, the best of those written after all of Dickinson's poems were available is Richard B. Sewall, *The Life of Emily Dickinson*. Also valuable are Thomas H. Johnson, *Emily Dickinson: An Interpretive Biography*, and Albert J. Gelpi, *Emily Dickinson: The Mind of the Poet*. Earlier important studies are George Frisbie Whicher, *This Was a Poet: A Critical Biography of Emily Dickinson*, and Richard Chase, *Emily Dickinson*. Brita Lindberg-Seyerstad has elucidated Dickinson's poetics in *The Voice of the Poet: Aspects of Style in the Poetry of Emily Dickinson*. A number of articles and essays have been conveniently collected in Richard B. Sewall, ed., *Emily Dickinson: A Collection of Critical Essays*. See also Willis J. Buckingham, ed., *Emily Dickinson: An Annotated Bibliography*.

¹¹ Gelpi, *Emily Dickinson: The Mind of the Poet*, pp. 183–184; Henry W. Wells, "Romantic Sensibility," in *Emily Dickinson: A Collection of Critical Essays*, ed. Sewall, pp. 48–49; Johnson, *Emily Dickinson: An Interpretive Biography*, pp. 155–180.

¹² See, especially, Ruth Flanders McNaughton, *The Imagery of Emily Dickinson*, pp. 11–12. The use of domestic imagery by American women poets has never been examined. Dickinson's imagery is only one aspect of an imaginative exploration which begins with Bradstreet and continues quite obviously today in the verse of Mona Van Duyn (especially *To See, To Take*) and Erica Jong (*Fruits and Vegetables*), among others. Unlike their English sisters, American women have never hesitated to make poetic use of domestic images. A thorough understanding of such imagery would, I believe, alter certain critical theories and would also prevent such statements as this: in her weekly cleaning, "The housewife awakens furniture that was asleep"—a contention from Gaston Bachelard's

otherwise valuable and provocative *The Poetics of Space*, trans. Maria Jolas, p. 68.

13 Yvor Winters, "Emily Dickinson and the Limits of Judgment," in *Emily Dickinson: A Collection of Critical Essays*, ed. Sewall, p. 34.

14 Austin Warren, "Emily Dickinson," in *Emily Dickinson: A Collection of Critical Essays*, ed. Sewall, p. 116.

15 Johnson, *Emily Dickinson: An Interpretive Biography*, p. 156. Jackson is, in fact, the only woman whom Johnson considers a "qualified judge" who did evaluate Dickinson's poetry. Following Johnson's judgment of Jackson is Sewall, *The Life of Emily Dickinson*, 2: 577–592.

16 Gelpi, *Emily Dickinson: The Mind of the Poet*, p. 36.

17 Johnson, *Emily Dickinson: An Interpretive Biography*, pp. 244–245.

18 Richard Wilbur, " 'Sumptuous Destitution,' " in *Emily Dickinson: A Collection of Critical Essays*, ed. Sewall, p. 130.

19 Warren, "Emily Dickinson," p. 111.

20 John Crowe Ransom, "Emily Dickinson: A Poet Restored," in *Emily Dickinson: A Collection of Critical Essays*, ed. Sewall, p. 97. Other critics have since refuted Ransom. To add another dimension to all the speculation concerning the identity of her "lover(s)," it should be pointed out that many unmarried women at this time wrote passionate amatory verse, while at the same time defending fiercely in their poetry their virginal status. An obvious example is the verse of Phoebe Cary.

21 The interpretation of this particular poem has been a subject of some controversy. See, for example, the three different readings in *The Explicator Cyclopedia*, ed. Charles Child Walcutt and J. Edwin Whitesell, 1: 68–70. My interpretation is closest to that of Kate Flores.

22 Whicher, *This Was a Poet*, p. 162.

23 "Faith" and "Annihilation" are from Rufus Griswold, ed., *The Female Poets of America*, p. 193.

24 An almost exact contemporary of Dickinson, Lucy Larcom (1824–1893), offers an even closer parallel in this kind of poem. Larcom graduated from the mills of Lowell, Massachusetts, taught school on the Illinois prairies in the 1840's, and then returned to Massachusetts, where she was editor from 1865 to 1873 of *Our Young Folks* (later *St. Nicholas Magazine*) and, with John Greenleaf Whittier, edited poetry anthologies (some of them for children). Her poems were highly popular and contain images such as "Grief is a tattered tent" and "That haunting dream of Better." I should also add that Larcom's nature verse offers several parallels to Dickinson's, although Larcom was more influenced by Emerson. Like Dickinson, Larcom preferred to remain single. In two poems, "Unwedded" and "Her Choice," she defended single women and questioned the "happiness" of marriage. Her (nearly) complete poems and some biographical material are contained in *The Poetical Works of Lucy Larcom* (1884).

25 I am citing categories from Sarah Josepha Hale, ed., *Flora's Interpreter; or, The American Book of Flowers and Sentiments*, 6th ed. (1838), but a large number of similar anthologies were published in the early nineteenth century. Sewall, for one, is aware of Dickinson's wide reading of contemporary fugitive verse. See *The Life of Emily Dickinson*, 2: 671.

26 Hale, ed., *Flora's Interpreter*, p. 209. It is interesting that, in a later

poem ("Untold Feelings"), Dinnies decided that it would be best not to reveal such inner states: "Let no cold observation tell/Where the limpid offering [the 'hidden feeling'] fell" (Coggeshall, ed., *The Poets and Poetry of the West*, p. 200). It is just such "cold observation," of course, which marks the best verse of Dickinson.

[27] As, for example, Sherman Paul has shown us in *The Shores of America: Thoreau's Inward Exploration*.

[28] It has also been suggested that Sara Teasdale committed suicide, but so far as I can tell the facts are uncertain.

[29] Poems of incipient madness are not uncommon among women writing in the early nineteenth century; for example, Lucretia Maria Davidson's "The Fear of Madness," which begins "There is something which I dread;/It is a dark, a fearful thing;/It steals along with withering tread,/Or sweeps on wild destruction's wing" (George B. Cheever, ed., *The Poets of America with Occasional Notes*, p. 125).

[30] Another relationship between Dickinson's verse and children's poetry has been examined by W. E. Stephenson, "Emily Dickinson and Watts's Songs for Children," *English Language Notes* 3 (June 1966): 278–281.

[31] James Gray, *Edna St. Vincent Millay*, p. 18.

[32] Adrienne Rich, *Poems: Selected and New, 1950–1974*, pp. 84–85.

[33] Elizabeth Bogart's poems are collected in *Driftings from the Stream of Life: A Collection of Fugitive Poems* (1866). Most of them had been previously published in the *New York Mirror* under her pseudonym, "Estelle."

[34] The negative image of the American businessman, of course, developed just at this time. Melville's Peleg and Bildad in *Moby Dick* led eventually to Christopher Newman of Henry James's *The American*. In general, American women poets have been less antagonistic toward the businessman than have the male poets. In fact, Millay's *Conversation at Midnight* (1937) is an obvious defense of the businessman, as are certain of Gertrude Stein's works in the 1930's. In the course of the poetry of American women, it is not "materialism" which has been disturbing to them, but rather that they have not been allowed to share or to participate in this world.

[35] Alfred Kreymborg, *A History of American Poetry: Our Singing Strength*, pp. 240–241.

[36] Lowell also praised Sappho and Elizabeth Barrett Browning. Baldwin's verse was apparently published too late for consideration in Stedman and Hutchinson's *Library*. As far as I can tell, the English women poets did not reject their own tradition until the twentieth century, when Edith Sitwell decided that only the verses of Sappho, one poem by Christina Rossetti, and a few poems by Emily Dickinson were competent (letter to Maurice Bowra, January 24, 1944); later she added Marianne Moore to her list (letter to John Lehmann, April 12, 1949) (*Edith Sitwell: Selected Letters (1919–1964)*, ed. John Lehmann and Derek Palmer).

[37] There is no modern edition of her poems, but a 1909 selection of her verse, *Happy Ending: The Collected Lyrics of Louise Imogen Guiney*, was republished in 1927. Several of her essays are collected in *Patrins, To Which is added An Inquirendo Into the Wit & Other Good Parts of His Late Majesty King Charles the Second* (1897). There are three twentieth-

century biographies: Alice Brown, *Louise Imogen Guiney*; Eva Mabel Tenison, *Louise Imogen Guiney: Her Life and Works, 1861–1920*; and Henry G. Fairbanks, *Louise Imogen Guiney*. See also *Letters of Louise Imogen Guiney*, ed. Grace Guiney.

38 Guiney, "Animum non Coelum," in *Patrins*, pp. 109–114. In keeping with her general trend toward "internationalism," Guiney made a special point of praising an English woman poet critically ("Appreciatory Note," in *Katherine Philips, "the Matchless Orinda": Selected Poems*, pp. 5–8) and examined the life of Margaret Danvers, the mother of George Herbert and a friend of John Donne ("Lady Danvers [1561–1627]," in *A Little English Gallery*, pp. 1–51). To urge less than total Americanism at this time was not unusual but was, of course, a reversal of the general thrust of American criticism and male literary achievement in the nineteenth century. See Van Wyck Brooks, "The European Scene," in *The Confident Years: 1885–1915*, pp. 423–448. It should be pointed out that this late-nineteenth-century thrust toward a more general humanism was necessary before Americans (especially the male poets) could express their own variety of Imagism.

39 See Guiney, "Open Letter to the Moon," in *Patrins*, pp. 170–178.

40 Teasdale's poems are now available in a modern, inexpensive paperback edition, *Collected Poems of Sara Teasdale*, with an introduction by Marya Zaturenska.

41 Allen Tate, *Sixty American Poets, 1896–1944*, rev. ed., p. 134.

42 See Zaturenska's introduction to *Collected Poems of Sara Teasdale*.

43 Jackson's *Poems* were posthumously collected in 1900. A modern critical biography is Ruth Odell's *Helen Hunt Jackson (HH)*.

44 Johnson, *Emily Dickinson: An Interpretive Biography*, p. 158. On the other hand, if Jackson is viewed only in the context of the male critics and poets of her day, she is "independent."

45 Edwin Fussell, "The Meter-Making Argument," in *Aspects of American Poetry: Essays Presented to Howard Mumford Jones*, ed. Richard M. Ludwig, pp. 3–31.

46 Kreymborg, *A History of American Poetry*, pp. 254–255.

47 Louise Bogan, *Achievement in American Poetry, 1900–1950*, p. 24.

48 There is no full-length biographical-critical study of her life nor any complete collection of her works. The widest selection of her verse is *The Selected Poems of Lizette Woodworth Reese* (1926).

49 Hyatt H. Waggoner, *American Poets from the Puritans to the Present*, p. xiv.

50 David M. Robinson, "Lizette Woodworth Reese, the Poet," in *Lizette Woodworth Reese, 1856–1935*, pp. 16–17. See also Hervey Allen's introduction to Reese's *The Old House in the Country* (1936).

6. 1900–1945: A Rose Is A Rose with Thorns

1 Jessie Belle Rittenhouse, *The Younger American Poets* has been reprinted in the Essay Index Reprint Series (1968). Rittenhouse (1869–1948) is another of those important American women editors and anthologists. A founder of the Poetry Society of America, she herself wrote poetry, best represented in *The Moving Tide: New and Selected Lyrics* (1939).

² The argument is, of course, still rumbling. See M. L. Rosenthal's *Poetry and The Common Life.*

³ Peabody is best known for her plays, among them *Portrait of Mrs. W* (1922) concerning Mary Wollstonecraft. For her work, see Josephine Preston Peabody, *The Collected Poems*, and idem, *The Collected Plays.*

⁴ Edith M. Thomas, *The Dancers and Other Legends and Lyrics.* In this same volume is a section entitled "La Muse S'Amuse," a series of brief humorous and ironic poems which anticipate Millay's verse, such as "Mistaken Magnanimity": "The storm of words was past, the air was cleared,/ When 'I forgive you!' thus he volunteered./'If anyone forgives,' she said, ' 'tis I!'—/The storm approached, and murky grew the sky." The echoes of the kind of poem Osgood wrote in the early nineteenth century are unmistakable. Thomas's *Selected Poems*, ed. Jessie Belle Rittenhouse, represents a broad spectrum of her verse.

⁵ An excellent modern text has been edited with an introduction by Bernice Slote: *April Twilights (1903): Poems by Willa Cather.*

⁶ Alfred Kazin, *On Native Grounds: An Interpretation of Modern American Prose Literature*, p. 78.

⁷ In *Edith Wharton: A Biography*, R. W. B. Lewis also notes her metrical consciousness in *Artemis to Actaeon* and emphasizes her respect for Whitman, Emerson, and Poe (pp. 236–237). Along with Guiney and Lazarus, Wharton seems to represent a bridge between Poe, Emerson, and Whitman and H. D.

⁸ There is no modern edition of her poetry, nor any definitive critical biography. Her poems written before 1925 have been collected: *Collected Poems of H. D.* A selection of her poems, *Selected Poems of H. D.*, has been published in an inexpensive edition, as have *Helen in Egypt, Hermetic Definition*, and the War Trilogy (*The Walls Do Not Fall, Tribute to the Angels*, and *The Flowering of the Rod.*) The best full-length biographical-critical study is Vincent Quinn, *Hilda Doolittle.*

⁹ See, for example, Hyatt H. Waggoner, *American Poets from the Puritans to the Present*, pp. 358–364.

¹⁰ William Pratt, introduction to *The Imagist Poem: Modern Poetry in Miniature*, ed. idem, p. 16.

¹¹ Hugh Kenner, *The Pound Era*, p. 191.

¹² See Harvey Gross, *Sound and Form in Modern Poetry: A Study of Prosody from Thomas Hardy to Robert Lowell*, especially pp. 100–129, 174–175. Also N. Christoph de Nagy, *Ezra Pound's Poetics and Literary Tradition*, pp. 83–86.

¹³ Amy Lowell was, of course, quite wrong when she stated that H. D.'s poems "show no slightest trace of those influences which until recently ruled American art" (*Tendencies in Modern American Poetry*, p. 279). Lowell was looking on the wrong side of "American art."

¹⁴ As quoted by Norman Holmes Pearson in his foreword to H. D.'s *Hermetic Definition*, p. vi.

¹⁵ See M. L. Rosenthal, *The New Poets: American and British Poetry since World War II*, p. 20.

¹⁶ See, for example, Michel Benamou, "Wallace Stevens: Some Relations between Poetry and Painting," in *The Achievement of Wallace Stevens*, ed. Ashley Brown and Robert S. Haller, pp. 232–248; and Emily Stipes Watts, *Ernest Hemingway and the Arts.*

[17] The art historians have to some extent noted this situation. See James Thomas Flexner, *That Wilder Image: The Painting of America's Native School from Thomas Cole to Winslow Homer,* pp. 61, 128. James T. Callow's *Kindred Spirits: Knickerbocker Writers and American Artists, 1807–1855* deals only with male writers. His chapters on "Genre" and "The Home and Its Environs" are amazing in their absolutely nonfeminine perspective.

[18] I should also note, at least in passing, the typographical techniques with which H. D. and others (especially the French) were experimenting at this time. However, for H. D., such experiments were limited because of her underlying loyalty to the iambic line and syntactical structure.

[19] Amy Lowell's *Complete Poetical Works* was published in 1955. *Selected Poems of Amy Lowell,* ed. John Livingston Lowes, appeared in 1928. *A Shard of Silence: Selected Poems,* ed. G. R. Ruihley (1957), contains a brief critical introduction. The only full-length critical studies are Clement Wood, *Amy Lowell,* and Horace Gregory, *Amy Lowell: Portrait of the Poet in Our Time.* S. Foster Damon's *Amy Lowell: A Chronicle* is largely biographical.

[20] Adelaide Crapsey's one book is *Verse,* originally published in 1915.

[21] The year before this poem appeared, a similar poem, Harriet Monroe's "Myself," was published in *You and I*—a volume which contains her best poetry. Monroe (1860–1936) was only a limited poet (although an intelligent and generous editor), but she wrote several striking poems, all of which appear in this volume: besides "Myself," also "The Woman," a vicious attack on men and commercialism (in the Bogart-Baldwin line); and "The Mockery," a sardonic statement echoing Ella Wheeler Wilcox's "A Gray Mood." Monroe's *A Poet's Life: Seventy Years in a Changing World,* which was finished after her death by Morton Dauwen Zabel, is an interesting history of the literary world at this time.

[22] *The Complete Poems of Marianne Moore.* Her translation of *The Fables of La Fontaine* is available in a paperback edition. Full-length studies are George W. Nitchie, *Marianne Moore: An Introduction to the Poetry*; Jean Garrigue, *Marianne Moore*; and Bernard Francis Engel, *Marianne Moore.* Essays concerning her poetry have been conveniently collected in Charles Tomlinson, ed., *Marianne Moore: A Collection of Critical Essays.* See also Gary Lane, ed., *A Concordance to the Poems of Marianne Moore.*

[23] See also the list of quotations from men at the beginning of Chapter 7 of Nitchie's *Marianne Moore: An Introduction to the Poetry,* pp. 170–171.

[24] Important statements concerning Moore have been made by Elizabeth Drew (with John L. Sweeney), *Directions in Modern Poetry*; Louise Bogan, *Selected Criticism: Prose, Poetry*; Babette Deutsch, *Poetry in Our Time*; and Garrigue, *Marianne Moore.*

[25] Garrigue, *Marianne Moore,* p. 7.

[26] Roy Harvey Pearce, *The Continuity of American Poetry,* pp. 366–375; Waggoner, *American Poets from the Puritans to the Present,* pp. 364–368.

[27] Randall Jarrell, "Two Essays on Marianne Moore," in *Poetry and the Age,* p. 204. One of the two essays, "Her Shield," is reprinted in Tomlinson, ed., *Marianne Moore: A Collection of Critical Essays.*

[28] For her work left unpublished at her death, see *The Yale Edition*

of the Unpublished Writings of Gertrude Stein, ed. Carl Van Vechten; also, *Reflection on the Atomic Bomb,* ed. Robert Bartlett Haas, vol. 1 of a projected two-volume collection, *The Previously Uncollected Writings of Gertrude Stein.* There is no collected edition for the work published in her lifetime, but paperback editions of separate works are appearing in the bookstores continually (or even in PTA booksales, where I bought her children's book, *The World is Round*). The best generally available selection of her works is *Selected Writings of Gertrude Stein,* ed. Carl Van Vechten. There are three excellent critical studies: Richard Bridgman, *Gertrude Stein in Pieces*; Allegra Stewart, *Gertrude Stein and the Present*; Michael J. Hoffman, *The Development of Abstractionism in the Writings of Gertrude Stein.* James R. Mellow's *Charmed Circle: Gertrude Stein and Company* is largely biographical. See also Frederick J. Hoffman, *Gertrude Stein.*

29 Bridgman, *Gertrude Stein in Pieces,* p. 184. Other critics, as Bridgman notes, have understood this passage as a "mystical experience." If it is supposed to be a "mystical experience," it seems to be unique in the body of her work. *Four Saints in Three Acts* is included in Carl Van Vechten's edition of Stein's *Last Operas and Plays.*

30 William Van O'Connor, *Sense and Sensibility in Modern Poetry,* p. 49.

31 "Poetry and Grammar" is a lecture which Stein delivered several times in the 1930's; in *Gertrude Stein: Writings and Lectures, 1909–1945,* ed. Patricia Meyerowitz, pp. 125–147.

32 F. Hoffman, *Gertrude Stein,* p. 10. See also William Carlos Williams's intelligent essay, "The Work of Gertrude Stein," originally published in 1931 and recently reprinted in *The Poetics of The New American Poetry,* ed. Donald M. Allen and Warren Tallman, pp. 130–137. Several contemporary poets, among them Robert Creeley, have been influenced by Stein.

33 *Selected Writings of Gertrude Stein,* ed. Van Vechten, p. 258.

34 Laura Riding, *Collected Poems,* (1938) is the only inclusive collection of her work. *Selected Poems: In Five Sets* (1973) is a recent paperback. Besides *Contemporaries and Snobs* (1928), Riding wrote other critical studies, notably *A Survey of Modernist Poetry* (1927), with Robert Graves as coauthor. Also of note is her *Lives of Wives* (1939), "because the principal male characters are here written of as husbands rather than heroes," as Riding says. Curiously enough, her "husbands" are several of the same ones Bradstreet examined in her "Four Monarchies." With Harry Kemp and others, Riding is also a coauthor of *The Left Heresy in Literature and Life* (1939). Some critical discussion of her work is in Louise Cowan's *The Fugitive Group: A Literary History.* More recently, she has been ignored or treated with condescension, as in John L. Stewart's *The Burden of Time: The Fugitives and the Agrarians,* pp. 81–83.

35 As quoted in Rosalie Murphy, ed., *Contemporary Poets of the English Language,* p. 971.

36 Alfred Kreymborg, *A History of American Poetry: Our Singing Strength,* pp. 567–568.

37 Allen Tate, *Sixty American Poets, 1896–1944,* rev. ed., p. 104.

38 Thomas A. Gray, *Elinor Wylie,* p. 114.

39 *Collected Poems of Elinor Wylie* (1938) seems to contain the entire

body of her verse. The only full-length study is Gray's *Elinor Wylie*. Her prose writings are gathered in *Collected Prose*, ed. William Rose Benét (1933).

40 Waggoner, *American Poets from the Puritans to the Present*, pp. 459–464.

41 Edna St. Vincent Millay's *Collected Poems*, ed. Norma Millay, appeared in 1956. There are paperback editions of most of her poetry available: *Collected Lyrics* (1965) and *Collected Sonnets* (1967). Even her letters are available in paperback: *Letters of Edna St. Vincent Millay*, ed. Allan Ross MacDougall (1952). A recent biography is Jean Gould's *The Poet and Her Book: A Biography of Edna St. Vincent Millay*. There are several major studies of her work: Norman A. Brittin, *Edna St. Vincent Millay*; James Gray, *Edna St. Vincent Millay*; Elizabeth Atkins, *Edna St. Vincent Millay and Her Times*. See also Karl Yost, *A Bibliography of the Works of Edna St. Vincent Millay*, and John J. Patton, "A Comprehensive Bibliography of Edna St. Vincent Millay," *The Serif* 5 (1968): 10–32.

42 Gray, *Edna St. Vincent Millay*, p. 8.

43 Kreymborg, *A History of American Poetry*, pp. 438–446.

44 See Norma Millay's introduction to *Collected Lyrics*, p. vi.

45 For a discussion of those images, see Joseph Warren Beach, *Obsessive Images: Symbolism in the Poetry of the 1930's and 1940's*, ed. William Van O'Connor. Beach was apparently unaware of Millay's mockery of these images in *Conversation at Midnight*.

46 See George Watson, "Were the Intellectuals Duped? The 1930's Revisited," *Encounter* (December 1973): 20–30.

47 The best selection of poems by women from this period is *No More Masks! An Anthology of Poems by Women*, ed. Florence Howe and Ellen Bass.

48 M. L. Rosenthal has also noted Rukeyser's pioneering tendencies, but our emphases are somewhat different. See *The New Poets: American and British Poetry since World War II*, p. 329.

49 Lola Ridge's *Sun-Up, and Other Poems* (1920) is an interesting collection of very diverse poems, ranging from poems of mother love ("Mama," part 3 of the title poem) to those of the city ghetto ("Time-Stone") and of radical political involvement ("Emma Goldman").

Bibliography

Works by American Women Poets

Baldwin, Emily Foote. *Flora and Other Poems, Grave and Humorous, for the Domestic Circle*. Hartford: Brown and Gross, 1879.

Bishop, Elizabeth. *The Complete Poems*. New York: Farrar, Straus and Giroux, 1969.

Bleecker, Ann Eliza. *The Posthumous Works of Ann Eliza Bleecker, in Prose and Verse: To which is added, A Collection of Essays, Prose and Poetical, by Margaretta V. Faugères*. New York: Printed by T. and J. Swords, 1793.

Bogan, Louise. *Achievement in American Poetry, 1900–1950*. Chicago: H. Regnery Co., 1951.

———. *Collected Poems, 1923–53*. New York: Noonday Press, 1954.

———. *Selected Criticism: Prose, Poetry*. New York: Noonday Press, 1955.

Bogart, Elizabeth. *Driftings from the Stream of Life: A Collection of Fugitive Poems*. New York: Hurd and Houghton, 1866.

Bradstreet, Anne. *Poems of Anne Bradstreet*. Edited by Robert Hutchinson. New York: Dover Publications, 1969.

———. *The Tenth Muse (1650) and, from the Manuscripts: Meditations Divine and Morall, Together with Letters and Occasional Pieces*. Facsimile reproduction. Edited by Josephine K. Piercy. Gainesville, Fla.: Scholars' Facsimiles and Reprints, 1965.

———. *The Works of Anne Bradstreet*. Edited by Jeannine Hensley. Cambridge, Mass.: Harvard University Press, Belknap Press, 1967.

Brewster, Martha. *Poems on Divers Subjects*. New London, Conn.: Printed by John Green, 1757.

Brooks, Gwendolyn. *Selected Poems*. New York, Evanston, and London: Harper and Row, 1963.

———. *The World of Gwendolyn Brooks*. New York: Harper and Row, 1971.

Brooks, Maria Gowen. *Judith, Esther, and Other Poems*. Boston: Cummings and Hilliard, 1820.

———. *Zóphiël; or, The Bride of Seven*. Edited by Zadel Barnes Gustafson. Boston: Lee and Shepard, 1879.

Cary, Alice and Phoebe. *The Poetical Works of Alice and Phoebe Cary with a Memoir of Their Lives*, by Mary Clemmer. Boston: Houghton Mifflin, 1881.

Cather, Willa. *April Twilights (1903): Poems by Willa Cather*. Edited by Bernice Slote. Lincoln: University of Nebraska Press, 1962.

Crapsey, Adelaide. *Verse*. Rochester, N.Y.: Manas Press, 1915.

Dickinson, Emily. *The Complete Poems of Emily Dickinson*. Edited by Thomas H. Johnson. Boston: Little, Brown, 1960.

———. *The Letters of Emily Dickinson*. 3 vols. Edited by Thomas H. Johnson. Cambridge, Mass.: Harvard University Press, Belknap Press, 1958.

———. *The Poems of Emily Dickinson*. 3 vols. Edited by Thomas H. Johnson. Cambridge, Mass.: Harvard University Press, Belknap Press, 1955.

Faugères, Margaretta V. *Belisarius: A Tragedy*. New York: Printed by T. and J. Swords, 1795.

————. *The Ghost of John Young, the Homicide Who was Executed the 17th of August last for the MURDER of Robert Barwick, a Sherif's Officer.* New York, 1797.

————. "Ode." In *An Oration Delivered on the Fourth of July, etc., 1798 by George Clinton, Junior.* New York, 1798.

————. *See also* Bleecker, Ann Eliza.

Fuller, Margaret. *Woman in the Nineteenth Century.* New York: W. W. Norton and Co. 1971. [Originally published in 1845.]

Gilman, Caroline. *Verses of a Life Time.* Boston and Cambridge: J. Munroe and Co., 1849.

Gould, Hannah F. *Poems by Miss H. F. Gould.* 2 vols. Boston: Hilliard, Gray, and Co., 1839–1841.

Guiney, Louise Imogen. "Appreciatory Note." In *Katherine Philips, "the Matchless Orinda": Selected Poems,* edited by idem, pp. 5–8. Cottingham near Hull: J. R. Tutin, 1904.

————. *Happy Ending: The Collected Lyrics of Louise Imogen Guiney.* Boston and New York: Houghton Mifflin, 1927. [Originally published in 1909.]

————. *Letters of Louise Imogen Guiney.* Edited by Grace Guiney. New York and London: Harper and Brothers, 1926.

————. *A Little English Gallery.* New York: Harper and Brothers, 1894.

————. *Patrins, To Which is added An Inquirendo Into the Wit & Other Good Parts of His Late Majesty King Charles the Second.* Boston: Printed for Copeland and Day, 1897.

————. *A Roadside Harp: A Book of Verses.* Boston and New York: Houghton Mifflin, 1893.

Harper, Frances Ellen Watkins. *Poems on Miscellaneous Subjects.* Reprint of 1857 ed. Afro-American History Series, edited by Maxwell Whiteman, no. 242. Philadelphia: Rhistoric Publications, 1969.

Hayden (or Haiden), Anna Tompson. Two poems. In *Handkerchiefs from Paul . . . ,* edited by Kenneth B. Murdock, pp. 6–7, 20–22. Cambridge, Mass.: Harvard University Press, 1927.

Hayden, Esther. Poem. In *A Short Account of the Life, Death and Character of Esther Hayden, the Wife of Samuel Hayden of Braintree.* Boston, 1759.

H. D. (Hilda Doolittle Aldington.) *Collected Poems of H. D.* New York: Boni and Liveright, 1925.

————. *The Flowering of the Rod.* New York: Oxford University Press, 1946.

————. *Helen in Egypt.* New York: Grove Press, 1961.

————. *Hermetic Definition.* New York: New Directions, 1972.

————. *Hymen.* New York: H. H. Holt and Co., 1921.

————. *Palimpsest.* Paris: Contact Editions, 1926.

————. *Red Roses for Bronze.* London: Chatto and Windus, 1931.

————. *Sea Garden.* London: Constable and Co., 1916.

————. *Selected Poems of H. D.* New York: Grove Press, 1957.

————. *Tribute to the Angels.* New York: Oxford University Press, 1945.

————. *The Walls Do Not Fall.* New York: Oxford University Press, 1944.

Hewitt, Mary E. *Poems: Sacred, Passionate, and Legendary.* New York: Lamport, Blakeman, and Law, 1853.

Howarth, Ellen Clementine. *The Wind Harp, and Other Poems.* Philadelphia: W. P. Hazard, 1864.

Jackson, Helen Hunt. *Poems.* Boston: Little, Brown, 1900.

Knight, Sarah Kemble. *The Journal of Madam Knight.* Boston: D. R. Godine, 1972.

Larcom, Lucy. *The Poetical Works of Lucy Larcom.* Boston and New York: Houghton Mifflin, 1884.

Lazarus, Emma. *Emma Lazarus: Selections from Her Poetry and Prose.* 3d rev. ed. Edited by Morris U. Schappes. New York: Emma Lazarus Federation of Jewish Women's Clubs, 1967.

———. *The Poems of Emma Lazarus.* 2 vols. Cambridge, Mass.: Riverside Press, 1889.

———. *Songs of a Semite.* Reprint. Upper Saddle, N.J.: Literature House, 1970. [Originally published in 1882.]

Lowell, Amy. *Complete Poetical Works.* Boston: Houghton Mifflin, 1955.

———. *A Critical Fable* [by "A Poker of Fun"]. Boston and New York: Houghton Mifflin, 1922.

———. *A Dome of Many-Coloured Glass.* New York: Houghton Mifflin, 1915.

———. *Pictures of the Floating World.* New York: Macmillan, 1919.

———. *Selected Poems of Amy Lowell.* Edited by John Livingston Lowes. Boston and New York: Houghton Mifflin, 1928.

———. *A Shard of Silence: Selected Poems.* Edited by G. R. Ruihley. New York: Twayne Publishers, 1957.

———. *Tendencies in Modern American Poetry.* New York: Macmillan, 1917.

Menken, Adah Isaacs. *Infelicia.* Philadelphia: J. B. Lippincott and Co., 1868.

Millay, Edna St. Vincent. *Collected Lyrics.* New York: Washington Square Press, 1965.

———. *Collected Poems.* Edited by Norma Millay. New York: Harper, 1956.

———. *Collected Sonnets.* New York: Washington Square Press, 1967.

———. *Conversation at Midnight.* New York and London: Harper and Brothers, 1937.

———. *Letters of Edna St. Vincent Millay.* Edited by Allan Ross MacDougall. New York: Grosset and Dunlap, 1952.

———. *Mine the Harvest: A Collection of New Poems.* New York: Harper, 1954.

Monroe, Harriet. *A Poet's Life: Seventy Years in a Changing World.* With Morton Dauwen Zabel. New York: Macmillan, 1938.

———. *You and I.* New York: Macmillan, 1914.

Moore, Marianne. *The Complete Poems of Marianne Moore.* New York: Macmillan, 1967; London: Faber and Faber, 1968.

———, trans. *The Fables of La Fontaine.* New York: Viking Press, 1964.

Morton, Sarah Wentworth. *Beacon Hill: A Local Poem, Historic and Descriptive.* Boston: Printed by Manning and Loring, 1797.

———. *My Mind and Its Thoughts, in Sketches, Fragments, and Essays.* Boston: Wells and Lilly, 1823. Facsimile reproduction. Delmar, N.Y.: Scholars' Facsimiles and Reprints, 1975.

————. *Ouâbi, or The Virtues of Nature: An Indian Tale in Four Cantoes.* Boston: Printed by Thomas and Andrews, 1790.

Murray, Judith Sargent Stevens. *The Gleaner: A Miscellaneous Production.* 3 vols. Boston: Printed by Thomas and Andrews, 1798.

Osgood, Frances Sargent Locke. *Poems.* New York: Clark, Austin and Co., 1850.

————, ed. *The Poetry of Flowers and the Flowers of Poetry.* New York: J. C. Riker, 1841.

Peabody, Josephine Preston. *The Collected Plays.* Boston and New York: Houghton Mifflin, 1927.

————. *The Collected Poems.* Boston and New York: Houghton Mifflin, 1927.

Peirson, Lydia Jane. *Forest Leaves.* Philadelphia: Lindsay and Blakiston, 1845.

————. *The Forest Minstrel.* Edited by Rev. B. S. Schneck. Philadelphia: J. W. Moore, 1846.

Piatt, Sarah Morgan Bryan. *Poems in Company with Children.* Boston: D. Lothrop and Co., 1877.

————. *That New World, and Other Poems.* Boston: J. R. Osgood and Co., 1877.

————. *A Voyage to the Fortunate Isles.* Boston: J. R. Osgood and Co., 1874.

Plath, Sylvia. *Ariel.* New York: Harper and Row, 1966.

————. *The Colossus and Other Poems.* New York: Random House, 1966.

Read, Harriette Fanning. *Dramatic Poems.* Boston: William Crosby and H. P. Nichols, 1848.

Reese, Lizette Woodworth. *A Branch of May.* Portland, Maine: Thomas B. Mosher, 1887.

————. *The Old House in the Country.* Introduction by Hervey Allen. New York: Farrar and Rinehart, 1936.

————. *A Quiet Road.* Portland, Maine: Thomas B. Mosher, 1896.

————. *The Selected Poems of Lizette Woodworth Reese.* New York: George H. Doran Co., 1926.

————. *Spicewood.* Baltimore: Norman, Remington Co., 1921.

————. *A Wayside Lute.* Portland, Maine: Thomas B. Mosher, 1916.

————. *Wild Cherry.* Baltimore: Norman, Remington Co., 1923.

Rich, Adrienne. *Poems: Selected and New, 1950–1974.* New York: W. W. Norton and Co., 1974.

Ridge, Lola. *Sun-Up, and Other Poems.* New York: B. W. Huebsch, 1920.

Riding, Laura. *Collected Poems.* New York: Random House, 1938.

————. *Contemporaries and Snobs.* London: J. Cape, 1928.

————. *Lives of Wives.* New York: Random House, 1939.

————. *Selected Poems: In Five Sets.* New York: W. W. Norton and Co., 1973.

Riding, Laura, and Robert Graves. *A Survey of Modernist Poetry.* London: W. Heinemann, 1927.

Riding, Laura, Harry Kemp, et al. *The Left Heresy in Literature and Life.* London: Methuen, 1939.

Rittenhouse, Jessie Belle. *The Moving Tide: New and Selected Lyrics.* Boston: Houghton Mifflin, 1939.

——. *The Younger American Poets (1904).* Essay Index Reprint Series. Freeport, N.Y.: Books for Libraries Press, 1968.

Rowson, Susanna Haswell. *Miscellaneous Poems.* Boston: Printed by Gilbert and Dean, 1804.

——. *Slaves in Algiers; or, a Struggle for Freedom.* Philadelphia: Printed by Wrigley and Berriman, 1794.

Rukeyser, Muriel. *Beast in View.* Garden City, N.Y.: Doubleday, Doran and Co., 1944.

——. *The Life of Poetry.* New York: Current Books, 1949.

——. *Theory of Flight.* New Haven: Yale University Press, 1935.

——. *A Turning Wind: Poems by Muriel Rukeyser.* New York: Viking Press, 1939.

——. *U.S. 1.* New York: Covici, Friede, 1938.

Sigourney, Lydia Huntley. *Moral Pieces, in Prose and Verse* [by Lydia Huntley]. Hartford: Shelden and Goodwin, 1815.

——. *Poems.* Philadelphia: Key and Biddle, 1834.

——. *Select Poems.* 5th ed. Philadelphia: E. C. and J. Biddle, 1845.

Smith, Elizabeth Oakes. *Bertha and Lily.* New York: J. C. Derby and Jackson, 1858.

——. "Characterless Women." *Graham's Magazine* 21, no. 4 (October 1842): 199–200.

——. *The Poetical Writings.* Edited by Rufus Griswold. New York: Redfield, 1845.

——. *Selections from the Autobiography of Elizabeth Oakes Smith.* Edited by Mary Alice Wyman. Lewiston, Maine: Lewiston Journal Co., 1924.

——. *The Sinless Child and Other Poems.* Edited by John Keese. New York: Wiley and Putnam, 1843.

Stein, Gertrude. *Gertrude Stein: Writings and Lectures, 1909–1945.* Edited by Patricia Meyerowitz. Baltimore: Penguin Books, 1967.

——. *Gertrude Stein on Picasso.* Edited by Edward Burns. New York: Liveright Publishing Corp., 1970.

——. *Last Operas and Plays.* Edited by Carl Van Vechten. New York and Toronto: Rinehart and Co., 1949.

——. "Many, Many Women." In *Matisse, Picasso, and Gertrude Stein with Two Shorter Stories.* Paris: Plain Edition, 1933.

——. *Reflection on the Atomic Bomb.* Edited by Robert Bartlett Haas. Vol. 1 of a projected two-volume *The Previously Uncollected Writings of Gertrude Stein.* Los Angeles: Black Sparrow Press, 1973.

——. *Selected Writings of Gertrude Stein.* Edited by Carl Van Vechten. New York: Random House, 1962.

——. *Three Lives.* New York: Modern Library, 1933. [Originally published in 1909.]

——. *The World is Round.* New York: Avon Books, 1972.

——. *The Yale Edition of the Unpublished Writings of Gertrude Stein.* 8 vols. General editor, Carl Van Vechten. New Haven: Yale University Press, 1951–1958.

Teasdale, Sara. *Collected Poems of Sara Teasdale.* London: Collier-Macmillan, 1966.

Thomas, Edith M. *The Dancers and Other Legends and Lyrics.* Boston: R. G. Badger, 1903.
———. *Selected Poems.* Edited by Jessie Belle Rittenhouse. New York and London: Harper and Brothers, 1926.
———. *The White Messenger, and Other War Poems.* Boston: R. G. Badger, 1915.
Turell, Jane Colman. *Reliquiae Turellae et Lacrymae Paternae. Two Sermons Preach'd at Medford, April 16, 1735 . . . To Which are added some long memoirs of her life and death.* Boston: Printed by S. Kneeland and T. Green for J. Edwards and H. Foster, 1735.
Walker, Margaret. *For My People.* New Haven: Yale University Press, 1942. Reissued 1968.
Warren, Mercy Otis. *The Adulateur* (1773). Reprinted in *The Magazine of History with Notes and Queries,* Extra Number 63 (1918): 225–259.
———. *The Group: A Farce.* Facsimile edition. Ann Arbor: William L. Clements Library, University of Michigan, 1953.
———. *History of the Rise, Progress, and Termination of the American Revolution, Interspersed with Biographical and Moral Observations.* 3 vols. Boston: Printed by Manning and Loring, for E. Larkin, 1805.
———. *Observations on the New Constitution, and on the Federal and State Conventions* [by "A Columbian Patriot"]. Boston, 1788.
———. *Poems, Dramatic and Miscellaneous.* Boston: Printed by I. Thomas and E. T. Andrews, 1790.
Welby, Amelia. *Poems.* New York: D. Appleton and Co., 1850.
Wharton, Edith. *Artemis to Actaeon and Other Verse.* New York: Charles Scribner's Sons, 1909.
Wheatley, Phillis. Five poems. In "Some Unpublished Poems of Phillis Wheatley," by Robert C. Kuncio. *New England Quarterly* 43 (June 1970): 287-297.
———. *Phillis Wheatley (Phillis Peters): Poems and Letters (1915).* Edited by Charles F. Heartman. Miami, Fla.: Mnemosyne Publishing Co., 1969.
———. *The Poems of Phillis Wheatley.* Edited by Julian D. Mason, Jr. Chapel Hill: University of North Carolina Press, 1966.
———. *Poems on Various Subjects, Religious and Moral.* Boston: Printed for A. Bell, 1773.
Whitman, Sarah Helen. *Poems.* Boston: Houghton, Osgood and Co., 1879.
Wilcox, Ella Wheeler. *Maurine, and Other Poems.* Chicago: W. B. Conkey Co., 1888.
———. *Poems of Passion.* Chicago: W. B. Conkey Co., 1883.
———. *Poems of Pleasure.* Chicago: Morrill, Higgins and Co., 1892.
———. *Three Women.* Chicago: W. B. Conkey Co., 1897.
Wylie, Elinor. *Collected Poems of Elinor Wylie.* New York: Alfred A. Knopf, 1938.
———. *Collected Prose.* Edited by William Rose Benét. New York: Alfred A. Knopf, 1933.

Anthologies

Beatty, Richard Croom, Floyd C. Watkins, Thomas Daniel Young, and Randall Stewart, eds. *The Literature of The South.* Chicago: Scott, Foresman and Co., 1952.

Bethune, George Washington, ed. *The British Female Poets*. Philadelphia: Lindsay and Blakiston, 1848.

Bode, Carl, ed. *American Life in the 1840's*. New York: New York University Press, 1967.

Cheever, George B., ed. *The Poets of America with Occasional Notes*. New York: Manhattan Publishing Co., 1847.

Coggeshall, William T., ed. *The Poets and Poetry of the West: With Biographical and Critical Notices*. Columbus: Follett, Foster, and Co., 1860.

The Columbian Muse: A Selection of American Poetry, from Various Authors of Established Reputation. New York: Printed by J. Carey, 1794.

Gallagher, William D., ed. *Selections from the Poetical Literature of the West*. Gainesville, Fla.: Scholars' Facsimiles and Reprints, 1968. [Originally published in 1841.]

Griswold, Rufus, ed. *The Female Poets of America*. Philadelphia: Carey and Hart, 1849.

Gross, Theodore L., ed. *The Literature of the Jews*. New York: Free Press, 1973.

Hale, Sarah Josepha, ed. *Flora's Interpreter; or, The American Book of Flowers and Sentiments*. 6th ed. Boston: Marsh, Capen, and Lyon, 1838.

Herringshaw, Thomas W., ed. *Local and National Poets of America*. Chicago: American Publishers Association, 1890.

Hewitt, Mary E., ed. *The Memorial: Written by Friends of the Late Mrs. Osgood*. New York: George P. Putnam, 1851.

Howe, Florence, and Ellen Bass, eds. *No More Masks! An Anthology of Poems by Women*. Garden City, N.Y.: Doubleday, 1973.

Kettell, Samuel, ed. *Specimens of American Poetry*. 3 vols. Boston: S. G. Goodrich and Co., 1829.

May, Caroline, ed. *The American Female Poets*. Philadelphia: Lindsay and Blakiston, 1848.

Meserole, Harrison T., ed. *Seventeenth-Century American Poetry*. New York: New York University Press, 1968.

Murdock, Kenneth B., ed. *Handkerchiefs from Paul: Being Pious and Consolatory Verses of Puritan Massachusetts . . .* Cambridge, Mass.: Harvard University Press, 1927.

Patterson, Samuel White, ed. *The Spirit of the American Revolution As Revealed in the Poetry of the Period*. Boston: R. G. Badger, 1915.

Read, Thomas Buchanan, ed. *The Female Poets of America*. Philadelphia: E. H. Butler and Co., 1849.

Robinson, William Henry, Jr., ed. *Early Black American Poets*. Dubuque, Iowa: W. C. Brown Co., 1969.

Sladen, Douglas, ed. *Younger American Poets, 1830–1890*. New York: Cassell Publishing Co., 1891.

Smith, Elihu H., ed. *American Poems, Selected and Original*, vol. 1. [No further volumes appeared.] Litchfield, Conn.: Printed by Collier and Buell, 1793.

Smith, Elizabeth Oakes, ed. *The Mayflower*. Boston: Saxton and Kelt, 1847.

Stedman, E. C., ed. *An American Anthology, 1787–1900: Selections Illustrating the Editor's Critical Review of American Poetry in the Nineteenth Century*. Boston: Houghton Mifflin, 1900.

Stedman, E. C., and Ellen Mackay Hutchinson, eds. *A Library of American Literature from the Earliest Settlement to the Present Time.* 11 vols. New York: C. L. Webster and Co., 1888–1891.

Other References

Note: Brief biographical and bibliographical information for many of the American women poets can be found in *Notable American Women: A Biographical Dictionary*, edited by Edward T. James, Janet Wilson James, and Paul S. Boyer, 3 vols. (Cambridge, Mass.: Harvard University Press, Belknap Press, 1971).

Aldridge, Alfred Owen. *Benjamin Franklin and Nature's God.* Durham, N.C.: Duke University Press, 1967.

Allen, Hervey. *Israfel: The Life and Time of Edgar Allan Poe.* New York: Farrar and Rinehart, 1934.

Anthony, Katharine. *First Lady of the Revolution: The Life of Mercy Otis Warren.* Garden City, N.Y.: Doubleday, 1958.

Ariés, Philippe. *Centuries of Childhood: A Social History of Family Life.* Translated by Robert Baldick. New York: Vintage, 1962.

Armens, Sven. *Archetypes of the Family in Literature.* Seattle: University of Washington Press, 1966.

Atkins, Elizabeth. *Edna St. Vincent Millay and Her Times.* Chicago: University of Chicago Press, 1936.

Bachelard, Gaston. *The Poetics of Space.* Translated by Maria Jolas. Boston: Beacon Press, 1964.

Beach, Joseph Warren. *Obsessive Images: Symbolism in the Poetry of the 1930's and 1940's.* Edited by William Van O'Connor. Minneapolis: University of Minnesota Press, 1960.

Benamou, Michel. "Wallace Stevens: Some Relations between Poetry and Painting." In *The Achievement of Wallace Stevens*, edited by Ashley Brown and Robert S. Haller, pp. 232–248. Philadelphia: Lippincott, 1962.

Bercovitch, Sacvan, ed. *Typology and Early American Literature.* Amherst: University of Massachusetts Press, 1972.

Booth, Bradford A. "Taste in the Annuals." *American Literature* 14 (November 1942): 299–302.

Bridgman, Richard. *Gertrude Stein in Pieces.* New York: Oxford University Press, 1970.

Brittin, Norman A. *Edna St. Vincent Millay.* New York: Twayne Publishers, 1967.

Brooks, Van Wyck. *The Confident Years: 1885–1915.* New York: Dutton, 1955.

———. *The Writer in America.* New York: Dutton, 1953.

Brown, Alice. *Louise Imogen Guiney.* New York: Macmillan, 1921.

———. *Women of Colonial and Revolutionary Times: Mercy Warren.* New York: Charles Scribner's Sons, 1903.

Brown, Clarence, ed. *The Achievement of American Criticism: Representative Selections from Three Hundred Years of American Criticism.* New York: Ronald Press Co., 1954.

Brown, Dee. *The Gentle Tamers: Women of the Old Wild West*. New York: Putnam, 1958.

Bryant, William Cullen. *The Poetical Works of William Cullen Bryant*. Edited by Parke Godwin. 2 vols. New York: Russell and Russell, 1967. [Reprint of the 1883 edition.]

Buckingham, Willis J., ed. *Emily Dickinson: An Annotated Bibliography*. Bloomington: Indiana University Press, 1970.

Burtt, Edwin A. *The Metaphysical Foundations of Modern Physical Science*. London: K. Paul, Trench, Trubner and Co., 1925.

Callow, James T. *Kindred Spirits: Knickerbocker Writers and American Artists, 1807–1855*. Chapel Hill: University of North Carolina Press, 1967.

Charvat, William. *The Profession of Authorship in America, 1800–1870*. Edited by Matthew J. Bruccoli. Columbus: Ohio State University Press, 1968.

Chase, Richard. *Emily Dickinson*. New York: Sloane, 1951.

Cody, John. *After Great Pain: The Inner Life of Emily Dickinson*. Cambridge, Mass.: Harvard University Press, Belknap Press, 1971.

Commager, Henry Steele. *The American Mind: An Interpretation of American Thought since the 1880's*. New Haven: Yale University Press, 1950.

Cowan, Louise. *The Fugitive Group: A Literary History*. Baton Rouge: Louisiana State University Press, 1959.

Dacier, Anne Lefèvre. *See* Lefèvre, Anne.

Damon, S. Foster. *Amy Lowell: A Chronicle*. Boston and New York: Houghton Mifflin, 1935.

Deutsch, Babette. *Poetry in Our Time*. New York: Columbia University Press, 1956.

Drew, Elizabeth. With John L. Sweeney. *Directions in Modern Poetry*. New York: W. W. Norton Co., 1940.

DuPee, F. W. "General Introduction." In *Selected Writings of Gertrude Stein*, edited by Carl Van Vechten. New York: Random House, 1962.

Earnest, Ernest. *The American Eve in Fact and Fiction, 1775–1914*. Urbana: University of Illinois Press, 1974.

Edwards, Jonathan. *Jonathan Edwards: Representative Selections*. Edited by Clarence H. Faust and Thomas H. Johnson. Rev. ed. New York: Hill and Wang, 1962.

Eliot, T. S. *The Complete Poems and Plays*. New York: Harcourt, Brace and Co., 1952.

Ellman, Mary. *Thinking about Women*. New York: Harcourt, Brace and World, 1968.

Emerson, Ralph Waldo. *The Complete Works*. Edited by Edward W. Emerson. Centenary ed. 12 vols. Boston and New York: Houghton Mifflin, 1903–1904.

Engel, Bernard Francis. *Marianne Moore*. New York: Twayne Publishers, 1964.

Fairbanks, Henry G. *Louise Imogen Guiney*. New York: Twayne Publishers, 1973.

Falk, Bernard. *The Naked Lady; or, Storm over Adah*. London: Hutchinson and Co., 1934. Rev. ed. *The Naked Lady: A Biography of Adah Isaacs Menken*. London: Hutchinson, 1952.

Fiedler, Leslie. *Love and Death in the American Novel.* Rev. ed. New York: Dell Publishing Co., 1966.

———. *The Return of the Vanishing American.* New York: Stein and Day, 1968.

Field, Vena Bernadette. *Constantia: A Study of the Life and Works of Judith Sargent Murray, 1751–1820.* University of Maine Studies, 2d ser. 17. Orono: University of Maine Press, 1931.

Flexner, James Thomas. *That Wilder Image: The Painting of America's Native School from Thomas Cole to Winslow Homer.* Boston: Little, Brown, 1962.

Flint, F. Cudworth. *Amy Lowell.* University of Minnesota Pamphlets on American Writers, no. 82. Minneapolis: University of Minnesota Press, 1969.

Flint, F. S. "Imagisme." *Poetry* 1, no. 6 (March 1913): 198–200.

Franklin, Benjamin. *The Papers of Benjamin Franklin.* Edited by Leonard W. Larabee et al. New Haven: Yale University Press, 1959–.

———. *The Writings of Benjamin Franklin.* Edited by A. H. Smyth. 10 vols. New York. MacMillan, 1905–1907.

Free, W. J. *The Columbian Magazine and American Literary Nationalism.* Paris and The Hague: Mouton, 1968.

Freneau, Philip. *Poems of Freneau.* Edited by Harry Hayden Clark. Reprint. New York: Harcourt, Brace and Co., 1960.

Fussell, Edwin. *Lucifer in Harness: American Meter, Metaphor, and Diction.* Princeton, N.J.: Princeton University Press, 1973.

———. "The Meter-Making Argument." In *Aspects of American Poetry: Essays Presented to Howard Mumford Jones,* edited by Richard M. Ludwig, pp. 3–31. Columbus: Ohio State University Press, 1962.

Garrigue, Jean. *Marianne Moore.* University of Minnesota Pamphlets on American Writers, no. 50. Minneapolis: University of Minnesota Press, 1965.

Gelpi, Albert J. *Emily Dickinson: The Mind of the Poet.* Cambridge, Mass.: Harvard University Press, 1965.

Gould, Jean. *The Poet and Her Book: A Biography of Edna St. Vincent Millay.* New York: Dodd, Mead, 1969.

Gray, James. *Edna St. Vincent Millay.* University of Minnesota Pamphlets on American Writers, no. 64. Minneapolis: University of Minnesota Press, 1967.

Gray, Thomas A. *Elinor Wylie.* New York: Twayne Publishers, 1969.

Gregory, Horace. *Amy Lowell: Portrait of the Poet in Our Time.* Edinburgh and New York: T. Nelson, 1958.

Griswold, Rufus Wilmot. "Frances Sargent Osgood." In *The Memorial: Written by Friends of the Late Mrs. Osgood,* edited by Mary E. Hewitt, pp. 13–30. New York: George P. Putnam, 1851.

Gross, Harvey. *Sound and Form in Modern Poetry: A Study of Prosody from Thomas Hardy to Robert Lowell.* Ann Arbor: University of Michigan Press, 1964.

Haight, Gordon S. *Mrs. Sigourney: The Sweet Singer of Hartford.* New Haven: Yale University Press, 1930.

Hayne, Paul H. "Literature at the South: The Fungous School; 'Christian Reid's' Novels." *Southern Magazine* 14, no. 6 (June 1874): 651–655.

Hemans, Felicia. *The Works of Mrs. Hemans: With a memoir by her sis-*

ter and an essay on her genius by Mrs. Sigourney. 7 vols. Philadelphia: Lea and Blanchard, 1840.

Hildebrand, Anne. "Anne Bradstreet's Quaternions and 'Contemplations.' " *Early American Literature* 8 (Fall 1973): 117–125.

Hoffman, Frederick J. *Gertrude Stein.* University of Minnesota Pamphlets on American Writers, no. 10. Minneapolis: University of Minnesota Press, 1961.

Hoffman, Michael J. *The Development of Abstractionism in the Writings of Gertrude Stein.* Philadelphia: University of Pennsylvania Press, 1965.

Howard, Leon. *Literature and the American Tradition.* Garden City, N.Y.: Doubleday, 1960.

Howells, William Dean. *Literary Friends and Acquaintance: A Personal Retrospect of American Authorship.* New York and London: Harper and Brothers, 1901.

Hubbell, Jay B. *The South in American Literature, 1607–1900.* Durham, N.C.: Duke University Press, 1954.

James, Edward T., Janet Wilson James, and Paul S. Boyer, eds. *Notable American Women: A Biographical Dictionary.* 3 vols. Cambridge, Mass.: Harvard University Press, Belknap Press, 1971.

Jantz, Harold S. "The First Century of New England Verse." *Proceedings of the American Antiquarian Society,* n.s. 53, pt. 2 (October 1943): 219–523.

Jarrell, Randall. *Poetry and the Age.* New York: Knopf, 1953.

Johnson, Thomas H. *Emily Dickinson: An Interpretive Biography.* Cambridge, Mass.: Harvard University Press, Belknap Press, 1955.

Jones, Howard Mumford. *The Theory of American Literature.* Ithaca, N.Y.: Cornell University Press, 1965.

Kazin, Alfred. *On Native Grounds: An Interpretation of Modern American Prose Literature.* New York: Reynal and Hitchcock, 1942.

Kenner, Hugh. *The Pound Era.* Berkeley: University of California Press, 1971.

Kramer, Aaron. *The Prophetic Tradition in American Poetry, 1835–1900.* Rutherford, N.J.: Fairleigh Dickinson University Press, 1968.

Kreymborg, Alfred. *A History of American Poetry: Our Singing Strength.* New York: Tudor Publishing Co., 1934.

Lane, Gary, ed. *A Concordance to the Poems of Marianne Moore.* New York: Haskell House, 1972.

Laughlin, Rosemary M. "Anne Bradstreet: Poet in Search of Form." *American Literature* 42 (March 1970): 1–17.

Lefèvre, Anne. *Poësies d'Anacréon et de Sapho.* Paris, 1681.

Lesser, Allen. *Enchanting Rebel.* Philadelphia: Jewish Book Guild, 1947.

Lewis, R. W. B. *The American Adam: Innocence, Tragedy, and Tradition in the Nineteenth Century.* Chicago: University of Chicago Press, 1955.

———. *Edith Wharton: A Biography.* New York: Harper and Row, 1975.

Lifton, Robert J., ed. *The Woman in America.* Boston: Houghton Mifflin, 1965.

Lindberg-Seyerstad, Brita. *The Voice of the Poet: Aspects of Style in the Poetry of Emily Dickinson.* Cambridge, Mass.: Harvard University Press, 1968.

Longfellow, Henry Wadsworth. *The Complete Poetical and Prose Works of Henry Wadsworth Longfellow*. Riverside ed. 11 vols. Boston: Houghton Mifflin, 1886.

Lowell, Robert. *Imitations*. New York: Farrar, Straus and Cudahy, 1961.

McNaughton, Ruth Flanders. *The Imagery of Emily Dickinson*. University of Nebraska Studies, no. 4. Lincoln: University of Nebraska, 1949.

Maddison, Carol. *Apollo and the Nine: A History of the Ode*. Baltimore: Johns Hopkins Press, 1960.

Marx, Leo. *The Machine in the Garden: Technology and the Pastoral Ideal in America*. New York: Oxford University Press, 1964.

Matthiessen, F. O. *American Renaissance*. London and New York: Oxford University Press, 1941.

Meigs, Cornelia, Anne Thaxter Eaton, Elizabeth Nesbitt, and Ruth Hill Vigeurs. *A Critical History of Children's Literature: A Survey of Children's Books in English from Earliest Times to the Present*. New York: Macmillan, 1953.

Mellow, James R. *Charmed Circle: Gertrude Stein and Company*. New York: Praeger, 1974.

Melville, Herman. *Collected Poems of Herman Melville*. Edited by Howard P. Vincent. Chicago: Packard and Co., 1947.

Mersand, Joseph. *Traditions in American Literature: A Study of Jewish Characters and Authors*. New York: Modern Chapbooks, 1939.

Miller, Perry. Foreword to *Margaret Fuller: American Romantic*. Garden City, N.Y.: Doubleday, 1963.

Morison, Samuel Eliot. *The Intellectual Life of Colonial New England*. New York: New York University Press, 1965.

Murdock, Kenneth B. *Literature and Theology in Colonial New England*. Cambridge, Mass.: Harvard University Press, 1949.

Murphy, Rosalie, ed. *Contemporary Poets of the English Language*. Chicago: St. James Press, 1970.

Nagy, N. Christoph de. *Ezra Pound's Poetics and Literary Tradition*. Cooper Monographs, no. 11. Bern: Francke Verlag, 1966.

Nason, Elias. *A Memoir of Susanna Rowson*. Albany, N.Y.: J. Munsell, 1870.

Nitchie, George W. *Marianne Moore: An Introduction to the Poetry*. New York: Columbia University Press, 1969.

O'Connor, William Van. *Sense and Sensibility in Modern Poetry*. Chicago: University of Chicago Press, 1948.

Odell, Ruth. *Helen Hunt Jackson (HH)*. New York and London: D. Appleton-Century Co., 1939.

Parrington, Vernon Louis. *Main Currents in American Thought: An Interpretation of American Literature from the Beginnings to 1920*. 3 vols. New York: Harcourt, Brace and Co., 1930.

Pattee, Fred Lewis. *The Feminine Fifties*. New York and London: D. Appleton-Century Co., 1940.

————. *The History of American Literature since 1870*. New York: Century Co., 1915.

Patton, John J. "A Comprehensive Bibliography of Edna St. Vincent Millay." *The Serif* 5 (1968): 10–32.

Paul, Sherman. *The Shores of America: Thoreau's Inward Exploration*. Urbana: University of Illinois Press, 1958.

Pearce, Roy Harvey. *The Continuity of American Poetry*. Princeton, N.J.: Princeton University Press, 1961.
————. *The Savages of America: A Study of the Indian and the Idea of Civilization*. Rev. ed. Baltimore: Johns Hopkins Press, 1965.
Pendleton, Emily, and Milton Ellis. *Philenia: The Life and Works of Sarah Wentworth Morton, 1759–1846*. University of Maine Studies, 2d ser. 20. Orono: University of Maine Press, 1931.
Petter, Henri. *The Early American Novel*. Columbus: Ohio State University Press, 1971.
Philips, Katherine. *Katherine Philips, "the Matchless Orinda": Selected Poems*. Edited by Louise Imogen Guiney. Cottingham near Hull: J. R. Tutin, 1904.
Piercy, Josephine K. *Anne Bradstreet*. New York: Twayne Publishers, 1965.
Poe, Edgar Allan. *The Poems of Edgar Allan Poe*. Edited by Floyd Stovall. Charlottesville: University Press of Virginia, 1965.
————. *The Works of the Late Edgar Allan Poe: With a memoir by Rufus Wilmot Griswold, and notices of his life and genius by N. P. Willis and J. R. Lowell*. 4 vols. New York: Redfield, 1853–1856.
Pound, Ezra. "The Audience." *Poetry* 5, no. 1 (October 1914): 29–30.
Pratt, William. Introduction to *The Imagist Poem: Modern Poetry in Miniature*, ed. idem, pp. 11–39. New York: Dutton, 1963.
Quinn, Arthur Hobson. *Edgar Allan Poe: A Critical Biography*. New York and London: D. Appleton-Century Co., 1941.
————. *A History of the American Drama from the Beginning to the Civil War*. 2d ed. New York: Appleton-Century-Crofts, 1951.
Quinn, Vincent. *Hilda Doolittle*. New York: Twayne Publishers, 1967.
Ransom, John Crowe. *Selected Poems*. 3d ed. rev. and enlarged. New York: Alfred A. Knopf, 1969.
————. *The World's Body*. New York: Charles Scribner's Son, 1938.
Requa, Kenneth A. "Anne Bradstreet's Poetic Voices." *Early American Literature* 9 (Spring 1974): 3–18.
Robinson, David M. "Lizette Woodworth Reese, the Poet." In *Lizette Woodworth Reese, 1856–1935*, pp. 11–20. Baltimore: Enoch Pratt Free Library, 1944.
Rosenthal, M. L. *The New Poets: American and British Poetry since World War II*. New York: Oxford University Press, 1967.
————. *Poetry and the Common Life*. New York: Oxford University Press, 1975.
Sewall, Richard B. *The Life of Emily Dickinson*. 2 vols. New York: Farrar, Strauss and Giroux, 1974.
————, ed. *Emily Dickinson: A Collection of Critical Essays*. Englewood Cliffs, N.J.: Prentice-Hall, 1963.
Sherman, Joan R. *Invisible Poets: Afro-Americans of the Nineteenth Century*. Urbana: University of Illinois Press, 1974.
Sitwell, Edith. *Edith Sitwell: Selected Letters (1919–1964)*. Edited by John Lehmann and Derek Palmer. New York: Vanguard Press, 1970.
Smith, Page. *Daughters of the Promised Land: Women in American History*. Boston: Little, Brown, 1970.
Smith, William R. *History as Argument: Three Patriotic Historians of the American Revolution*. The Hague: Mouton and Co., 1966.

Spencer, Benjamin T. *The Quest for Nationality: An American Literary Campaign.* Syracuse, N.Y.: Syracuse University Press, 1957.

Stafford, John. *The Literary Criticism of "Young America": A Study in the Relationship of Politics and Literature, 1837–1850.* Berkeley: University of California Press, 1952.

Stanford, Ann. "An Annotated Check-List of Works by and about Anne Bradstreet." *Early American Literature* 3 (Winter 1968–1969): 217–228.

Stephenson, W. E. "Emily Dickinson and Watts's Songs for Children." *English Language Notes* 3 (June 1966): 278–281.

Stewart, Allegra. *Gertrude Stein and the Present.* Cambridge, Mass.: Harvard University Press, 1967.

Stewart, John L. *The Burden of Time: The Fugitives and the Agrarians.* Princeton, N.J.: Princeton University Press, 1965.

Tate, Allen. *Sixty American Poets, 1896–1944.* Rev. ed. Washington, D.C.: Library of Congress, 1954.

Taylor, Edward. *The Poetical Works of Edward Taylor.* Edited by Thomas H. Johnson. Princeton, N.J.: Princeton University Press, 1943.

Tenison, Eva Mabel. *Louise Imogen Guiney: Her Life and Works, 1861–1920.* London: Macmillan, 1923.

Teunissen, John J. "Blockheadism and the Propaganda Plays of the American Revolution." *Early American Literature* 7 (Fall 1972): 148–161.

Ticknor, Caroline, ed. *Hawthorne and His Publisher.* Boston and New York: Houghton Mifflin, 1913.

Tomlinson, Charles, ed. *Marianne Moore: A Collection of Critical Essays.* Englewood Cliffs, N.J.: Prentice-Hall, 1969.

Vail, R. W. G. "Susanna Haswell Rowson, the Author of *Charlotte Temple:* A Bibliographical Study." *Proceedings of the American Antiquarian Society,* n.s. 42 (April–October 1932): 47–160.

Waggoner, Hyatt H. *American Poets from the Puritans to the Present.* Boston: Houghton Mifflin, 1968.

Walcutt, Charles Child, and J. Edwin Whitesell. *The Explicator Cyclopedia.* 3 vols. Chicago: Quadrangle Books, 1966–1968.

Watson, George. "Were the Intellectuals Duped? The 1930's Revisited." *Encounter* (December 1973): 20–30.

Watts, Emily Stipes. *Ernest Hemingway and the Arts.* Urbana: University of Illinois Press, 1971.

Wertenbaker, Thomas Jefferson. *The Puritan Oligarchy: The Founding of American Civilization.* New York: Grosset and Dunlap, 1947.

Weston, Jessie L. *From Ritual to Romance.* Cambridge: The University Press, 1920.

Whicher, George Frisbie. *This Was a Poet: A Critical Biography of Emily Dickinson.* New York: Charles Scribner's Sons, 1938.

White, Elizabeth Wade. *Anne Bradstreet: "The Tenth Muse."* New York: Oxford University Press, 1971.

Whitman, Walt. *The Collected Writings of Walt Whitman.* Edited by Gay Wilson Allen and E. Sculley Bradley. New York: New York University Press, 1961–.

———. *Complete Poetry and Selected Prose.* Edited by James E. Miller, Jr. Boston: Houghton Mifflin, 1959.

Whittier, John Greenleaf. *The Writings of John Greenleaf Whittier.* Edited by Horace C. Scudder. Riverside ed. 7 vols. Boston and New York: Houghton Mifflin, 1888–1889.

Williams, William Carlos. "The Work of Gertrude Stein." [Originally published in 1931.] Reprinted in *The Poetics of the New American Poetry*, edited by Donald M. Allen and Warren Tallman, pp. 130–137. New York: Grove Press, 1973.

Winthrop, John. *History of New England, 1630–1649*. Edited by James Savage. Boston: Little, Brown, 1853.

——. *Winthrop's Journal: "History of New England," 1630–1649*. Edited by James Kendall Hosmer. 2 vols. Original Narratives of Early American History, vol. 7, pts. 1–2. New York: Charles Scribner's Sons, 1908. Reprint. New York: Barnes and Noble, 1959.

Wood, Clement. *Amy Lowell*. New York: H. Vinal, 1926.

Wyman, Mary Alice. *Two American Pioneers: Seba Smith and Elizabeth Oakes Smith*. New York: Columbia University Press, 1927.

Yost, Karl. *A Bibliography of the Works of Edna St. Vincent Millay*. New York: Harper and Brothers, 1937.

Index